Cool-climate
white wine
oenology

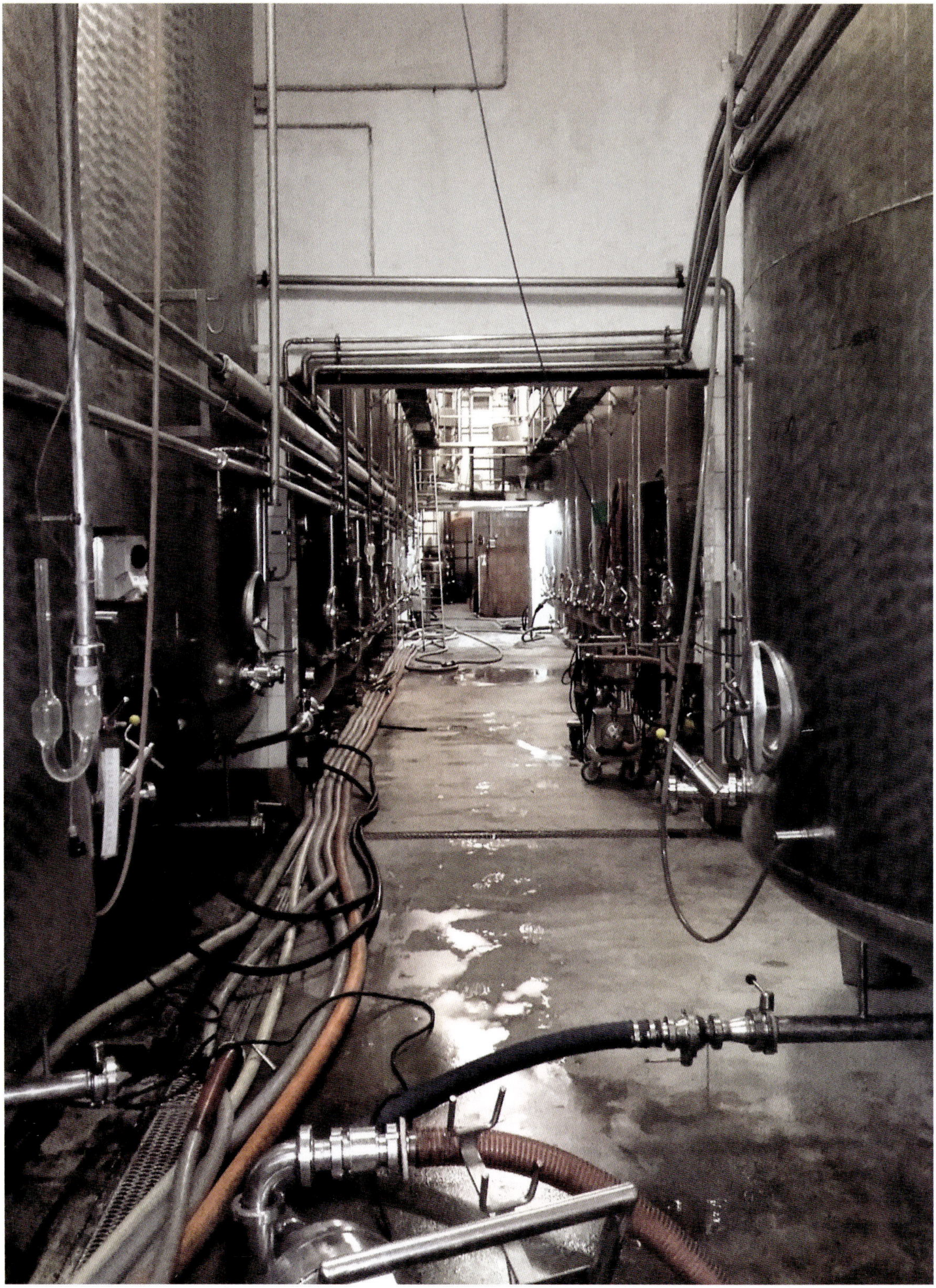

Volker Schneider
& Mark Tracey

Cool-climate white wine
oenology

✳ THE CROWOOD PRESS

First published in 2024 by
The Crowood Press Ltd
Ramsbury, Marlborough
Wiltshire SN8 2HR

enquiries@crowood.com

www.crowood.com

© Volker Schneider and Mark Tracey 2024

All rights reserved. No part of this publication may be reproduced or transmitted in any form or by any means, electronic or mechanical, including photocopy, recording, or any information storage and retrieval system, without permission in writing from the publishers.

British Library Cataloguing-in-Publication Data
A catalogue record for this book is available from the British Library.

ISBN 978 0 7198 4370 9

The right of Volker Schneider and Mark Tracey to be identified as authors of this work has been asserted by them in accordance with the Copyright, Designs and Patents Act 1988.

Frontispiece: bulk storage area of a contemporary winery.

Typeset by Envisage IT
Cover design by Sergey Tsvetkov
Printed and bound in India by Nutech Print Services

CONTENTS

	Preface	6
1	**Assessing Fruit Ripeness**	**9**
1.1	Beyond Sugar Levels and Acidity: Physiological Ripeness	9
1.2	Sensory Assessments of Fruit Maturity	12
2	**Pre-Fermentation Strategies**	**15**
2.1	Must Acidification and the Issue of Safe pH	15
2.2	Reductive vs Oxidative Grape Processing	17
2.3	Skin Contact	28
2.4	Pressing	31
2.5	Juice Treatments	36
3	**Fermentation Strategies**	**47**
3.1	Optimising Fermentation Conditions	47
3.2	Spontaneous Fermentations	59
4	**Acidity Corrections**	**63**
4.1	Biological Deacidification by Malolactic Fermentation	63
4.2	Spontaneous Acidity Losses by Potassium Bitartrate Precipitation	68
4.3	Chemical Deacidification	71
5	**Use and Effect of Reducing Agents During Storage**	**85**
5.1	Sulphur Dioxide	85
5.2	Ascorbic Acid	93
5.3	Hydrolysable Tannins	96
5.4	Inactive Dry Yeast Preparations	96
5.5	Post-Fermentation Yeast Lees	100
6	**Practical Use of Yeast Lees**	**107**
6.1	Avoiding Counterproductive Interventions on Fruity Wines	107
6.2	Barrel Ageing, Sur-Lie and Bâtonnage	110
6.3	Wines without Added Sulphites	114
7	**Limiting Oxygen Uptake**	**117**
7.1	Sensory Impact of Oxygen Uptake in Filtered Wines	117
7.2	Sources of Oxygen Uptake	119
7.3	Importance and Measures of Gentle Wine Treatment	124
8	**Preparing Wine for Bottling**	**131**
8.1	Bentonite Fining for Protein Stabilisation	131
8.2	Final Corrections of Taste, Flaws and Faults	135
8.3	Crystal Stabilisation	139
8.4	Adjusting Free Sulphur Dioxide Before Bottling	141
	Bibliography	**148**
	Index	**155**

PREFACE

This book is dedicated exclusively to the oenology of white wines, with a particular focus on those from cool-climate growing areas and the sparkling wines obtained from them. It is the authors' view that many of the latest developments in white wine oenology are often poorly appreciated by practising winemakers. In particular, their integration with current techniques to optimally vinify cool-climate fruit, such as that of the rapidly developing British wine industry, is frequently little understood. Accordingly, we seek to address this issue in a science-based but approachable manner.

Whilst the oenological concepts of red winemaking hardly apply to white winemaking, those of cool-climate white wines diverge even more from common oenological principles. Apart from their long-lasting aftertaste, freshness, and lively but often too high acidity, they are strongly associated with their aromatic properties. However, these aromas are fragile and easily lost by inappropriate grape and juice processing, unsuitable cellar operations and storage conditions, or due to poor wine stabilisation with regard to post-bottling shelf life. Hence there is need for detailed discussion of topical aspects such as grape maturity assessments, grape processing, juice treatments, acidity corrections, fermentation strategies, sur-lie treatments, stabilisation procedures, and the complex role of oxygen and reducing agents. Discussion extends to often confusing stylistic options such as oak barrels and alternatives, clay amphorae, and spontaneous fermentation. All issues are explained with care, traced back to their scientific fundamentals, and illustrated by extensive original data obtained from more than 40 years of the authors' experience in commercial winemaking conditions, quality control and research in various countries. Numerous practical hints, technical details of hands-on winery work and solutions to typical engineering issues complete the picture.

However, winemaking is more than process technology. After decades of a tendency to technocracy and even over-processing, a growing number of winemakers embrace a trend towards minimal or non-interventionist winemaking in order to respect consumer expectations and traditions. Recent research has allowed us to understand why some ancient techniques, evolved through experience, can be beneficial. It has provided knowledge, insights, and carefully selected strategies that can even improve the fine heritage of traditional winemaking. Examples such as the utilisation of oxygen in must, working with yeast lees after fermentation and the challenge of winemaking without added sulphites are discussed in detail.

Ultimately, this book seeks to present a valuable insight into the inherently cross-disciplinary nature of cool-climate white winemaking, unifying knowledge scattered across chemistry, microbiology and technology. It is written for professional winemakers, hobby winemakers with some proficiency in school-level chemistry, grape growers considering moving their whole winemaking process in-house, consultants and oenology students. The listing of comprehensive bibliographical references allows for deepening up-to-date expertise on specific subject areas. The authors hope that the readers will find *Cool-Climate White Wine Oenology* both edifying and enjoyable, and that it will be considered a valuable resource for years to come.

Volker Schneider and Mark Tracey

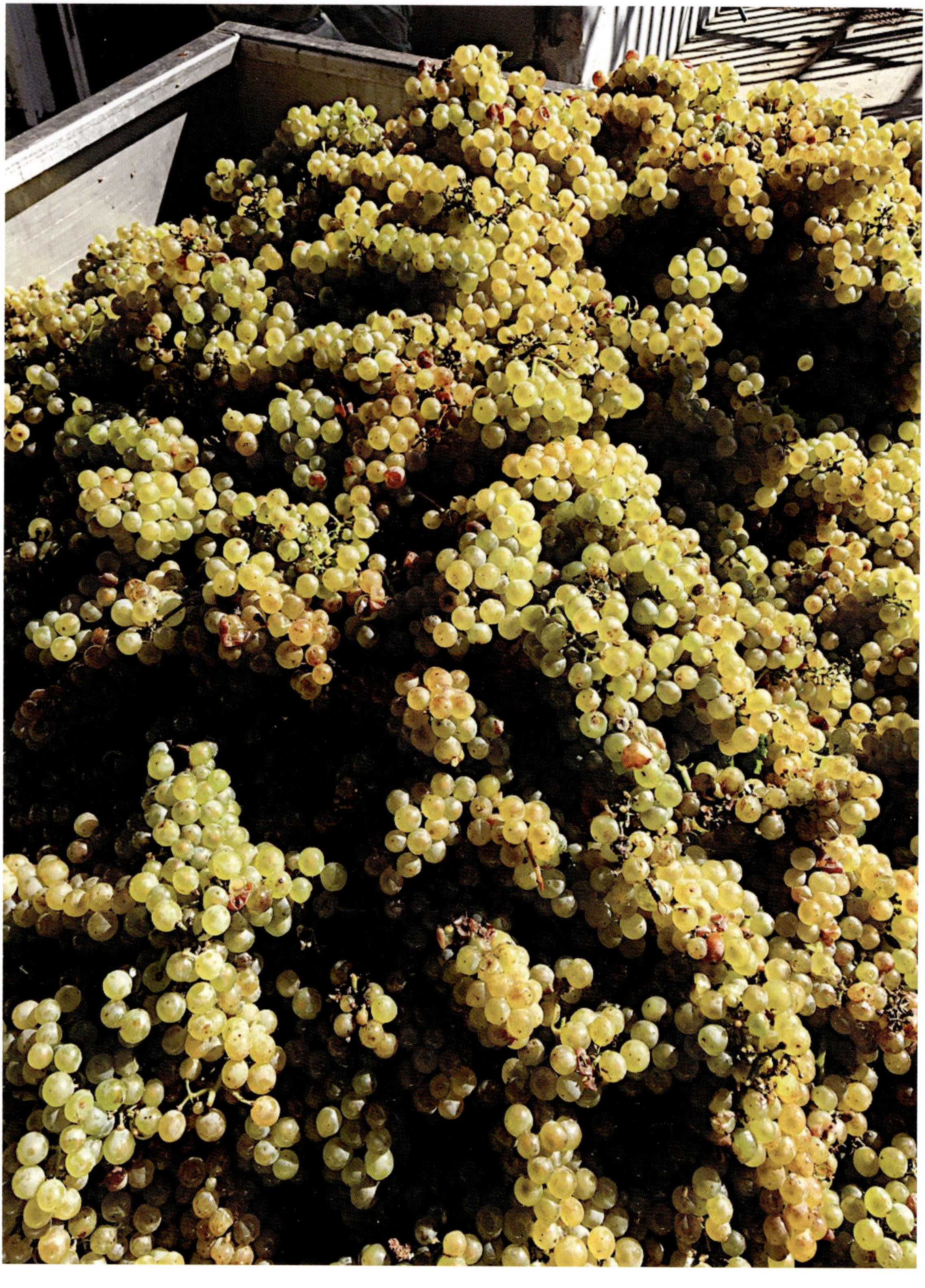

CHAPTER 1

ASSESSING FRUIT RIPENESS

In cool-climate growing regions, wine growers traditionally aimed to harvest their grapes when sugar levels were as high as possible and acidity reasonably low. It could be assumed that at this point all other grape constituents, specifically the aroma compounds (and in red grapes, also the tannins), had reached their optimal qualitative expression, also referred to as physiological ripeness. However, in our times of global climate change, the process of physiological ripeness has become increasingly uncoupled from increasing sugar levels and lagging behind them. Wines made from physiologically underripe fruit display an aroma reminiscent of freshly cut grass, green pepper, or no aroma at all, regardless of grape sugar. This is the reason that trivial sugar measurements have lost much of their former importance, to be replaced instead by an assessment of physiological ripeness. After all, sugar and acidity levels can be adjusted in the cellar, but deficient aromatics cannot. However, the chemical complexity of aroma makes its analytical measurement practically impossible. Accordingly, this chapter explains how aromatic ripeness of grapes can be assessed using smell, taste, visual appearance and tactile sensations.

1.1 Beyond Sugar Levels and Acidity: Physiological Ripeness

At the beginning of any winemaking process are the grapes. Their ripeness and health determine the quality of the wine at least as much as the oenological processes involved in winemaking. Therefore, no book on oenology can begin without considering the grapes and their evaluation before harvest. This results in harvest decisions, but also affects oenological decision-making in the subsequent steps of must and wine processing.

Sugar level, titratable acidity (TA) and pH are standard measurements every grape grower and winemaker is familiar with. They stand in the foreground during the monitoring of grape ripeness because they are easy to assess by simple technical means. As ripeness progresses, sugar increases and TA decreases, whilst pH is inversely related to TA. However, wine is more than an aqueous solution of alcohol and acids. Ripeness in the sense of grape sugar alone does not guarantee a pleasurable drinking experience. Nonetheless, there is still a widespread erroneous belief that quality can be determined solely by grape sugar content measured as specific gravity (SG) or Oechsle, possibly in combination with a moderate TA. Most winemakers claim that they do not depend on such figures, but it's a rare one who does not rely on SG, TA and pH readings when it comes to determining whether the grapes are ripe to pick.

Only recently has yeast-assimilable nitrogen (YAN) been increasingly measured in musts. Whilst not

OPPOSITE: **Ripe grapes are the most important prerequisite for serious wine quality.**

directly related to ripeness, it is crucial for a smooth fermentation. This will be discussed in more detail in chapter 3.

The Concept of Aromatic Ripeness

Grape sugar content exclusively determines alcoholic ripeness, that is, the potential alcohol content. However, beyond that, one can also identify a physiological ripeness, comprising aromatic ripeness and, in the case of red grapes, phenolic ripeness. It is not directly associated with alcoholic ripeness, at least not in accordance with the contemporary understanding of ripeness, and even less as global climate change progresses. Therefore, one can find completely unimpressive and one-dimensional wines obtained from high-gravity juices from physiologically unripe grapes.

The concept of aromatic ripeness is often ignored. In reality, long after the increase of sugar content has come to a standstill, the synthesis of highly valuable aromatic compounds in the berries continues. These are the compounds that, at comparable grape sugar and acidity levels, allow us to differentiate between white wines, especially between a cheap table wine and a complex vintage wine expressing its identity in terms of origin and variety. Otherwise wine description would be reduced to a monotonous repetition of the five basic tastes – sweet, sour, bitter, salty and umami – and possibly the tactile sensation of astringency.

Since aromatic ripeness and crop yield are interdependent, overcropping can be a reason for deficient aromatic ripeness. However, not only high harvest yields, but also extraordinary weather events may explain why aromatic ripeness does not run proportionally to alcoholic ripeness. Under humid climate conditions, grey rot often brings the development of desirable aroma compounds to a complete standstill. Conversely, as global climate change progresses, even cool-climate growing areas can be affected by deficient aromatic ripeness due to drought. In extreme cases, this can cause a wine made from 1.0105 SG grapes to remind us of one with an aroma profile of 1.0060 SG fruit.

Deficiency in aromatic ripeness may present in three ways:

- A shortage or complete absence of any aroma.
- The appearance of an aroma defect called 'atypical ageing' at a relatively early stage of white wine development, sometimes quite soon after fermentation. The olfactory feature of those wines is reminiscent of mothballs, naphthalene, soap, acacia blossom, or similar. Its underlying cause is a hormonal stress in the vines that might be induced

Overcropped vineyard with more grapes than leaves. The desirable leaf-to-fruit ratio depends on a plethora of viticultural variables, but less than ten leaves per grape cluster, as shown in this image, barely allows for physiological ripeness of the grapes.

by premature harvest, overcropping, or drought (Schneider 2014).
- Vegetal-green aromas, the distinguishing mark of unripe grapes or any other fruits and deriving from a group of compounds designated as methoxypyrazines, colloquially referred to as 'MPs'. They are most often responsible for deficient aromatic ripeness under cool-climate conditions.

Vegetal-Green Aroma Caused by Methoxypyrazines (MPs)

The vegetal-green or herbaceous fraction of wine aroma caused by MPs is reminiscent of cut green grass and green capsicum. Everybody is familiar with this kind of smell from their daily lives, but optimistic expectancy or the emotional investment people might have in their own wines can prevent them from identifying it in them. Some also euphemistically describe it as 'vibrant green fruits'. It can be so intense that it eventually dominates the overall aroma such that one can no longer discern the desired, pleasurable aroma attributes such as ripe fruits, flowers, or minerals.

In some wine, such as those obtained from Sauvignon, MPs are accepted to contribute to varietal flavour, provided that their concentration does not exceed a certain limit and their contribution to total aroma is in balance with other aromatic compounds (Allen and Lacey 1993). If there is not such a balance, they dominate the flavour by their green-vegetative characteristics. Besides smell, they also adversely affect in-mouth sensations by sensory synergisms, feigning more acidity than the wine actually contains. In cool-climate growing areas, such a flavour feature can become a serious issue in bad years or after premature harvest

MPs are stored in the grapes before véraison, and their synthesis is accelerated under humid growing conditions. After crossing a concentration peak, they decrease continuously during ripening. This decrease is due to the impact of sunlight and correlates with the breakdown of acidity. All viticultural factors contributing directly or indirectly to a better exposure of the grapes to sunlight, including leaf removal, accelerate the decrease. Regardless of this photo-degradation induced by sun exposure, high temperatures during ripening act in the same way. However, high yield and humid climate act inversely. Leaf removal and cluster thinning are more effective means for decreasing MPs than a low number of buds during pruning. Fungal infection of unripe grapes yields higher concentrations not only because it mandates an early harvest, but also by promoting MP extraction from the prematurely destroyed skin tissue (Kotseridis et al. 1999).

Skins, seeds and stems contain more MPs than the respective juice fraction. As they are highly soluble, they are easily carried over from the grape tissues into the must, where they reach their maximum concentration after one day of skin contact. The presence of leaves and harsh mechanical grape processing such as excessive pumping and pressing give rise to a further enhancement, while removal of the last pressing fractions may lower their concentration. Furthermore, in freshly pressed juices, a certain amount of MPs are bound to solids. Thus, a proper juice clarification (*see* section 2.5) may help reduce them. However, there are no oenological measures able to completely avoid the appearance of vegetal-green flavour if this is an intrinsic feature of fruit quality.

Chemically, MPs are quite stable molecules. Common must and wine treatments related to finings, oxidation or reduction during vinification and storage hardly affect their concentration. In particular, the lack of any reactions with adsorbing materials is responsible for their stability against fining agents and filtration media. Their only reaction with practical importance is their photo-degradation discussed previously – that is, their breakdown under the influence of light. This reaction can also take place slowly after bottling in white glass. However, standard storage conditions in the dark do not facilitate any reduction of herbaceous flavour.

While there are no oenological means of efficiently reducing MP levels, yeast-derived aroma compounds can mitigate their vegetal-green flavour to a certain extent in very young wines. However, these secondary metabolites of yeasts have a relatively short life span. After approximately one year, and under improper cellar operations and storage conditions significantly faster, the yeast's impact on overall aroma has disappeared to a great extent (*see* section 3.1). Therefore, viticultural tools for exploiting the full aroma potential of ripe grapes and lowering their MP levels during ripening are of utmost importance. The most important of these tools is to postpone the time of picking as far as possible. Under cool-climate conditions, extending hang time rarely leads to what, in hot-climate areas, is pejoratively called an 'overripe' type of wine. Furthermore, whereas sugar levels and acidity can be easily corrected in the winery, a lack of aromatic ripeness cannot. Hence, it makes little sense attempting to preserve natural acidity as it is sought for sparkling wines when this is achieved at the expense of aromatic ripeness.

1.2 Sensory Assessments of Fruit Maturity

Since viewing sugar levels as the sole quality criterion has become unsatisfactory and obsolete, there have been significant efforts to replace it by a direct measurement of grape aroma potential. One analytical approach led to the determination of the so-called glycosyl-glucose. It is based on the assumption that the grape-derived aroma compounds, initially odourless and far too diverse for their individual measurement, are predominantly bound to glucose, from which they are gradually released during the winemaking process to become odour-active (Williams et al. 1995). Another method of determining aromatic ripeness is based on the fact that the aroma of most grape cultivars consists overwhelmingly of terpenols, which can be distilled off and measured in the distillate (Dimitriadis and Williams 1984).

Although results of such measurements correlate to some degree with sensorially perceived quality, unfortunately their routine use is far too cumbersome under commercial winemaking conditions. Therefore, the sensory evaluation of physiological ripeness remains of outstanding importance. Such an evaluation uses the human senses of touch, taste, smell and sight, as detailed below.

Ripe grape berries display a yellow-green and slightly transparent skin.

Visual Assessment of Grape Quality

- Lightly transparent, yellowish-green-coloured skins with golden shades indicate ripeness of white grapes; green skins reveal its lack.
- Behind the skins of the intact berries one can see the seeds.
- When perfect ripeness is reached, the berries can be easily removed from the stems, which are partially lignified and display a brown colour.
- Rotten grapes are easy to recognise and should be discarded at harvest. However, this becomes a problem when rot spreads strongly in rainy years. Musts from grapes with more than 10 per cent rotten berries require specific treatment, which is discussed in section 2.5.

The skin of ripe berries clearly reveals the seeds inside.

The seeds of ripe berries display a brown colour and can be easily detached from the pulp.

Grapes lacking physiological ripeness can be easily identified by their green and opaque skins.

Squeezing the Berries
- Ripe berries remain deformed after mild squeezing with the fingers, but unripe berries are elastic and turn back to their initial shape.
- When the berries are completely crushed, brown and hard seeds are easy to detach from the pulp if the grapes are ripe.
- If only a little juice can be squeezed out of a gelatinous pulp with adhering seeds, the grapes are underripe.
- Gelatinous adherence of the pulp to the skin or seeds goes along with a lack of ripeness.
- In unripe fruit, the seeds are green, soft or mealy; they also have a bitter flavour.

Smelling and Chewing the Berries
- It is easy to distinguish unripe berries from ripe ones only by smell. To be ripe, the pulp should be free of herbaceous notes and viscosity.
- In most aromatic cultivars (Bacchus, Ortega, Muscat varieties), the varietal aroma is already clearly recognisable in the smell of the squeezed berries, but hardly so in Sauvignon, in which it is only released by yeast during fermentation.
- The skins should be crumbly after chewing and not tough.

Fruit Sampling
The simple sensory assessments described above can yield very useful indicators of grape ripeness, but only if the sample tested is really appropriate. Conclusions about grape ripening status are often drawn from too small and unrepresentative grape samples. In practice, varieties and even blocks of the same variety are likely to have quite different ripening patterns. Hence, a systematic fruit sampling strategy is crucial to overcome the variability of ripeness within a vineyard block. It requires blind picking berries from numerous separate grape clusters, from different parts of the clusters, and from different parts of the canopy each time one walks through the rows. Generally, more than one sampling will need to be performed in each vineyard when the anticipated harvest date comes closer, in particular when there are weather changes affecting fruit quality expected.

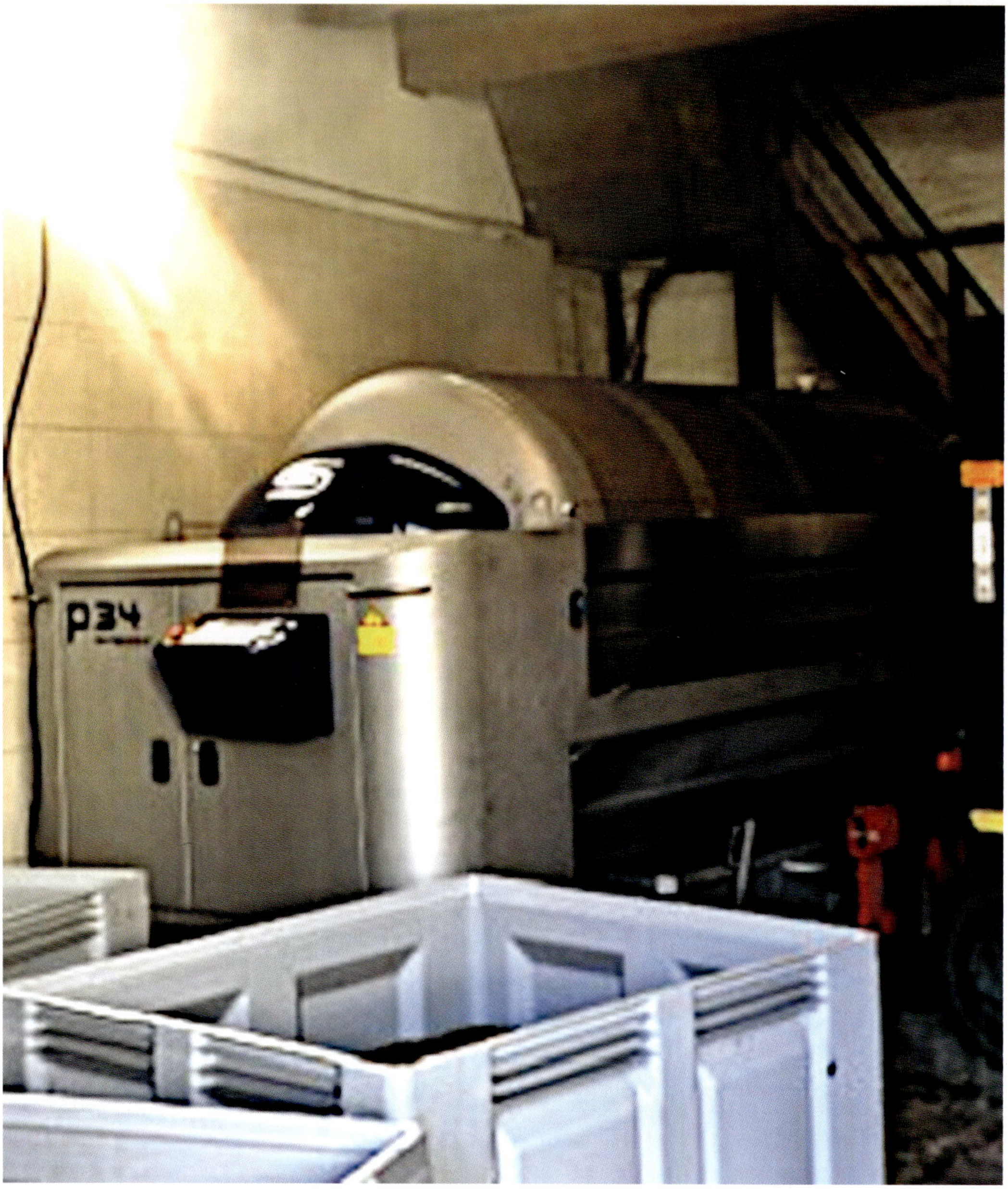
p34

CHAPTER 2

PRE-FERMENTATION STRATEGIES

Pre-fermentation operations performed between the grapes' crushing and the start of fermentation have a widely underestimated impact on wine quality and its sensory stability during storage. A skin contact period of up to one day is frequently used to enhance aromatics by their extraction from the skins, provided that the grapes are perfectly ripe. More important than the technical modalities of pressing is the issue of the generally recommended addition of sulphur dioxide to must. The oxidation and browning of must resulting from omitting it is not related to the oxidation of wine, and even mitigates it by lowering detrimental phenols, thus improving the wine's shelf life and reducing its astringency. Aroma losses frequently attributed to it only occur in a few specific grape varieties. Protein stabilisation by bentonite fining and any acidity corrections deemed necessary are already useful at this stage. Another important measure to achieve flawless wines with pristine aroma is juice clarification. Choice of clarification procedure is not decisive, but rather the level of clarification obtained, evaluated as residual turbidity. The use of pectolytic enzymes is strongly recommended for this purpose.

2.1 Must Acidification and the Issue of Safe pH

From a historical perspective, until the end of the twentieth century, must acidification had never played a major role in cool-climate growing areas. The acidity was usually high enough and often too high, so that deacidification was more important. High acidity was also accompanied by low pH, although this inverse correlation is weak. As is generally known in the wine industry, a low pH contributes to microbial safety. Hence, no thought had ever been given to microbial hazards caused by high pH levels. However, this situation has changed in the meantime, and the pH has become a hotly debated topic of conversation even in cool-climate areas. There are two reasons for that.

The first reason can be found in the development of the New World wine industry in the second half of the twentieth century. Most of their wine growing areas sprouted in hot regions that yielded low acidity and high pH figures. Therefore, acidification became a necessity to achieve a balanced taste and, at the same time, a decrease in pH to improve microbial safety.

OPPOSITE: **Closed-cage membrane press awaiting its next load of grapes.**

Since absolute safety was considered paramount, much importance was and still is attached to the lowering of pH to values considered safe through the addition of tartaric acid. As these countries quickly became opinion-leading in the global wine industry, the fear of supposedly too high pH levels spread to Old World wine-producing countries as well.

The second reason is global climate change. It has led to the fact that even in cool-climate growing areas, hot and dry vintages occur more often, providing musts with low acidity and actually high pH figures. That is why most of the countries concerned have now legalised must and wine acidification. This raises the question of how far the pH should be lowered and the acidity increased.

Interpreting pH Correctly

With a few exceptions, pH in musts ranges from 3.0 to 4.0. Some very conservative schools of thought continue advocating lowering pH to 3.5 for safety reasons and to add as much tartaric acid as necessary to achieve this goal regardless of the sensory outcome. As a consequence, many winemakers are terrified by higher pH figures, because they mean more risk of adverse microbial activity since SO_2 is less effective in the higher pH wine. This is absolutely true. The molecular gaseous fraction of free SO_2, which alone is responsible for microbial protection, decreases logarithmically with increasing pH (Figure 5.1).

Other winemakers have learnt to handle high pH musts and wines by using modern techniques such as cooling, filtration and sterile bottling that were not available some decades ago. These winemakers feel quite comfortable vinifying and bottling particularly high-end wines with pH in the range from 3.5 to 3.8, stating that wines acidified according to pH taste thin, harsh and tough. This is also true. Many of the great wines of the world would be considered undrinkable by contemporary quality standards if their pH was lowered to 3.5. Unpleasant wines that have been distorted by overacidification just for pH concerns are easy to find.

Factors Affecting pH

It is frequently believed that low titratable acidity (TA) automatically leads to high pH and vice versa. However, this relationship is not that clear, as shown in Figure 1.1. Indeed, pH is also affected by potassium. It is the most common alkali mineral cation in wine and neutralises acids. Just as acids drive pH down, potassium drives it up (Figure 4.4). Thus, the pH actually measured is the result of an interaction between acids and potassium. Musts with high TA from bad rainy years do not necessarily display low pH figures, because they also tend to have high potassium levels. However, the reverse can also become true when, in the course of global climate change, hot and dry growing conditions yield musts with little potassium (section 4.2).

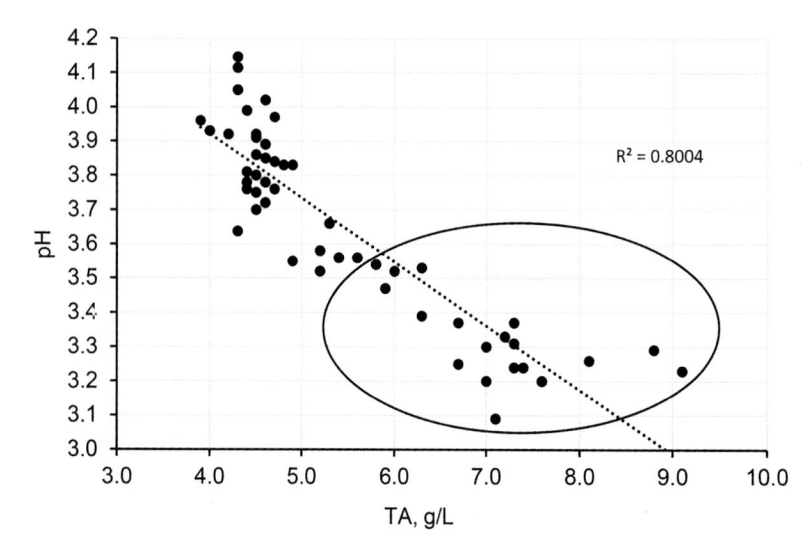

Figure 1.1: Relationship between titratable acidity (TA) and pH. Data in the oval circle represent white wines.

When Lowering pH Through Acidification is Really Necessary

Generally, a TA in the range of 7–9g/L and a pH of 3.2–3.6 is preferred in white musts. Somewhat higher acidity levels can be useful for the production of sparkling base wines. After the precipitation of potassium bitartrate during and after fermentation, wines generally display a lower TA and also a lower pH than the musts they have been obtained from (section 4.2). This counterintuitive behaviour, that despite less TA the pH is also lower, is partially explained by the decrease of potassium that accompanies this process. The pH decrease always occurs unless the initial must pH is above 4.1, which is practically never the case. Older theories, according to which the initial pH only decreases when it is below 3.65 and increases when it is above, are based on aqueous solutions that do not take into account the impact of alcohol content and ionic strength of wines (Boulton et al. 1996).

The pH drop due to potassium bitartrate precipitation relativises the significance of high pH figures in must. Only when must is actually high in pH (>3.8) or very low in acidity (for example, less than 6g/L TA), should these numbers be corrected by acidification at this early stage. For that purpose, tartaric acid is used, usually in amounts of 1 or 2g/L. It is the organic acid that gives the greatest reduction in pH. An addition of 1.0g/L tartaric acid leads to a reduction of pH by 0.15–0.20, depending on how much of it remains in solution and on the buffering capacity of the individual must. It is important to note in this context that about 80 per cent of sensorially perceived sourness is determined by TA, whilst pH only contributes approximately 20 per cent. Therefore, TA must be given at least the same importance as pH (Schneider and Troxell 2022).

Special Features of Acidification with Tartaric Acid

Tartaric acid differs from the other acids contained in wine in that it can precipitate as insoluble salts. This results in the following peculiarities of its application:

- The addition of 1.0g/L tartaric acid only temporarily increases TA by 1.0g/L, because a significant part of it precipitates together with potassium as a potassium bitartrate after some days or weeks.
- If the added tartaric acid were to precipitate completely as potassium bitartrate, an addition of 1.0g/L would only result in a permanent increase in TA of 0.5g/L. In practice, this value is usually around 0.6g/L.
- Potassium in wine contributes to sensory sensations that are described as volume, weight and body on the palate. Its inevitable decrease by addition of tartaric acid makes the wine thinner. Details are outlined in section 4.2.

These properties indicate that any acidification of must, if really necessary, should be approached with caution. Under cool-climate conditions, questions about acidity and pH management arise primarily in connection with deacidification. Whether this is performed on the must or in the wine depends on numerous factors. This issue will be discussed in detail in Chapter 4. Furthermore, it is not admissible to state in a simplified way, as so often happens in the lay press, that low pH or high TA improve the shelf life of wines. On the contrary, shelf life and aroma stability are primarily determined by variables such a phenolic composition and must treatment (section 2.2), oxygen uptake post-fermentation (Chapter 7) and storage temperature.

2.2 Reductive vs Oxidative Grape Processing

When white grapes are crushed without previous SO_2 additions, the juice they release undergoes rapid browning and displays a smell reminiscent of fresh bread. Many winemakers are startled by this appearance and believe it will remain in their later wine. Therefore, they immediately add SO_2 to the grapes or, at the latest, to the juice.

Grapes and wine contain polyphenolic compounds that easily oxidise to brown pigments when the juice picks up atmospheric oxygen. This oxidation is an enzymatic one caused by grape-derived enzymes called polyphenoloxidase (PPO) or, more specifically, tyrosinase. It results in a profound quantitative and

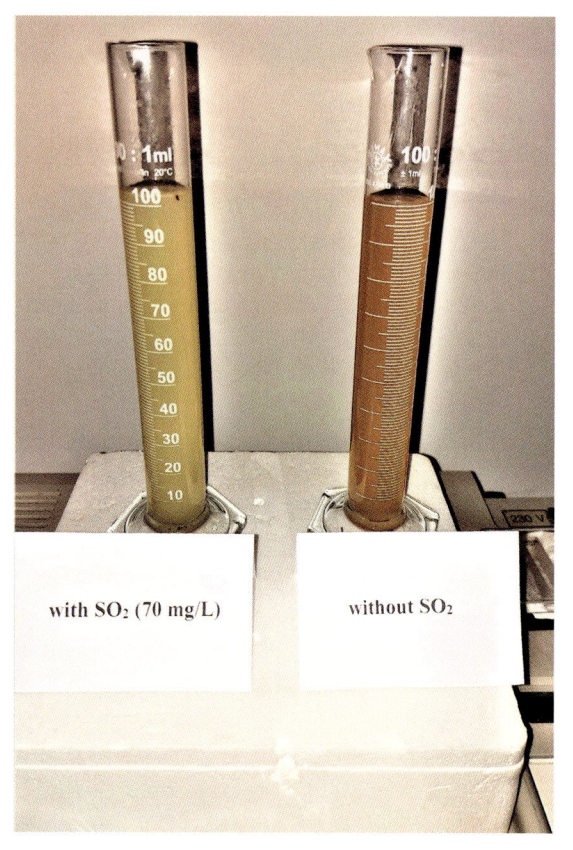

Juices without SO$_2$ added rapidly undergo browning during and after pressing.

qualitative change in the phenolic constitution of the juice. The process ends up with the oxidation and polymerisation of flavonoid phenols to larger molecular aggregates, which are insoluble in the aqueous environment of juice and precipitate as brown, solid particles.

Flavonoid phenols are also designated as flavonoids, flavanols or catechins. Together with their much larger counterpart in white wines, the nonflavonoid phenols, they constitute the total phenol content. While grape-derived nonflavonoids do not play a major sensory role, flavonoid levels describe very precisely the content of 'bad' phenols or tannins that the wine industry aims at minimising in white wines. Thanks to a relatively simple spectrophotometric method, they can be specifically measured in routine analysis and expressed as mg/L catechin equivalents, or CE (Zironi et al. 1992, Schneider 2019).

Back to the crush pad. Musts can keep up to 8mg/L oxygen in solution. To the extent that this dissolved oxygen is consumed by phenols before, during and after pressing, the must can absorb further amounts of it, which are also consumed. At some point, after sufficient oxygen has been taken up and consumed by the phenols, flavonoid phenols are almost all precipitated. This is illustrated in Figure 2.1 on the basis of four musts.

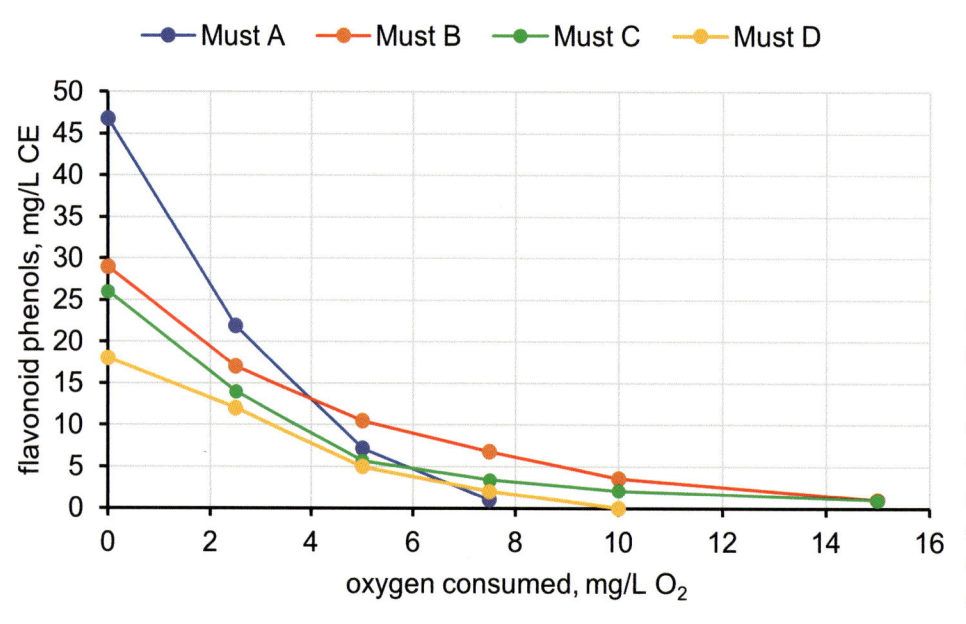

Figure 2.1: Precipitation of flavonoid phenols during oxidation of four white grape musts as a function of the amount of oxygen consumed.

When solid brown flavonoid particles are removed from the juice by filtration, the juice left behind displays the normal green-yellow colour of standard white wines. In practice, the particles are removed during juice clarification via settling or otherwise. The smell of fresh bread disappears at the latest on the second day of fermentation due to the reductive strength of the yeast (Schneider 1998).

Interestingly, there is no direct correlation between the amount of oxygen consumed and the extent of flavonoid phenol precipitation. One of the reasons is variable levels of glutathione, a peptide that acts as a reducing agent (section 5.4) and interferes in the reaction (Singleton et al. 1985). However, it can be stated that in about 90 per cent of all juices, the oxygen absorbed during and after pressing (Cheynier et al. 1993, Day et al. 2019) is sufficient to precipitate the great majority of flavonoids in a few hours if the process is not stopped beforehand by the addition of SO_2.

Sensory Properties of Flavonoid Phenols

Since the primary sensory results of must oxidation derive from the depletion of flavonoids, a closer look at their sensory properties is helpful to understand fully the impact of oxidative or reductive grape processing on the resulting wine.

Colour

Flavonoids are the only phenols in white wine able to produce significant browning under conditions of oxygen uptake. Their concentration correlates with the browning rate and intensity (Schneider 1998, Lee and Jaworski 1988, Salacha et al. 2008).

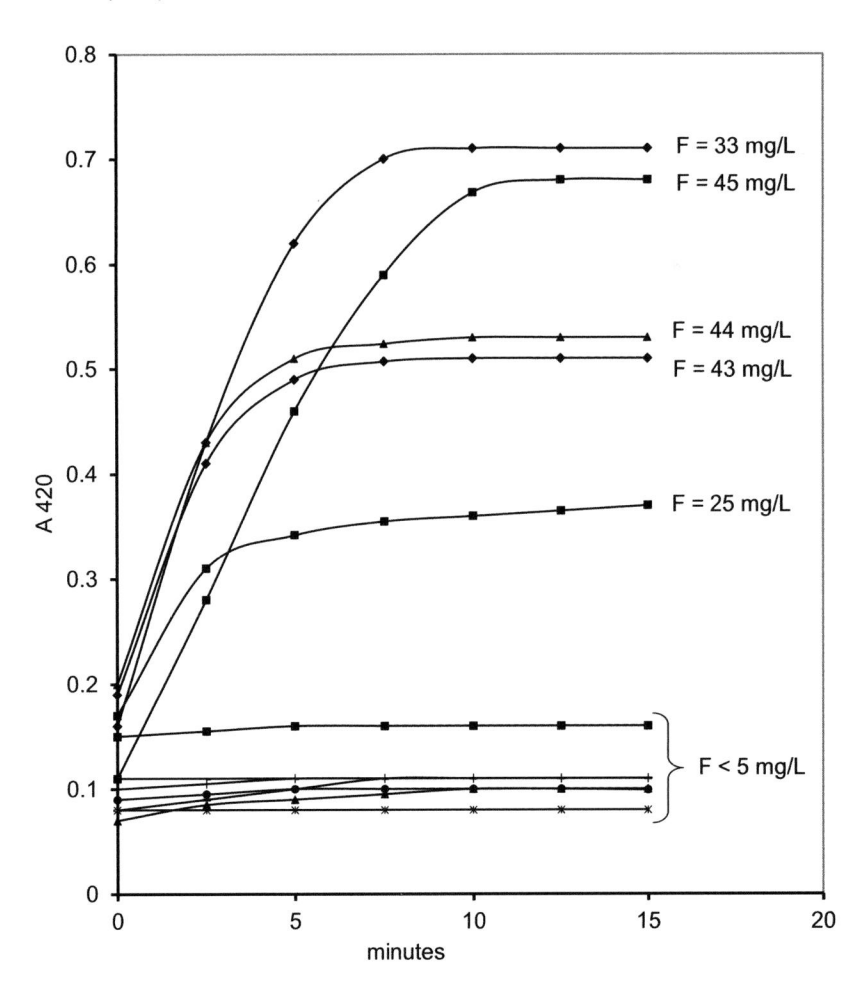

Figure 2.2: Time course of browning (A 420) in young filtered white wines exposed to air without SO_2 additions as a function of their content of flavonoid phenols (F).

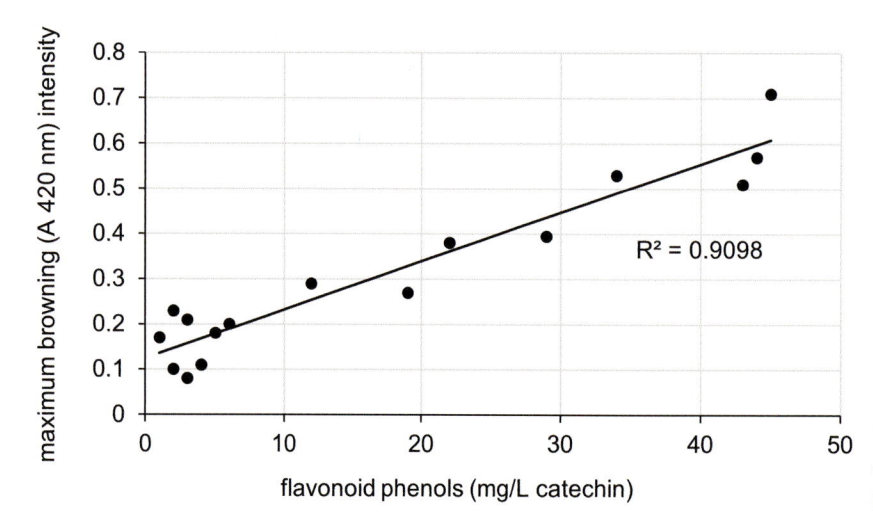

Figure 2.3: Relationship between flavonoid content and maximum browning intensity in white wines.

Figure 2.2 depicts the course of browning over time in young filtered white wines kept under air without any SO_2 additions. Under these conditions, wines containing less than 5mg/L of flavonoids remain almost stable in colour. Browning was measured spectrophotometrically as the absorbance at 420nm (A 420).

The higher the flavonoid content, the more intense is the resulting browning, as clearly shown in Figure 2.3. This browning potential is the direct visible evidence of a wine's propensity to undergo drastic chemical changes upon oxygen uptake. The underlying reaction of browning is the polymerisation of monomeric flavonoids to polymeric pigments. Before analytical methods for flavonoid measurements were available, the sensory stability of the wine was estimated visually, based on the browning intensity in the absence of free SO_2.

The same applies when juices from red grapes intended for the elaboration of rosé or Blanc de noir wines are oxidised. After juice clarification, their slightly red colour reappears, although some anthocyanins responsible for that colour will inevitably have been destroyed by oxidation. However, these losses are generally not strong enough to completely remove red colour as is required for Blanc de noir production. Instead, the use of charcoal, bentonite or a specific enzyme will be required for that purpose (section 2.5).

Taste

With regard to taste, flavonoids are by far the most important drivers of astringency, bitterness, and what is called 'phenolic taste'. When they undergo polymerisation during wine ageing, their astringency and colour increase (Lea et al. 1979, Delcour et al. 1984, Robichaud and Noble 1990). Hence, astringency of white wines also depends on their age. The increasing astringency of white wines displaying relatively high flavonoid levels is a phenomenon widely known by practitioners. When it occurs, it is usually noticed long before any visible browning can be observed. Table 1

Table 1: Sensory assessment and technological evaluation of flavonoid concentrations in white wines

Concentration (mg/L catechin)	Interpretation
1	Lowest value ever measured
3–5	White wines with long shelf life
~ 10	Astringency caused by flavonoids can be perceived
15–25	White wines obtained by consistently reductive grape and juice processing
≥20	Accentuated astringency, which is always perceived as such

gives an overview of the evaluation of flavonoid phenol concentrations in white wines. Of course, the hedonic appraisal of astringency depends on that one is used to and on the cultural context.

Odour
With regard to odour, flavonoids are non-volatile and odourless. Nevertheless, they affect aroma perceived by smell, long-term aroma stability, and white wine shelf life in general when they interact with oxygen. The odour changes occurring thereby are designated as oxidative or typical ageing. It is reminiscent of dry herbs, boiled potatoes, canned mushrooms, corn, boiled vegetables, honey, toasted bread, nuts, among others. These aroma attributes appear long before any taste and colour changes can be observed. They

Figure 2.4: Impact of flavonoid phenols on oxidative ageing as perceived by smell of two bottled white wines sealed with cork after eighteen months' bottle storage. n = eighteen tasters.

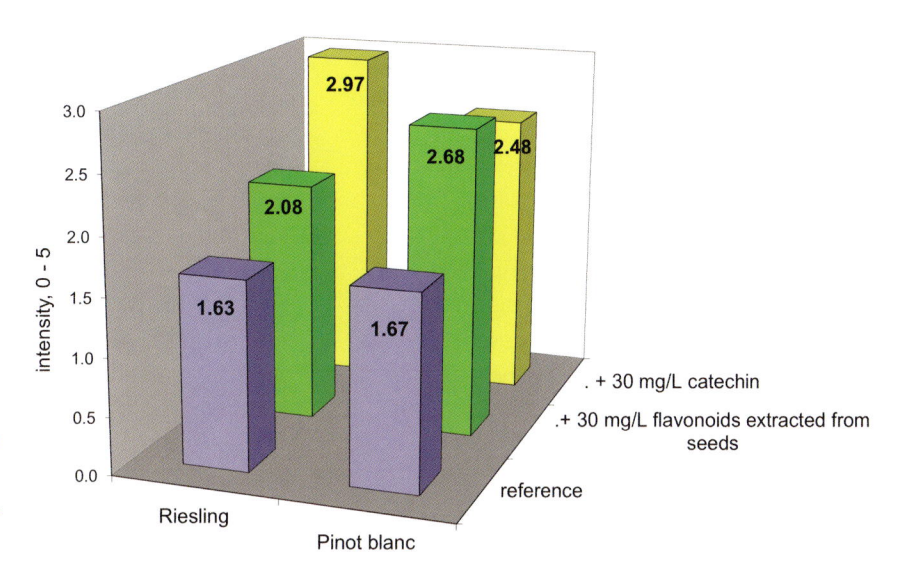

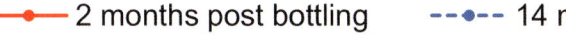

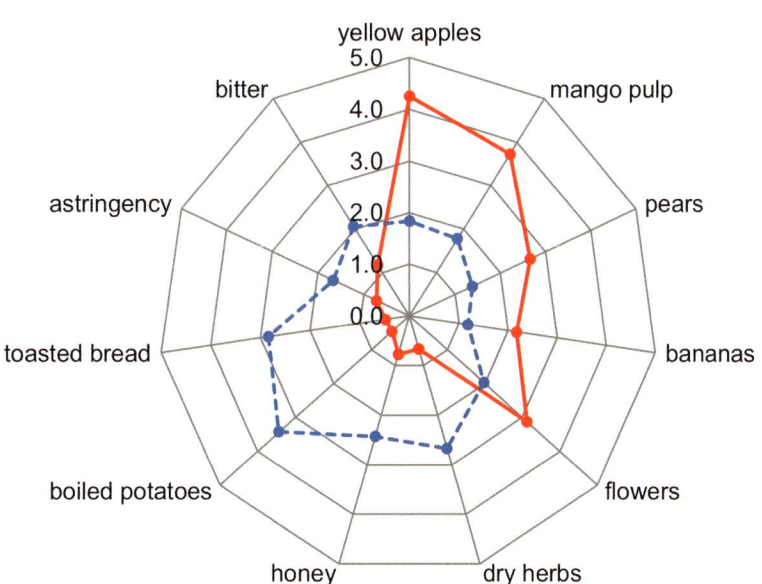

Figure 2.5: Example of accelerated typical ageing of an unoaked Chardonnay sealed with cork during twelve months of bottle storage at 18°C.

also occur in the presence of free SO_2, but are greatly accelerated when free SO_2 is no longer present. Any increase in colour indicates that profound flavour modifications have already taken place.

Ultimately, there is a close relationship between the content of flavonoid phenols and oxidative ageing as perceived by smell when white wines are aged under conditions of mild oxygen uptake as it can occur through certain bottle closures (section 8.4). Figure 2.4 shows this effect on two white varietal wines supplemented with flavonoid phenols extracted from grape seeds and the same amount of a pure flavonoid, (+)-catechin. Similar results can be expected when commercial grape tannins are added to white wines. However, these effects are largely absent if the wine is stored under oxygen exclusion.

When this effect of odourless flavonoids on aroma stability was documented for the first time (Schneider 1989), it was hypothesised that flavonoids act as a sort of catalyst in the formation of oxidative ageing perceived by smell to an extent not known from other grape-derived phenols. It would take another quarter of a century before this phenomenon was substantiated by analytical data: for three chemical markers of oxidative ageing – methional, phenylacetaldehyde and sotolon – an increased formation was shown in the presence of elevated contents of flavonoids under conditions of nanooxygenation, prevailing when bottles are sealed with oxygen-permeable closures (section 8.4). Oxidation products of flavonoids and acetaldehyde were hypothesised to be responsible for that formation. Out of 54 white wines bottled with cork closures, those displaying less than 3mg/L flavonoids showed no noticeable formation of sotolon, methional and phenylacetaldehyde during prolonged bottle ageing. The winery and winemaking techniques had a strong effect (Pons et al. 2015). Figure 2.5 gives an example of how this process of typical ageing affects both smell and taste in a way most consumers reject. White wine ageing is rarely perceived as positive.

It is important to emphasise that 2-aminoacetophenone, which is often listed in the context of white wine ageing, does not belong to the aforementioned group of oxidation markers. It is the impact molecule of a distinct kind of ageing denominated as 'atypical ageing', which in reality is an aroma defect reminiscent of mothballs and furniture varnish emerging sometimes in rather young wines a few weeks or months post-fermentation. It is induced by viticultural stress factors as the ultimate cause. Although oxygen is involved in its formation, it is only required in trace amounts that are far from sufficient to trigger oxidative ageing (Schneider 2014). Viticultural factors also are at the root of the so-called 'petrol flavour', which occurs primarily in aged Riesling wines regardless of oxygen exposure. These differences underline the importance of sensory discrimination between different types of ageing, precursors, and reaction mechanisms.

The Difference Between Typical Ageing and 'Premox'

Obviously, flavonoids are not the only driver of detrimental white wine ageing. Oxygen exposure, storage temperature and free SO_2 levels play an additional role. As odourless non-volatile phenols, flavonoids act as a catalyst accelerating the degradation of fruity varietal aroma only in the presence of oxygen when wine picks it up under inappropriate cellar storage conditions (section 7.2) or through certain bottle closures (section 8.4). The chemical reactions involved also occur in the presence of free SO_2 (section 5.1). Their sensory outcome is a progressive drift of the fruity or floral aroma attributes of young wines towards those previously discussed (Figure 2.5). This is what is designated as oxidative or typical ageing, but not yet as distinctive oxidation. When wine is stored under absolute oxygen exclusion, as happens in rare cases, flavonoids only act on the palate as the main driver of astringency and also contribute to bitterness.

When oxygen uptake causes the complete disappearance of free SO_2 by oxidation, this adverse development is accelerated. Concomitantly, acetaldehyde is released from its SO_2-bound form and dominates the aroma profile with its typical smell of sherry and bruised apples (section 5.1). This equates to a complete oxidative breakdown and is called 'premature oxidation' or 'premox' when it occurs in a relatively early stage of wine ageing. The cause is that free SO_2 before bottling was not adjusted to the oxygen exposure of the wine (section 8.4).

Reductive Grape Processing Preserves Flavonoid Phenols

Returning from the sensory aspects of flavonoids to the basic outcome of must oxidation:

- Must oxidation leads to a depletion of flavonoid phenols, which are nothing but tannins with their well-known astringent and bitter flavour that is quite unpopular in white wines. Thus, sensory problems of that kind, as well as wine finings required for their rectification, are largely avoided.
- Flavonoids that are removed by must oxidation are no longer available for oxidation and browning in wine. The wine's susceptibility to ageing greatly diminishes.

However, traditional oenological teaching erroneously associates juice oxidation with wine oxidation. Accordingly, it advocates impeding juice oxidation by the addition of sulphur dioxide, thus preventing it from browning. The basic role of SO_2 in this context is to irreversibly inactivate polyphenol oxidase (PPO), which is a grape-derived enzyme that transfers oxygen to phenols. Consequently, dissolved oxygen (DO) is no longer depleted by PPO activity. For that purpose, the presence of only a small amount of less than 10mg/L free SO_2 is necessary, as shown in figure 2.6.

However, these tiny amounts of free SO_2 are misleading, because in order to obtain them, it is necessary to add at least twice the amount, since in musts within the standard SG range, about 55 per cent of the added SO_2 is loosely bound to glucose. Moreover, a much more important decrease of SO_2 results from its oxidation. This effect is highly variable and depends on the amount of oxygen picked up before, during and after pressing. Considering all these aspects, 50mg/L are usually added to must when the intention is to prevent its oxidation.

In commercial winemaking and due to SO_2 losses by oxidation, the last pressings of a press cycle frequently drain from the press without any free SO_2 at all. For this reason, some wineries have moved to increase the SO_2 addition to 70mg/L upon crushing in cases where must oxidation is to be completely prevented and flavonoid phenols preserved. Figure 2.7 shows the result. In this real-world example, oxidation was not measured as the DO consumption rate as in the previous figure, but as residual flavonoids before and after fermentation. Note that flavonoids decrease by about 20 per cent during fermentation due to adsorption by yeast.

If, as in the last case illustrated, the oxidation of the juice is completely prevented, phenols are protected

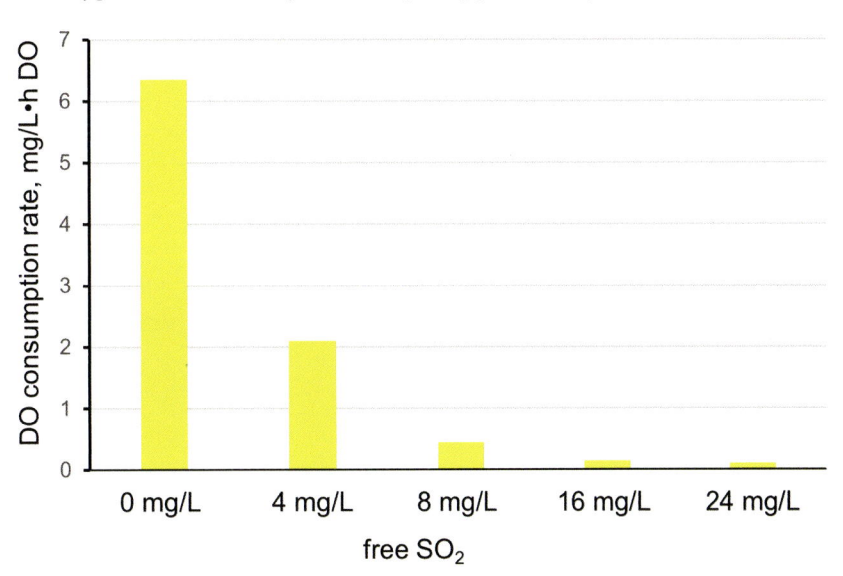

Figure 2.6: Effect of free SO_2 on the oxygen consumption rate of must.

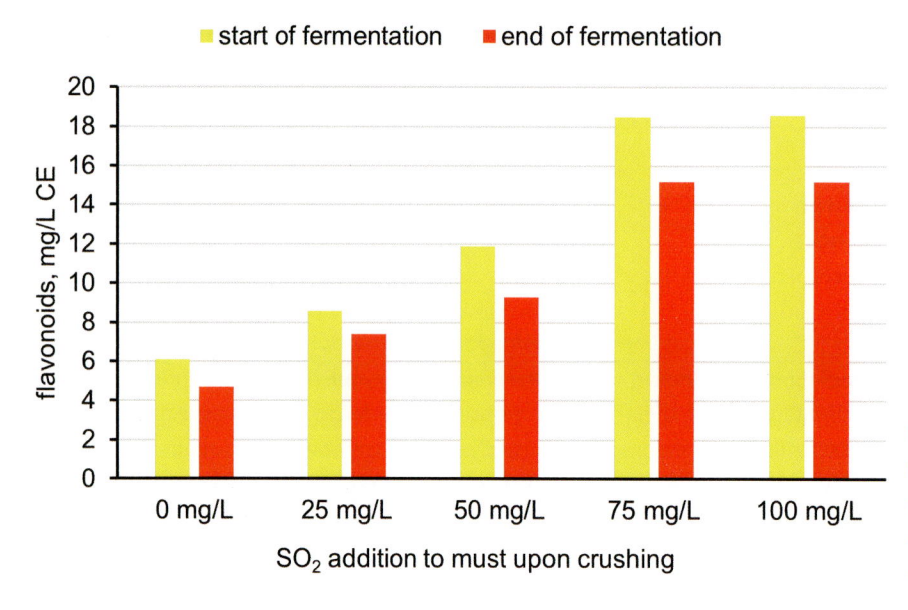

Figure 2.7: Flavonoid levels in white juice and young wine as a function of SO$_2$ additions upon crushing.

from oxidation, remain soluble in the juice, and find themselves in the resulting wine. Concomitantly, the juice remains green. Following this line of reasoning, adding SO$_2$ on the crush pad has become one of the central dogmas of oenological doctrine for generations of oenologists. Here and there, the effect of SO$_2$ is complemented by addition of ascorbic acid and the use of inert gases during grape processing and juice handling. Both additions are known to remove dissolved oxygen indispensable for oxidation. In doing so, one obtains wines with significant higher levels of total and flavonoid phenols, which are presented in section 2.4.

Different Levels of Must Oxidation

At the opposite extreme lies deliberate oxidative juice processing, going so far as to actively oxidise the juice by injecting air or pure oxygen. Between these

Table 2: Reductive vs oxidative juice processing in white wine production. Impact of SO$_2$ and oxygen prior to fermentation on the sensory stability of white wine during ageing

oxidation prior to fermentation ↓	Hyper-reduction	Extreme protection against oxidation by use of SO$_2$, ascorbic acid and inert gas on fruit, upon pressing, and during juice processing. No oxidation.
	Reductive vinification	Addition of SO$_2$ and perhaps ascorbic acid, limited oxygen uptake during juice processing. No oxidation.
	Standard vinification	Addition of SO$_2$ to fruit or juice without special measures to avoid oxygen uptake. Some oxidation.
	Oxidative vinification	No addition of SO$_2$ prior to fermentation, no measures to impede oxygen uptake. Passive oxidation.
	Active juice oxidation (hyper-oxidation)	No addition of SO$_2$ prior to fermentation, deliberate supply of air or pure oxygen to juice. Actively promoted oxidation. ↑ susceptibility of oxidative ageing

extremes, there is a broad range of gradual differences between reductive and oxidative juice processing, as illustrated in Table 2.

The term 'must hyperoxidation' as it is generally used to refer to oxidative juice processing is insufficient to precisely convey the gradual differences outlined in Table 2. Rather, it means the active oxidation of juice by a deliberate supply of air or pure oxygen. However, a certain level of juice oxidation is also achieved by passive oxygen uptake during grape and juice processing. For that purpose, it's sufficient to forgo any SO_2 additions prior to fermentation. Under these conditions, PPO's enzymatic activity is preserved so that it transfers dissolved oxygen to phenols, whose flavonoid fraction is depleted.

Typical Flavonoid Concentrations in White Wines

The critical concentration limits reported in Table 1 require a classification of their magnitude. Surveys on white wines in several countries yielded the following mean concentrations of flavonoids, each expressed as the sum of catechins:

- 15.1mg/L on 57 wines from France (Carando et al. 1999)
- 11.7mg/L on 29 wines from South Africa (de Villiers et al. 2005)
- 13.6mg/L on 41 wines from Portugal (Ribeiro de Lima et al. 2006)
- 18.1mg/L on 16 wines from Greece (Anastasiadi et al. 2009)
- 9.3mg/L on 37 wines from Austria (Schneider 2009)
- 15.3mg/L on 14 wines from the Czech Republic (Lampiř et al. 2013)

A more comprehensive survey (Goldberg et al. 1999) on 664 commercial white wines from all important varieties and growing areas of the world yielded averages of 5.9mg/L for Chardonnay, 6.1mg/L for Sauvignon, 4.6mg/L for Riesling and 5.2mg/L for Pinot gris and blanc, with differences related to country, climate, winemaking techniques and traditions.

The entirety of data shows that reductive or oxidative vinification is implemented to varying degrees, as shown in Table 2. It also reveals that in many wineries there is much room for improvement regarding shelf life and varietal aroma stability by lowering flavonoid phenols.

Differences Between Must and Wine Oxidation

As many winemakers are appalled by the browning of juice and associate it with browning of wine, we need to emphasise that these are two completely different reactions with different consequences. Their long-term effects are even diametrically opposed. The basic differences can be summarised as follows:

- The oxidation of juice is an enzymatic one, specific to phenols, and induced by grape-derived polyphenol oxidase as long as it is not inactivated by SO_2. In contrast, the oxidation of wine is a chemical one, nonspecific and affecting all wine compounds. It is only partially inhibited by SO_2.
- The by-product of enzymatic oxidation by tyrosinase in juice is only water (Solomon et al. 2001). Non-enzymatic oxidation of wine, however, generates hydrogen peroxide and oxygen radicals, both of which are extremely reactive with far-reaching consequences for wine aroma (section 5.1).
- In both cases, phenols oxidise. In juice, their oxidation products precipitate as brown solids. Conversely, in wine they are soluble and thus sensorially active in wine's alcoholic environment. Their insolubility in juice is easy to verify, as juice filtration yields a filtrate of the normal green-yellow colour of standard white wines.

The deliberate oxidation of white grape must was first investigated in the 1970s when the development of mechanical harvesting, associated with severe mechanical fruit treatment and long skin contact times, led to an increase in phenols that resulted in astringent, coarse white wines with short shelf life. In the intervening period, it has become disseminated to some extent in cool-climate growing areas, where low harvest temperatures make SO$_2$ additions pre-fermentation unnecessary for microbial control. The reasons for its uptake are superior sensory results and better shelf life of the resulting wines. However, when must oxidation in the absence of SO$_2$ is performed under hot harvest conditions, effective must cooling has to be ensured to avoid microbial spoilage.

Ultimately, the decision for or against must oxidation typically depends on the individual's professional training and environment. Hence, winemakers divide themselves into two distinct camps: the Green Juice Club, seeking to maintain 'healthy juice' by adding SO$_2$ at the crusher; and the Brown Juice Club, adding nothing at the crusher. The former are cherished by the oenological products industry, because they rely on fining agents to reduce the astringency caused by flavonoids and, sometimes, on additional supplements that are allegedly required to reinforce the reductive effect of SO$_2$. Meanwhile, members of the latter club get nervous when their juice doesn't become as brown as expected and question how it is possible that the supply industry dictates official teaching.

Sensory Effects of Must Oxidation

To the extent that oxidation is prevented pre-fermentation, the propensity to oxidise shifts to the wine stage with all the sensory consequences derived therefrom (Table 2 and Figure 2.4). Phenols are the primary oxygen acceptors in wine, and hence phenols that are removed by oxidation and clarification of juice are no longer available for oxidation in wine. The basic outcome is a better resistance of white wine to oxidative ageing under otherwise comparable conditions. Furthermore, the entire range of fining agents commercialised for decreasing phenols, astringency and bitterness (section 8.2) becomes superfluous. Wines made from properly oxidised musts rarely display astringent phenols, also known as tannins.

The better flavour stability, less or no browning potential, and greater resistance to oxidative ageing of wines obtained from oxidised musts have long been acknowledged. From this perspective, flavonoid levels of less than 5mg/L are considered desirable (Pons et al. 2015). They can always be achieved when must oxidation is performed, although variable

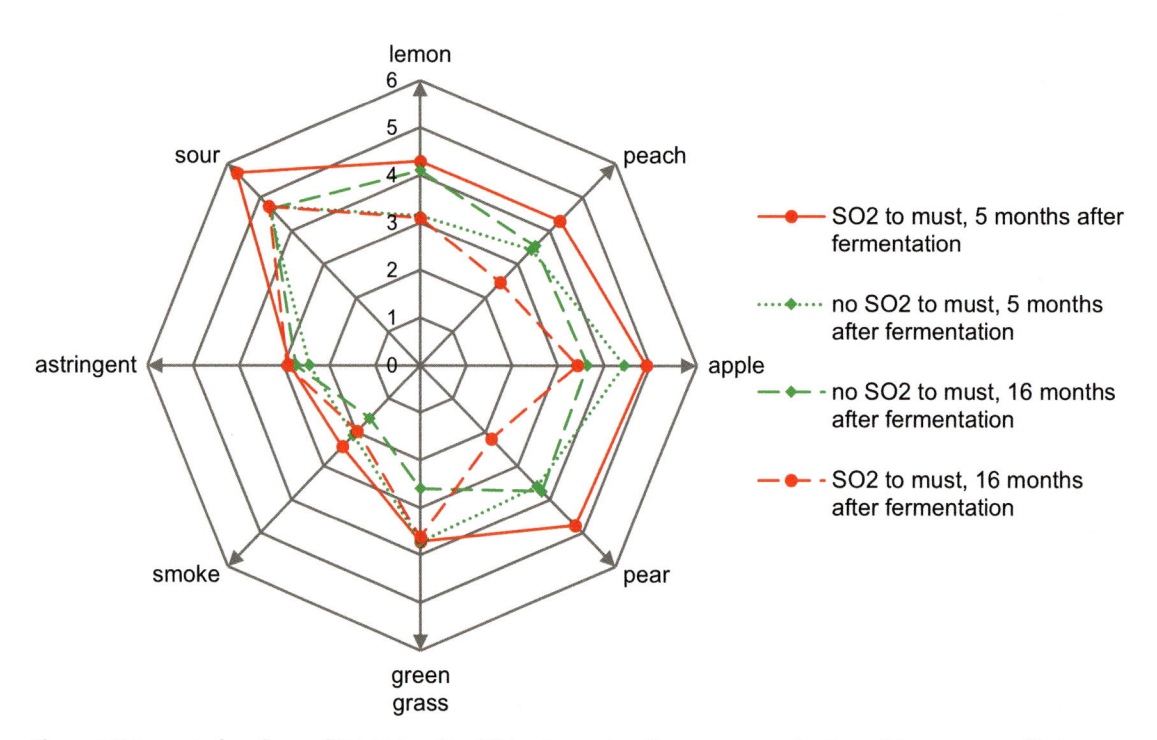

Figure 2.8: Impact of ageing and SO$_2$ (60mg/L) addition to must on the sensory evaluation of the aroma profile in Riesling. n = twelve panellists.

amounts of consumed oxygen might be required. Under cool-climate growing conditions, passive must oxidation fulfils this purpose in approximately 95 per cent of juices.

The major and enduring argument invoked against must oxidation is that it adversely affects wine aroma. This is certainly true for Sauvignon blanc and similar varieties in whose aroma thiols are involved (section 5.4). More often, however, psychological factors are more influential, when the oxidation of must is falsely associated with the oxidation of wine. Nonetheless, there are about 30 published peer-reviewed sensory studies on must oxidation from all over the world, the results of which have been summarised in a kind of meta-analysis (Schneider 1998, 2019). In simple terms, the totality of these comparative trials yielded sensory results that were positive for one third, negative for another third, and without difference for the remaining third of the wines obtained from oxidised musts. In the light of these findings, the often invoked, one-sided rejection of must oxidation is not justified. Nevertheless, results are indeed conflicting. These contradictions can be explained by variable boundary conditions such as variable oxygen supply, residual turbidity after juice clarification (section 2.5), yeast strains and fermentation kinetics (section 3.1), post-fermentation storage conditions (Chapter 7), sensory evaluation at different time points of wine ageing, different concepts of quality and so on. In particular, the time when the evaluation takes place will affect the result. An example is given in Figure 2.8.

Frequently, SO_2 addition to must enhances fruity or floral aroma attributes in very young wine. Over time, however, the result reverses, because these attributes are faster masked by increasing attribute intensities of oxidative ageing. In contrast, fruity varietal aroma is better preserved during ageing when wines are obtained from oxidised musts. In summary, must oxidation does not provide any short-term benefits in the young wine, but is primarily an investment in the future of the wine.

The Special Case of Sauvignon Blanc
However, there is agreement on systematic and irreversible aroma losses brought about by must oxidation on cultivars with sensorially significant levels of oxygen-sensitive aroma thiols. These cultivars primarily comprise Sauvignon blanc (Coetzee and du Toit 2012), followed at some distance by some other varieties of regional importance. In musts obtained from these cultivars, aroma thiols occur as bound to glutathione and cysteine. Only when they are released from these odourless precursors by a specific enzymatic activity of certain yeast strains do they become odour-active. Interestingly, the concentration of the precursors themselves is not affected by must oxidation since they are not sensitive to oxygen. On the other hand, addition of glutathione to the must induces an increase of the production of odour-active thiols in the resulting wine. Conversely, they are lowered when glutathione is removed by must oxidation (Roland et al. 2010). In short, losses of aroma thiols due to oxidative must processing of these varieties are not caused by their oxidation in the must but rather by the decrease of glutathione levels required to produce them on the crush pad and to protect them from oxidation in the later wine (section 5.4). In this context, it is crucial to note that the aroma intensity of other aroma-intensive varieties such as Gewürztraminer and Ortega, whose aroma is based on terpenols instead of thiols, is not affected by must oxidation. Bacchus falls somewhere in between.

Stabilisation and Storage of Very Reductively Produced Wines
Trials with extremely reductive must processing using high additions of SO_2, ascorbic acid and nitrogen blanketing before, during and after pressing are not a phenomenon of the modern age, but were already conducted in the 1970s in numerous European countries. They were quickly abandoned when serious problems with wine shelf life and astringency arose. Depending on zeitgeist and the prevailing winemaking doctrine, such trials are periodically repeated. One of the reasons is the global propagation of Sauvignon, whose aroma does indeed require rigorous oxidation protection from the moment grapes are crushed.

As previously shown, depending upon the extent to which oxidation is prevented before fermentation, the disposition to oxidise shifts to the stage of wine with all sensory consequences derived therefrom. Hence, very reductive must handling yields fragile wines intended for early consumption, but hardly white wines suitable for longer bottle ageing. It requires a similar markedly reductive handling of the wines during their stabilisation, storage and bottling, including careful protection against inadvertent oxygen uptake (section 7.2), in order to take account of their poor resistance to oxygen uptake. Depending on the wines' flavonoid content and the astringency derived therefrom, the use of adequate fining agents can become advisable (section 8.2). When such finings are performed, the rules of gentle wine treatment (section 7.3) must be respected. However, under real-world conditions, wine handling post-fermentation is not always gentle, often leading to oxygen uptake that is completely undesirable for such oxygen-sensitive wines. If the answer to premature oxidative ageing is an even more reductive must processing, a vicious circle closes.

2.3 Skin Contact

Most grape-derived aroma compounds are located in the berry skins. Hence, a skin contact period of several hours or even days is sometimes performed between crushing and pressing to enhance their extraction and improve varietal characteristics. The standard period for this purpose is one day or overnight, with longer durations rarely extracting additional positive aromatics. The sensory results largely depend on fruit quality, ripeness, and the maceration variables such as duration, temperature, and the presence or absence of sulphur dioxide. From a merely analytical perspective, the effects can be summarised as follows:

- Increase of potassium, pH and nitrogen, the latter including yeast-assimilable nitrogen (section 3.1).
- Decrease of tartaric acid and TA resulting from the increased potassium levels (section 4.2).
- Increase of all kinds of phenolics, in particular of sensorially relevant flavonoid phenols.
- Increase of aromatic components and their respective precursors, depending on their type and on the amount actually present in the grapes. Ripe fruit of aromatic varieties such as Gewürztraminer, Bacchus, Muscat and Sauvignon respond more strongly to skin contact than neutral varieties, though the differences are slight.

The latter point explains why it makes no sense to submit bad fruit to a maceration period. From underripe grapes, at best methoxypyrazines (section 1.1) are extracted, which enhance the vegetal-green aroma of the resulting wine. From grapes damaged by rot (>5 per cent), metabolic products of the fungi are extracted and convey an earthy, mouldy flavour that is difficult to tackle at a later stage. These considerations mean that only perfect fruit should be used for skin contact, and even then, the sensory results in terms of overall quality are highly variable. The primary reason is the simultaneous extraction of flavonoid phenols with sensory consequences discussed in the previous section. Thus, the sensory effect of aroma enhancement can be readily cancelled out or even reversed during storage.

Effect of Temperature and SO_2 During Skin Contact

Warmth facilitates extraction. Thus, the holding temperature during the skin contact period has considerable influence on the extraction of all kinds of grape compounds. This is especially true for the extraction of flavonoids, but there is no clear trend linking the much-sought aroma concentration with skin contact temperature. In order to limit flavonoid extraction, skin contact for enhancing aroma is frequently run as 'cold soak' after cooling the must. However, the extreme form of this approach, cryoextraction at approximately 5°C, does not bring any additional benefits. It is crucial to note that temperatures above 15°C as well as mechanical disintegration of the must by upstream pumping cycles strongly boost flavonoid extraction (Ramey et al. 1986, Marais 1998). Contemporary closed-cage horizontal membrane presses offer the useful facility to perform skin contact within the press and to proceed to pressing without further pumping.

When active cooling is required to prevent the onset of fermentation during skin contact, recirculation of the whole must through an external cooling unit should be avoided, since the mechanical strain imposed by this

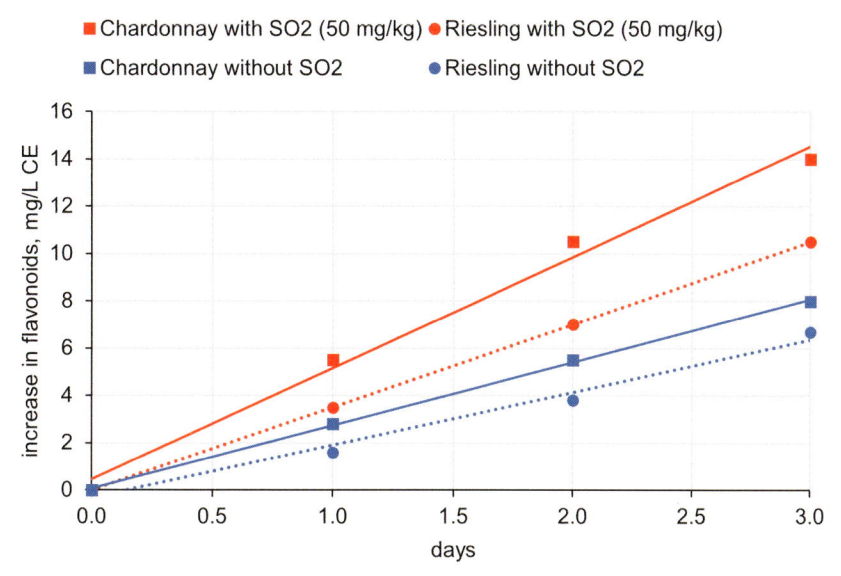

Figure 2.9: Extraction of flavonoid phenols as a function of SO_2 during skin contact (13°C, after destemming) of two varieties.

causes a strong increase of flavonoids and solids after pressing. Instead, double-jacketed cooling tanks or dry ice should be preferred. Dry ice must be added evenly when filling the maceration vessel. Whenever mixing is deemed necessary, it should be performed by injecting a gas rather than pumping over.

The absence or presence of SO_2 has the most decisive influence on the accumulation of flavonoids during a maceration period. If no SO_2 is present, flavonoid accumulation in the liquid phase is largely offset by their precipitation due to the effect of must oxidation. An example of this effect is shown for two varieties in Figure 2.9. For the same purpose, deliberate juice oxidation after skin contact was particularly recommended a long time ago (Cheynier et al. 1989).

When skin contact is limited to a couple of hours, previous destemming has only limited impact on flavonoid uptake since seeds continue to be present as a potential source of flavonoids. Selective extraction of stems, skins, and seeds of *Vitis vinifera* cultivars shows that approximately half of total flavonoids originate from the seeds.

Orange Wine, or Skin Contact to the Extreme

Consideration of duration of maceration offers the proper context to briefly discuss orange or amber

Orange wines acquire their amber colour from high levels of flavonoid phenols extracted during fermentation on the skins and post-fermentation maceration.

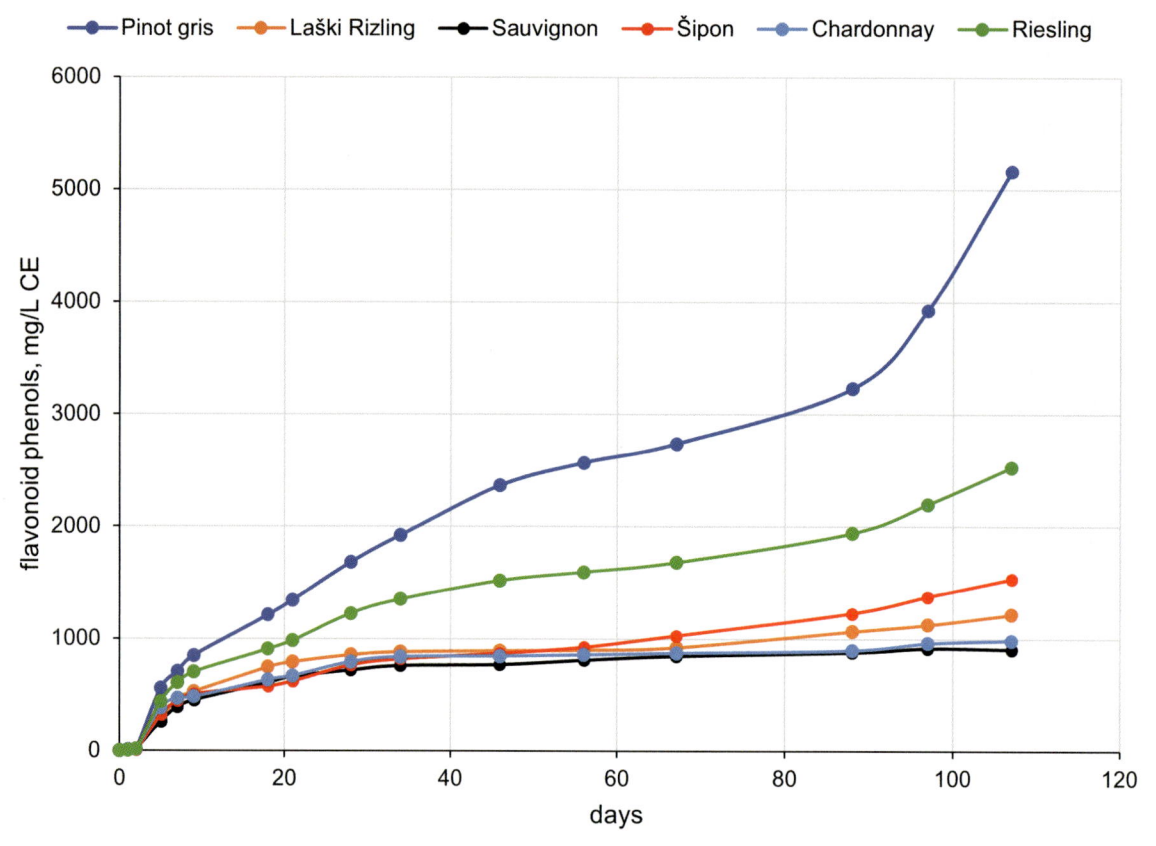

Figure 2.10: Extraction of flavonoid phenols during maceration of white grapes of different *V. vinifera* varieties intended for orange wine production. Must homogenisation is achieved by punching down three times per day during active fermentation.

wines. They are frequently referred to as 'amphora wines', though their storage in clay amphorae was only a technical necessity millennia ago when the first wines were produced in the area between the Black and Caspian seas. Contemporary containers do the job just as well, since the key element of orange wine production is an extended skin contact period of white varieties including fermentation on the skins and several months of post-fermentation maceration. This ancient way of winemaking has been adopted in the Western world with some variations as a means to create an alternative wine style to fruity or barrel-aged white wines.

The extended skin contact imparts typical orange wines with flavonoid phenols in concentrations ranging from 1,000 to more than 2,500mg/L CE, a brown to amber colour, and levels of astringency and bitterness close to those of light red wines. Besides the total amounts of flavonoids extracted, the extraction rate is also highly variable, depending on variety and fruit ripeness. Figure 2.10 gives an example.

Obviously, these data are in no way related to the kind of wines discussed in this book, because they have been obtained under conditions of an unusually extended maceration period. However, they illustrate that prolonged maceration periods exceeding one or two days, as sometimes performed for optimised aroma extraction, lead to high, extremely variable and hardly predictable levels of flavonoids; in most varieties, aroma extraction is completed in one or two days. The sensory outcome of such an approach is opposed to the pursuit of dry white wines of the fruity style. One of the reasons is the catalytic role of these flavonoid levels on aroma modulation (section 2.1). It explains why such wines inevitably present the aroma pattern of oxidative ageing, accompanied by a loss of fruity aroma attributes. Another reason is the astringency that orange wines elicit on the palate.

2.4 Pressing

In most wineries, presses are fed using pumps. However, each pumping cycle of grapes, especially of heavily crushed fruit or after longer skin contact, can be considered one too many. Any pressure resistance on the pump discharge side caused by pipe deflections, valves, small cross-sections or large differences in height exacerbates mechanical tearing and grinding of the fruit tissue. As a result, flavonoids are extracted more easily. Insoluble solids and juice turbidity increase concomitantly, thus complicating juice clarification. Conveying grapes and musts using dumping devices or gravity flow is much gentler than the use of pumps and screws. Slowly running pumps with large cross-sections are preferable when gravity flow cannot be used.

The Role of Stems During Pressing

Stems are a source of flavonoids, but destemming is not a reliable means to lower flavonoid uptake upon pressing. The presence of stems in the must facilitates the release of juice draining through the pomace cake. In contrast, destemmed fruit requires more mechanical load and more pressure acting in the press to extract the juice. As a result, pressing destemmed fruit can counterintuitively result in even higher flavonoid levels.

However, the outcome will be quite different when longer skin contact takes place. During that period, stems would act as an additional source of flavonoids and other undesirable compounds. This is one of the reasons for destemming. Hence destemmers are usually incorporated into the crusher.

The Role of the Press System

Batch presses are the standard in pressing technology, but there are differences between the various types of batch presses with regard to juice and wine quality. Primarily, the number of times the pomace cake is broken up and crumbled by depressurising and rotation has more impact on flavonoid extraction, insoluble juice solids and overall juice quality than the pressure applied.

Figure 2.11 depicts how juice flavonoid levels increase with increasing number of pressing fractions in two kinds of batch presses operated in the traditional aerobic mode, that is without using nitrogen to render the interior of the press inert. One of them is an old-style horizontal head press with chains connected between the two moving heads, and the other is a modern closed-cage membrane press with the membrane mounted horizontally on one side of the press between the two ends. Data refer to fruit supplied with 60mg/L SO_2 and pressed right after crushing and destemming. While there were no clear

Crusher-destemmer in a small winery.

Juice draining from the press.

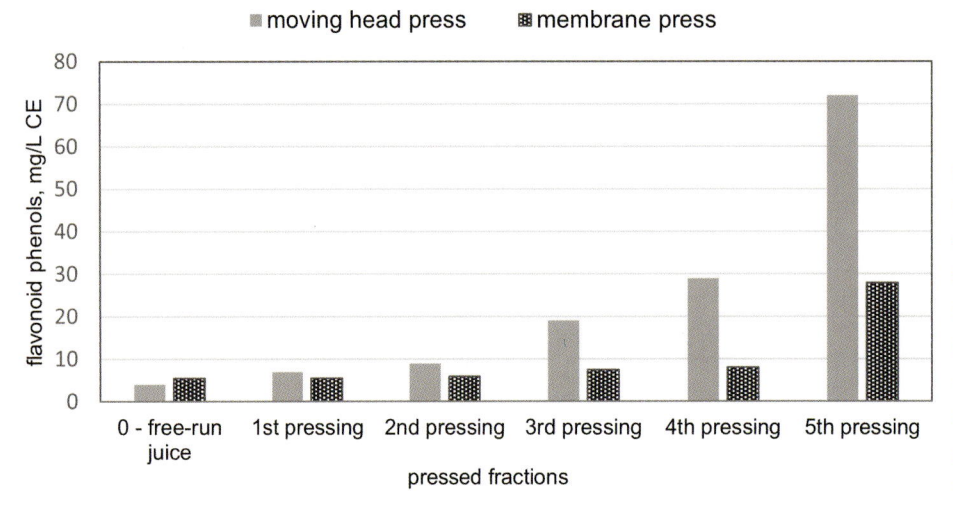

Figure 2.11: Impact of pressing fractions on flavonoid phenols. Comparison between a membrane press and a moving head press after addition of 60mg/L SO_2.

Hydro presses like the one shown here derive their pressure from the water supply.

differences between presses for free-run juice after the first two pressings, flavonoid levels sharply increased in further pressings produced by the moving head press, compared to the equivalent pressings delivered by the gentler membrane press.

Most winemakers are aware of the lower juice quality of heavy pressings. Therefore they keep the last pressings separate, with the option of improving them by additional oenological treatments, blending them back later according to the desired wine style, or bottling them under different labels for a lower price point blend. Under conditions of traditional grape processing with SO_2 addition, it depends on the individual winery, fruit quality, the pressing system and its handling if such an approach is beneficial. It might be worth reconsidering separating the pressings when modern membrane presses are used, considering the low amount of highly pressed juice to the total volume. Hydro presses and basket presses such as those frequently used for small volumes in home winemaking offer an even more gentle method of pressing, which makes press cuts useless. However, they require some manual crumbling of the pomace to obtain a satisfactory juice yield.

The way a press is operated is at least as important as its design. A more recent development of press systems has led to the introduction of presses that can function both aerobically and anaerobically. In classic aerobic mode, the presses suck in air when the membrane is deflated, which leads to oxidation of the must and the lowering of phenols of all kinds (section 2.2). In anaerobic or reductive mode, nitrogen is sucked in upon deflation instead of air. This prevents oxidation of the must in the press. Therefore juices obtained by reductive pressing display significantly higher levels of flavonoid and other phenols (Day et al. 2019), which does indeed suggest separate processing of the last press fractions.

When press fractions have been stored for a period of time after fermentation, it becomes an interesting benchtop exercise to determine by tasting whether press cuts should be added back or kept separate from the main lot. Measuring flavonoid phenols in the juice by use of a rapid method would be an easy approach to assess pressing quality as far as the specific aspect of phenol chemistry, astringency and shelf life is concerned. When flavonoids exceed some 50mg/L in the last 10 per cent of juice leaving the press, or when the inclusion of the pressings increases flavonoids by more than 20 per cent in the total juice volume, the pressing process should be rethought or pressings treated separately.

Impact of SO_2 During Pressing

Allowing the must to oxidise in the press in the absence of previous SO_2 additions completely changes the picture, as the reactions of must oxidation outlined in section 2.2 will occur. An example is shown in Figure 2.12. It reports juice flavonoid levels of the same lot of fruit pressed in the same membrane press both with and without previous SO_2 (70mg/kg) addition at crushing.

What applies to skin contact (section 2.3) also applies to pressing. When no SO_2 is present during a press run, enzymatic oxidation (section 2.2) of the must starts inside the press and removes a large portion of flavonoids, which precipitate as insoluble brown solids. This reaction continues during the holding time in the press pan and in the downstream juice tanks as long as it is not stopped by SO_2 additions. Thus, final flavonoid levels of 3–5mg/L CE can be easily achieved.

In contrast, when the same grapes are provided with 70mg/kg SO_2 upon crushing, this process is inhibited. As a result, flavonoid levels increase with increasing press cycles and remain in solution, at least as long as the SO_2 is not completely oxidised. In this example, after blending the pressings with the free-run juice, the juice blend obtained displayed flavonoid levels that were only about 10 per cent higher than in the free-run fraction. Juice handling until inoculation did not affect the initial flavonoid level as long as free SO_2 was present. Thus it is clear that the pre-fermentation redox regime (with SO_2 vs without SO_2) exerts a greater influence on must flavonoid content than the mechanical variables associated with crushing, destemming, press settings and separate processing of the press fractions.

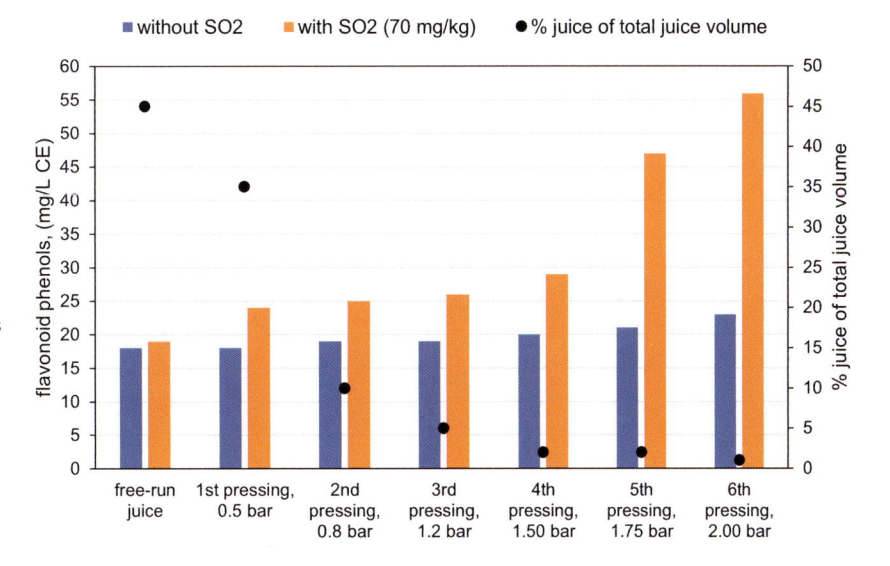

Figure 2.12: Impact of SO_2 (70mg/kg) addition to grapes on white juice flavonoid levels during pressing of a Chardonnay. Press system: horizontal closed-cage membrane press with axial feeding.

Considerable Oxygen Uptake Within the Press

In practice, losses of SO_2 by oxygen uptake during pressing frequently result in no free SO_2 remaining when the last juice fractions are released from the press. The oxygen uptake at the beginning of pressing with a membrane press was estimated as 9.6–12.8mg/L O_2 (Cheynier et al. 1993). It results from the air that is pulled into the press as the press membrane deflates for crumbling, with more frequent deflation cycles increasing the oxygen exposure in the press. In a subsequent study (Day et al. 2019) using in-press oxygen monitors fixed close to the juice screen, it was shown that aerobic pressing management, that is without inert gas protection, can cause an even higher oxygen uptake and a stronger impact on the resulting wine than the oxygen exposure during the subsequent steps of must handling until fermentation. These results suggest that when must is not consistently protected from oxidation during pressing, there is little benefit to be gained from protective practices during subsequent juice handling.

Reductive Winemaking Requires Monitoring of Free SO_2

As has been shown, oxygen uptake of must during pressing in the standard non-inert mode does not necessarily cause must oxidation. Indeed, the presence of SO_2 and the actual level of free SO_2 determine to what extent dissolved oxygen is enzymatically consumed and used for oxidation. Hence the pre-fermentation addition of SO_2 at variable amounts and time points is the traditional means of modulating must oxidation. This is shown in Figure 2.7, reporting data obtained under commercial winemaking conditions. In that case, the effect of must oxidation was measured as the concentration of flavonoid phenols in the juice right after pressing and in the wine after fermentation: the greater the reduction in flavonoids, the more must oxidation occurred. We observe that in that must undergoing specific processing conditions, the addition of at least 75mg/L SO_2 was required to ensure sufficient free SO_2 to completely inhibit must oxidation and stabilise flavonoids in solution throughout the whole must processing chain.

Unfortunately, such data are not transferable from one must to another or from one to another winery. SO_2 binding by sugars and unpredictable SO_2 losses by oxidation are the main causes. Hence it is advisable to control free SO_2 levels during the whole must processing chain, starting at the press pan, when the intention is to rigorously impede must oxidation. Figure 2.6 shows why a minimum of some 10mg/L free SO_2 should be constantly maintained for this purpose. For measuring free SO_2, there is no need to resort to the laboratory, as portable hand-held titrators allow a quick and approximate measurement at the crush pad. If the Ripper method with iodine titration is used, note that this method falsely suggests about 7–9mg/L more SO_2 in white juices than is really present.

Free-Run Juice Does not Ensure Low Flavonoid Levels

When free-run juices over three years and three varieties cultivated in Spain were obtained by a pneumatic press and subsequently supplemented with 60–90mg/L SO_2, they displayed average levels of 7.9mg/L flavonoids (Betés-Saura et al. 1996). Furthermore, the free-run fractions of the juice reported in Figure 2.12 showed a remarkable flavonoid level of 18 and 19mg/L CE respectively. This juice was part of a larger study on grape processing, including manual harvest, destemming/crushing, no skin contact time, axial feeding of horizontal pneumatic presses, and pressing with six press cycles up to 2.0 bar without inert gas protection. Six varieties from two Central European cool-climate countries and two years were included. In that real-world study, free-run juices sampled from the motionless presses yielded an average flavonoid content of 20.1mg/L CE with a fluctuation of ±42 per cent (Figures 2.11 and 2.12). These levels are considerably higher than those summarised in Table 1 for standard white wines and able to elicit astringency in such wines. However, in the absence of SO_2, they started to promptly decrease in the press pan, and continued doing so in the juice tank until a final level of 5±1mg/L CE was reached. During primary fermentation, a further decrease of approximately 20 per cent can be observed and attributed to absorption by yeast cells (Figure 2.7).

The crucial question in this context is where the 20mg/L flavonoids in the free-run juice come from. After all, free-run juices reflect the phenolic composition of the berries' pulp juice, which has never been assumed to contain significant amounts of flavonoids as long as the berries' tissue compartmentation remains intact, but only nonflavonoids dissolved in it (Somers and Pocock 1991). In other words, the presence of flavonoids in white grape juice would be the sole result of their extraction from the solid parts of the grape tissue during skin contact and mechanical loads as during pressing. Hence, in seeking to minimise flavonoids, free-run juice and juices obtained from whole-cluster pressing continue to be the preferred ones for sparkling wine production.

Flavonoid Levels in the Pulp Juice of Unprocessed Grapes

In order to clarify this contradiction and to consistently exclude any mechanical influence of grape processing from the vineyard to after pressing, grape pulp juice was analysed for flavonoids. For this purpose, five healthy grape bunches were taken from each of 38 plots of different *V. vinifera* varieties grown in three countries and three harvests. Each grape bunch was lightly pressed by hand according to the gentlest form of whole cluster pressing. SO_2 (100mg/L) was immediately added to the resulting juices, which were subsequently clarified and immediately analysed for their flavonoid content. A mean value of 18.5mg/L CE flavonoid phenols was found in the pulp juice of the total of 190 grape bunches. The mean standard deviation between the grapes of one plot was 24.5 per cent (Schneider and Kost 2021). These figures do not differ greatly from those of the free-run juices referred to above and obtained under commercial winemaking conditions. These values are corroborated by another study performed on grapes of Albariño grown in Spain, which succeeded in isolating 13.5±1mg/kg flavanols from the pulp of these grapes (di Lecce et al. 2014).

The flavonoid data obtained on manually squeezed pulp juice do not indicate a clear effect of grape variety or growing region, although such a dependency might exist. However, they show a positive correlation (r=0.63) with Brix numbers. This reflects the property of grapes to synthesise more flavonoid phenols with increasing ripeness or increasing sun exposure and store them in the solid parts of the grape (Somers and Pocock 1991). The occurrence of appreciable levels of flavonoids dissolved in the pulp juice of unprocessed white berries is a recent finding (Schneider and Kost 2021) with the potential to change widespread conceptions of whole-cluster pressing or of the exclusive use of free-run juice, as it is particularly recommended for sparkling wine production. If the purpose of such an approach is to obtain low flavonoid levels in sparkling base wines, must oxidation is clearly the better solution.

Higher TA and Lower pH in Free-Run Juices

On the other hand, there can be additional reasons for preferring free-run fractions for sparkling production, namely their lower pH, lower potassium levels, and higher TA. The TA difference between free-run and press fractions of around 1g/L could be another important consideration for some wines already at the low TA end of the target for a desired style of wine. Figure 2.13 gives an example from an industry trial.

Without doubt, TA, pH and the potassium content (section 4.2) associated therewith play an important role in mouthfeel. Their modulation over the whole press cycle, from free-run juice to the last pressings, as shown in Figure 2.13, confirms general experience and expectations. However, much less expected is the initial flavonoid level of 13mg/L CE in the free-run juice. According to Table 1, it is above its sensory threshold in white wines, higher than optimum for fruity white wines, and far away from the widely alleged absence of these phenols in free-run juice. It confirms previously reported results such as those illustrated in Figure 2.12.

These data clearly contradict the widespread assumption of wine professionals that free-run juices obtained without any previous skin contact do not contain significant amounts of flavonoids, which in industry lingo are referred to as astringent phenols or tannins. Contrarily, they do, and their levels are differentiated by SO_2 and oxygen management on the crush pad.

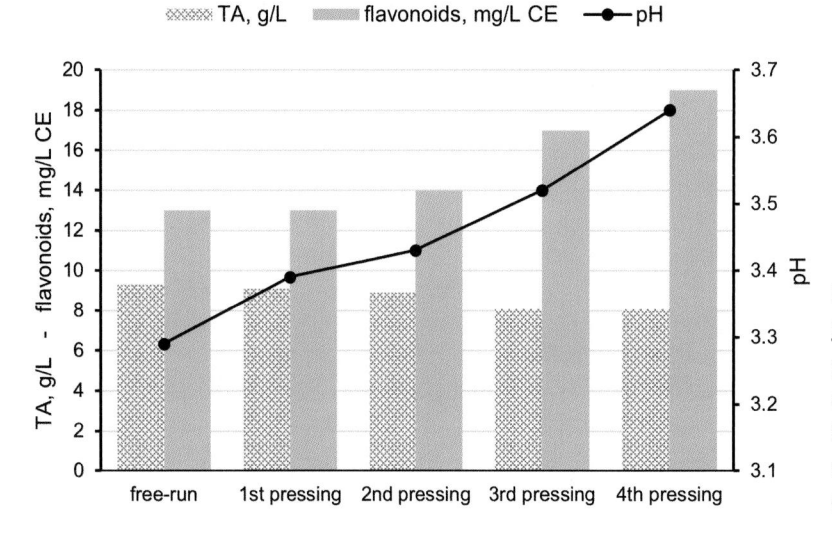

Figure 2.13: Effect of free-run juice and pressing on flavonoids, pH and titratable acidity (TA) in a Riesling juice. Press system: horizontal pneumatic closed-cage press, aerobic mode, with 60mg/L SO_2.

2.5 Juice Treatments

Juice treatments in their broadest sense comprise:

- Brix adjustment, if necessary, to the desired ABV. The increase of ABV by 1% requires the addition of 17g/L sugar. Under cool-climate conditions, lowering the ABV is unlikely to be necessary.
- SO_2 additions if necessary or desired.
- Acidity corrections that frequently require deacidification under cool-climate conditions. This wide field is discussed in detail in Chapter 4.
- Finings with the dual purpose of clarifying the juice and concomitantly removing detrimental compounds such as proteins. While this chapter focuses on the clarifying effect of fining agents on juice, details on their application and effect on wine will be dealt with in sections 8.1 and 8.2.
- Juice clarification, one of the most important steps in white winemaking. It is the topic of this section.

The Importance of Juice Clarification

Freshly pressed juices contain, among other things, residues of vineyard sprays, fragments of grape tissue, parts of insects and moulds, indigenous yeasts and bacteria, precipitated phenolic material, and precursors of off-flavours susceptible to appearing at a later stage of winemaking. Specifically, their presence causes:

- Lower concentrations of fruity esters produced by yeast during fermentation due to an esterase activity they contain, resulting in a global decrease of wine aroma.
- Higher concentrations of herbaceous alcohols and aldehydes of the C6 group responsible for green-vegetative aroma attributes.
- Elevated concentrations of more complex higher alcohols suppressing fruity varietal aroma by their alcoholic, solvent character.
- Higher concentrations of volatile sulphur compounds responsible for reductive taints.
- Methionol and other compounds that smell like meat or potato peelings, in some way comparable to the off-odour of typical ageing.

Less fruity and varietal aroma and less aroma stability are the ultimate sensory outcome of the aforementioned effects (Singleton et al. 1975, Williams et al. 1978, Vos and Gray 1979, Houtman et al. 1980a, Houtman et al. 1980b). Thus, juice clarification is a crucial means of optimising clean varietal aroma expression, fruitiness, and shelf life of white wines. It is at least as important as other oenological variables such as yeast strain, fermentation temperature and so on. However, the demands on the level of juice clarification are still widely underestimated. Poor juice clarification irreversibly affects wine quality and cannot be compensated for by any means during the subsequent stages of winemaking.

From the sole perspective of aroma purity, juice can never become clean enough when fruit-forward white wines are to be produced. Indeed, for three varieties cultivated in South Africa, juice filtration resulted in wines with the highest quality scores when adequate means of stimulating complete fermentation were taken (Houtman and du Plessis 1981). The sensory effect of juice turbidity is overwhelming. When one and the same juice is clarified to a variable extent so that three different juices are obtained and fermented under comparable conditions, one will obtain three different wines. Generally speaking, wine quality and purity increase with increasing juice clarity in an almost linear way.

The Level of Juice Clarification is Decisive, not the Technique

For a long time, the level of juice clarification has been the result of mere chance, mostly obtained by static settling overnight. Only the dissemination of modern pectolytic enzymes and the advent of appropriate filter and flotation units helped many wineries to achieve a reproducible and satisfactory degree of juice clarity. In some cases, juice clarity is even exaggerated to an extent that causes fermentation problems. Nonetheless, filtration or flotation are not mandatory for a perfect juice clarification. Cold settling continues to be a viable method for that purpose, though requiring separate processing of the bottoms to recover the appreciable amount of juice they still retain.

When winemakers are asked about intensity and outcome of their juice clarification, the usual response is how they execute it. Such a reply demonstrates that the kind of technical implementation is considered paramount, while little attention is given to the result. However, what is really decisive is the result obtained, expressed as juice limpidity. It can be measured and quantified as the amount of juice solids remaining in suspension – that is, as cloudiness or residual turbidity.

Many winemakers try to assess residual turbidity simply by eyeballing, determining that the clarified juice looks more or less milky or opalescent, like the appearance of an opal. However, winemakers have quite an individual judgement of what they consider a satisfactorily clarified juice. This complicates communication. In order to create a standardised assessment basis for decision making, the use of hard figures that can be measured objectively has a major benefit.

Measurement of Juice Turbidity

For measuring juice turbidity under commercial winemaking conditions, its photometric measurement

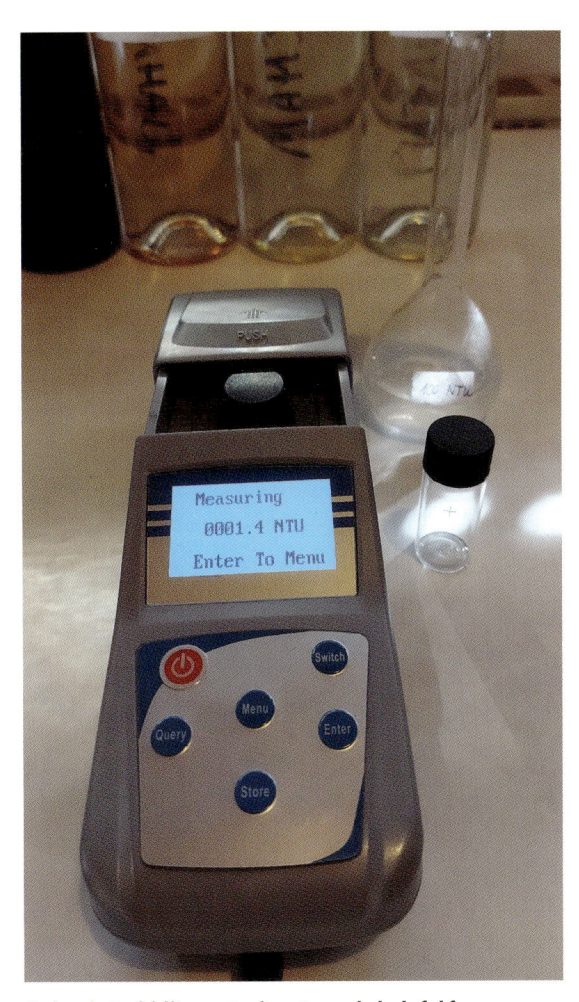

A simple turbidity meter is extremely helpful for controlling juice turbidity.

by means of a turbidity meter, also known as nephelometer, has become established. It measures the scattering of a beam of light as it gets reflected off the particles suspended in the liquid. No sample preparation is required other than perhaps dilution. This approach is characterised by high resolution, reproducibility and speed. Results are expressed as NTU (nephelometric turbidity units). They depend on careful collection of the samples to be tested. Juice from the top of the settling tank will always display less turbidity than at the bottom, but when the point is to settle the lees, there is no interest in mixing them up all over again. Instead, samples should be collected from the centre of the vessel, right after racking, or during the course of any other technique of clarification.

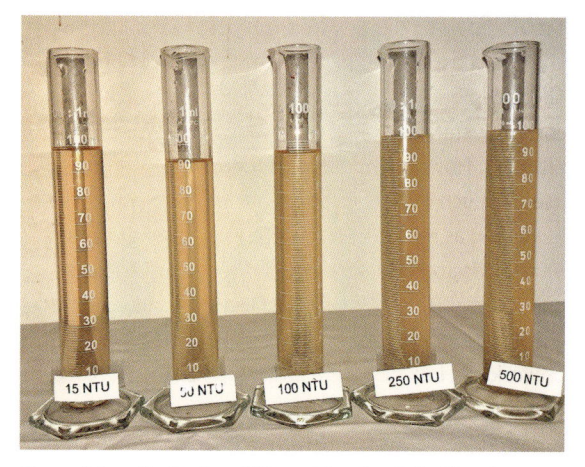

Grape juice displaying different levels of clarification. With some experience, NTU figures can be related to the visual impression of turbidity.

Interpretation of NTU Data as Related to Wine Quality and Fermentability

It is crucial to define what is meant by good or poor juice clarification and how much residual turbidity remaining after clarification, expressed as NTU, is acceptable. Although a residual turbidity of 0 NTU as obtained by filtration might result in the highest wine quality scorings when compared to lots fermented with juice of higher turbidity, elaborate measures must be taken to ensure complete fermentation of the filtered juice. In general, a residual turbidity of less than 20 NTU strongly increases the probability of fermentation problems able to nullify turbidity reduction's quality gains.

In fact, juice clarification negatively affects the nutritional status of the yeasts that ferment the juice. Hence the thorough clarification required for fine white wine production also leads to higher requirements for fermentation management and yeast nutrient supply if dry wines are to be achieved. However, care must be taken to grasp individual effects. Yeast assimilable nitrogen (YAN), frequently measured and essential for yeast growth, is not affected by juice clarification, because it consists of small molecules like amino acids and ammonium that are fairly well dissolved in the liquid. On the other hand, juice solids contain a finely emulsified fraction in which other essential yeast nutrients occur, in particular unsaturated fatty acids and sterols. These compounds, sometimes also designated as yeast survival factors, are particularly required for cell membrane integrity and cell viability at the end of fermentation. However, they decrease the better the juice is clarified (Houtman and du Plessis 1986, Casalta et al. 2019).

Details on yeast nutrition are outlined in section 3.1. In this context of juice clarification, it is worth mentioning a hands-on approach to overcome potential fermentation problems resulting from over-clarification: judiciously adding back of some of the sludge removed.

Ultimately, a residual turbidity of 80–100 NTU after clarification is deemed to be the acceptable upper limit for fruity white wines and the best compromise for obtaining fruity aroma notes and minimising languishing fermentation and off-flavours resulting therefrom. Below that level, changes in residual turbidity impacts wine quality less than the yeast strain inoculated. Above that level, one begins to perceive sensory differences with changes in turbidity, while the choice of the yeast strain loses importance. In particular, the production of volatile sulphur compounds causing reduction flavour rises when juice turbidity increases above 100 NTU (Nicolini et al. 2011).

Tools for Juice Clarification by Cold Settling

The techniques used to perform juice clarification comprise static settling, flotation, centrifugation and filtration. However, as shown above, the technique used is much less important than the outcome, evaluated as residual turbidity in NTU units. While filtration is an exaggerated and uneconomic means of juice clarification, centrifuges hardly achieve the currently required clarification levels without an unworkably low flow output. Thus static settling is still the most common method used globally, followed by flotation (which is discussed later).

There is nothing wrong with the ancient technique of static settling provided that some tools are correctly employed. Temperature control is one of these tools. While cooling is indispensable under hot winemaking conditions, it can become superfluous in cool-climate growing areas. The highest accepted must temperature should not exceed 18°C, but for must processing without SO_2, lower temperatures should be aimed for. The primary goal is to prevent the juice from starting fermentation before its clarification is achieved. Otherwise, it would be rendered impossible by the CO_2 bubbles released, without resorting to the costly process of juice filtration.

The Crucial Role of Pectolytic Enzymes

Satisfactory clarification by settling can hardly be achieved without using adjuvants unless one is prepared to keep the juice cooled for many days, thereby consuming a lot of energy. In this context, the use of pectolytic enzymes is key in most juices. Fining agents are barely able to provide the level of clarification they achieve, although the supply industry offers a plethora of them with eloquent names and multifaceted promises.

Pectolytic enzymes degrade pectins, which constitute a mix of high-molecular weight polysaccharides contained in the grape cell walls. After grape crushing, they act like a gelling or thickening agent that increases viscosity, lowers press yield and severely hampers sedimentation. Their enzymatic degradation reduces juice viscosity, facilitates pressing, increases juice yield, accelerates settling of solids (or indeed makes it possible at all), leads to a more compact deposit of juice solids, and facilitates the filtration of the future wine. Therefore their addition has become a standard in current commercial practice. Dispensing with them only makes sense in a very few juices obtained from ripe and sound fruit having undergone far-reaching pectin degradation on the vine. However, it is difficult to predict if this has happened when the fruit arrives at the crush pad.

Enzyme activity is a function of temperature and contact time. Recommended dosage rates are available from the manufacturer and vary considerably, depending on the activity of the product. Bentonite irreversibly inhibits pectolytic enzymes. Therefore, bentonite additions must be postponed by some 3–5 hours from the moment of the enzyme addition. Adding enzymes as early as possible upon crushing enables them to act during both maceration and pressing, thus considerably improving juice yield and the exchange of substances between the grapes and the juice. As a result, the juice is richer in sensorially important macromolecules and aroma precursors extracted from the grapes. Nonetheless, the primary objective of these enzymes is to improve juice extraction and clarification.

Pectin Test

A simple pectin test is available to check for whether the pectin has been completely degraded. For this purpose, 2.5mL of juice is mixed with 5mL of acidified ethanol (1mL hydrochloric acid 36 per cent in 99mL ethanol 96 per cent) in a test tube. Mix gently and let it stand before reading after 10 minutes. Read the result against a black background. The presence of pectin is confirmed by the presence of flakes. In contrast, the liquid will remain clear if depectinisation is complete. Any haze occurring after 5 minutes indicates proteins reacting and must not be mistaken as flakes.

Possible Side Activities of Commercial Pectolytic Enzymes

In reality, commercial pectolytic enzyme preparations comprise a large variety of different enzymes and activities such as pectin esterases, polygalacturonases, cellulases, and as side activities sometimes ß-glucanase and ß-glycosidase, for example. It can be useful to adapt these enzymes to the incoming fruit by blending different commercial formulations with different activities and side activities to achieve synergistic effects (Ridge et al. 2021).

When rot-infected fruit with more than some 20 per cent affected berries has to be processed, ß-glucanase as a side activity becomes important to degrade ß-glucane, which is a colloidal fungal polymer produced by *Botrytis cinerea* infesting the fruit but not occurring in sound grapes. As long as it is not broken down by an exogenous ß-glucanase, it considerably hampers juice clarification and, even more, the later filtration of the wine. However, since pure ß-glucanase is quite expensive and hardly available in pure form, it is added to pectolytic enzymes with relatively low activity. This requires a lot of time to take full effect, much longer than the few hours required to degrade the pectins, and often more than a week. In this case, if bentonite additions are planned for the juice, they must be postponed to the wine stage because they would inactivate ß-glucanase too early.

Another side activity with some interest is ß-glycosidase, not to be confused with ß-glucanase despite the similar name. Its function is to free grape aroma compounds, essentially glycosidically bound terpenols, and make them accessible to smell. However, its sensory effect is unpredictable. Only a few of the preparations advertised for this purpose provide a sensorially significant advantage in some wines. After addition to juice, they only become active after sugar depletion and in the absence of bentonite. Even after addition to wine, they require several weeks to show a sensorially significant effect, if at all.

Fining Agents Promote Juice Settling Less Effectively than Pectolytic Enzymes

Figure 2.14 illustrates the clarifying effect of frequently used fining agents on the settling of juices obtained from sound fruit grown under cool-climate conditions.

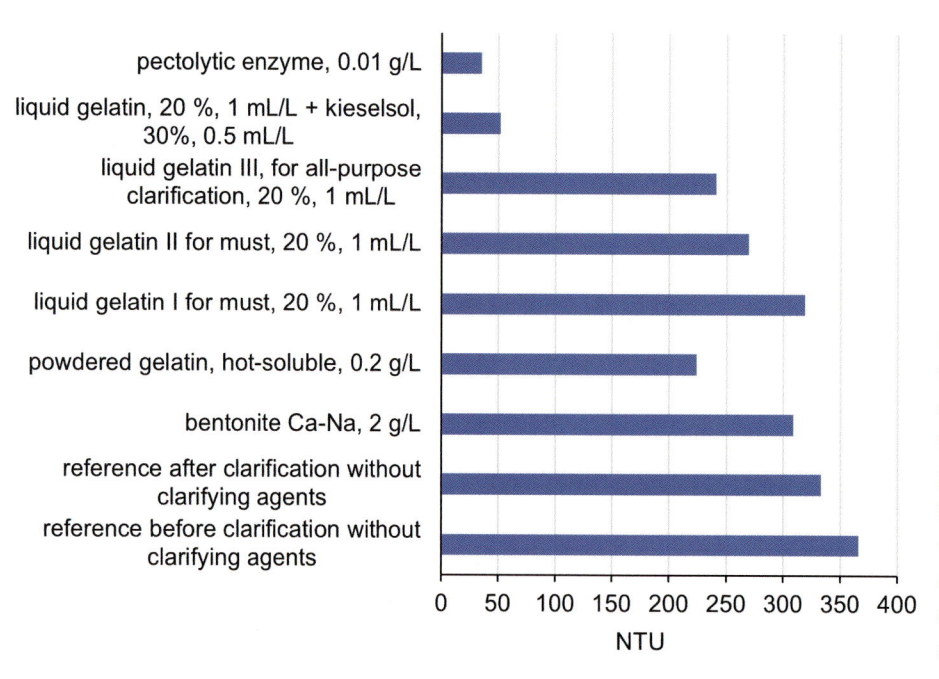

Figure 2.14: Residual turbidity (NTU) of settled juice after treatment with pectolytic enzyme, bentonite and various gelatins. Means of two juices after 12 hours' settling time at 14°C.

Leaving the juice on its own overnight without addition of any clarifying agent reduced turbidity only by a modest 9 per cent. The result provided by the bentonite addition, though on the higher side, yielded only slightly better and in any case unsatisfactory results. These results are repeatable for all kinds of bentonite regardless of their specification as Ca-bentonite, Na-bentonite, or Na-Ca mixed bentonite.

The primary purpose of bentonites is the adsorption of unstable proteins. Actually, they perfectly serve this purpose, and all the better the more sodium (Na) they contain (section 8.1). Conversely, pure calcium (Ca) bentonites display a lower protein adsorption capacity, though they have the advantage of producing less lees volume after sedimentation. However, solely from the perspective of clarification, this differentiation of bentonite composition is of little relevance. Bentonites are not able to contribute significantly to white juice clarification, although some of them are still promoted for this purpose.

The clarifying effect of gelatins works differently. To make them easier to use, some of them are commercialised in liquid form, usually at a concentration of 20 per cent. In order to be soluble in this form, they are first broken down into smaller gelatin fragments, which instead of reacting and producing the desired flocculation in white musts and wine, remain in solution and so contribute little to settling. At best, they increase the need for bentonite, as they represent proteins. However, the simultaneous addition of an equivalent amount of auxiliary silica sol, also known and commercialised as kieselsol, completely changes the picture. Charge balancing and mutual flocculation of both occurs. The fine granular suspension produced thereby attracts suspended must particles, thus achieving sufficient mass to settle quickly. In other words, the resulting flocs draw the must lees downward. Thus, a perfect clarification is achieved, more or less comparable to that of pectolytic enzyme.

A typical addition for promoting juice clarification is 50mL/hL kieselsol 30% in combination with 100mL/hL liquid gelatin 20%. Of course, the liquid gelatin can be replaced by a fifth of the amount in powdered form. The order of addition is not really important, but it is essential that both compounds are added one directly after the other under continuous stirring.

The good reputation of gelatin as a clarifying agent is due to its efficacy in red wines, whose tannins replace the silica sol. Gelatin alone only shows some impact on white juice settling in its high-bloom powdered form, which requires previous dissolution in hot (40–50°C) water. If the bloom number is higher than 150, it can also be used for flotation, where its use is indispensable.

Bentonite for Anticipated Protein Stabilisation in Juice

All white musts/wines contain unstable proteins causing cloudiness, and bentonite has until now been the only reliable means to achieve protein stability. So, despite its poor contribution to clarification, bentonite fining of juices is useful to exempt the later wine from the stress of fining operations. The reason is that high amounts of bentonite can absorb some wine aroma compounds (section 8.1). Furthermore, the operations associated with any wine fining such as mixing, pumping, filtration and so on lead almost inevitably to oxygen uptake that adversely affects wine aroma (Chapter 7). Since most sensorially relevant aroma compounds are generated only during fermentation, they cannot be removed by juice treatments.

For most varieties grown under cool-climate conditions in the northern half of Europe, standard bentonite additions of 200g/hL to juice have proven useful to achieve protein stability in more than 80 per cent of the resulting wines. In the remaining cases, the wine must be fined again, albeit with only minor amounts. Doubtless the dosage might appear excessively high in comparison with data cited in most textbooks, but it is crucial to understand that there are cultivars and humid growing areas that do not fit into internationally acknowledged standards. Details on bentonite fining and checking protein stability are given in section 8.1.

Many wineries remove bentonite added to juice in the course of juice clarification before fermentation, while others choose to add it after juice clarification. Its presence during fermentation is more efficient in achieving protein stability, reducing the amount required to stabilise the wine by approximately 30–50 per cent. Furthermore, it also increases the fermentation rate by acting as a support for yeast cells and facilitating CO_2 release. A major drawback of fermenting in contact with bentonite is the need of early racking post-fermentation, as most bentonites would release too much iron, causing iron instability in the long term, that is after more than a month contact time (section 8.1). Thus a prolonged ageing on the total lees (section 6.2) is precluded.

Charcoal Fining of Juices Obtained from Rotten Grapes

In a perfect world, one would only vinify grapes that one would also like to eat. However, as our world is not perfect, strong precipitations before harvest can cause serious rot damage to the grapes. When there is need to use such grapes for winemaking, care must be taken to avoid any mouldy off-flavour in the juice. This is where charcoal comes into play. As a rule of thumb, each per cent of rotten berries requires 1g/hL deodorising charcoal, which has to be removed with the settled juice solids. The juice must smell absolutely clean.

Note that juice responds quite robustly to charcoal, because most of the charcoal's adsorptive surface is engaged with juice solids and colloids. If comparable amounts of charcoal were applied after fermentation, serious quality losses would be the result.

Microbiological Considerations

Microbial risks are a serious concern impeding grape and must processing without SO_2 additions in many wineries. The risks increase as temperature rises. Thus temperature is a determining factor when assessing the possibility of conducting must oxidation. Harvest at low temperatures and efficient must cooling are the tools making it possible. It is also the way to gain time to achieve satisfactory juice settling.

Where SO_2 is deemed indispensable for microbiological reasons, this does not completely rule out must oxidation because SO_2 can also be added to the juice at a later stage instead of at crushing. However, it must be taken into account that while enzymatic oxidation of phenols is a fast reaction, their subsequent polymerisation and precipitation require 5–10 hours.

Thus, when SO_2 is added too early, polymerisation and precipitation steps are inhibited (section 2.2).

Juices are commonly settled over night. When they are racked the next morning, it is a good moment to smell the air in the emptied tank. A smell of ethyl acetate indicates that some undesirable but not necessarily detrimental microbial activity has taken place, suggesting more cooling or an earlier SO_2 addition might be advisable.

As soon as yeast starts fermentation, it strongly consumes dissolved oxygen (section 3.1), so there is no more oxygen available for fostering the growth of oxygen-dependent microorganisms producing volatile acidity and ethyl acetate. Thus a quick start of fermentation induced by inoculation immediately after clarification is the best way of creating microbial protection in musts without SO_2.

Flotation Instead of Settling

Flotation is a more recent technique of juice clarification that can be considered a kind of reverse settling. Rather than the solids slowly settling to the bottom of the tank, pressurised nitrogen or air (5–6 bar) is introduced in the juice. Gas bubbles form in the juice and adhere onto the surface of the solids, making them lighter than the juice and so carrying them up to the surface against gravity, where they initially form flocs and ultimately a foam. The clarified juice is then drained off from below this foam. Gelatin has to be added beforehand

Screw pump with gas inlet, gas flow meter and gas metering valve for flotation.

A flow sight glass for checking turbidity while juice racking.

to strengthen the flocs and help the gas bubbles to stick to them. Prior depectinisation under the action of a suitable pectolytic enzyme for at least three hours before the start of flotation is also required.

There are two methods of flotation: batch or continuous. Continuous flotation involves special tanks and a spacy set-up for large volumes. In contrast, batch flotation is more adapted to small and medium-scale wineries and typically processes up to 5,000L/h. It uses an adapted screw or centrifugal pump that recirculates approximately the entire volume of juice in the same tank, sucking it from the racking valve and returning it through the bottom valve. The outlet pressure of the pump is set to 5–6 bar by means of a valve, while the gas is sucked by the pump or injected into its suction pipe. Gas consumption (L/h), based on normal pressure, must be at least ten times that of the pump output (L/h). When the juice enters the tank, the normal atmospheric pressure is restored, and the gas dissolved under pressure in the pump expands as small bubbles that adhere to the juice solids, drawing them upwards. This process takes approximately one hour. Subsequently, the juice solids require several hours to aggregate on the juice surface and form a compact cake.

Generally, the clarified juice is drawn off from the bottom of the tank the next morning. When the solids cake reaches the bottom and the juice starts running off turbid, the pump is stopped. Unsatisfactory clarification results can usually be improved by more gas input.

The choice of the gas used for flotation is of importance to shape the wine style. Air is preferred in the context of must oxidation, since it enhances the oxygen consumption of the juice by some 2mg/L O_2, thus improving the decrease of flavonoid phenols. Flavonoid precipitation and the concomitant removal of the precipitate makes flotation with air a highly efficient technique for producing very fruity and delicate white wines. Conversely, nitrogen has to be used for varieties such as Sauvignon and Scheurebe with sensorially significant amounts of oxygen-sensitive aroma thiols in the overall aroma.

Preserving Unfermented Juice

It is always useful to have a certain stock of unfermented grape juice. It can be used for two purposes:

- For sweetening wines that are too dry for the intended market segment. However, the amount is decisive. For example, a 1 per cent addition of a typical juice with 200g/L sugar (1.082 SG) will provide approximately 2g/L of sugar to the base wine. If the wine is completely dry, this amount will not necessarily be perceived as sweetness, but rather as an increase of body and volume on the palate.
- For use as tirage liqueur and expedition liqueur in sparkling wine production. When it is added to the base wine as tirage liqueur, it has the advantage that the final alcohol content is not increased during secondary fermentation. In contrast, if sugar is added, the addition of 23g/L (as saccharose) required to achieve a typical pressure of 5.5 bar increases ABV by 1.44 per cent. The addition of juice to the base wine dilutes its ABV to the same extent that it is increased during fermentation of the sugar contained in that juice, so secondary fermentation does not increase final ABV. This is a great advantage when, as climate change progresses, more and more base wines have more alcohol than is desirable for the production of sparkling wine.

When storing juice, the question arises of how to prevent its fermentation. Clearly, the 0.8mg/L molecular SO_2 recommended for microbial stability (section 2.1) is not enough to prevent fermentation over a period of many months, nor is there any other minimal level of molecular SO_2 that could be recommended as 'safe' under these conditions. Instead, the juice collected after clarification should be adjusted to 50–100mg/L free SO_2 and submitted to coarse, fine, and eventually sterile, filtration before being stored completely topped and cold at approximately 0°C in steam-sterilised containers. Alternatively, glass carboys can be disinfected with an aqueous 2 per cent SO_2 solution. For small-scale wineries, the bag-in-box format offers an ideal solution.

Using the Juice Bottoms

When juice is clarified by flotation, the bottoms obtained are rather compact and rarely make up more than 5–6 per cent of the total juice volume. Thus, they do not necessarily justify any further treatment and are often discarded in the vineyard without major economic losses. This is one of the advantages of flotation. In contrast, when juices are clarified by static settling to a comparable degree of residual turbidity, the bottoms obtained are less dense and account for up to 25 per cent of the total volume. They require recovery of the juice they still contain. For that purpose, rotary vacuum filters or cross-flow filters with adapted modules for the filtration of dense sediments are used in larger operations. However, in small and medium-sized wineries, filter presses, also known as lees filters, are used. They require the use of diatomaceous earth or perlite for precoating. Hydropresses can also be used for even smaller operations. In this case, a bag made of synthetic material is filled with bottoms and pressed.

The high volume of juice bottoms after cold settling to less than 100 NTU residual turbidity is not a major drawback. If they were left in the juice, they would be found in the wine, where they proportionally increase the yeast lees volume during the first racking post-fermentation. Thus the problem would be postponed rather than resolved. In contrast, the volume of yeast lees in wines obtained from properly clarified juices rarely exceeds 1 per cent and makes further processing superfluous.

Nevertheless, the considerable amount of juice bottoms frequently leads winemakers to consider how to reduce that amount and hence dispense with its processing. In fact, the supply industry time and again proposes adjuvants that would better compact the juice

Lees filters allow the recovery of juice still contained in the juice bottoms or of wine contained in the yeast lees after racking.

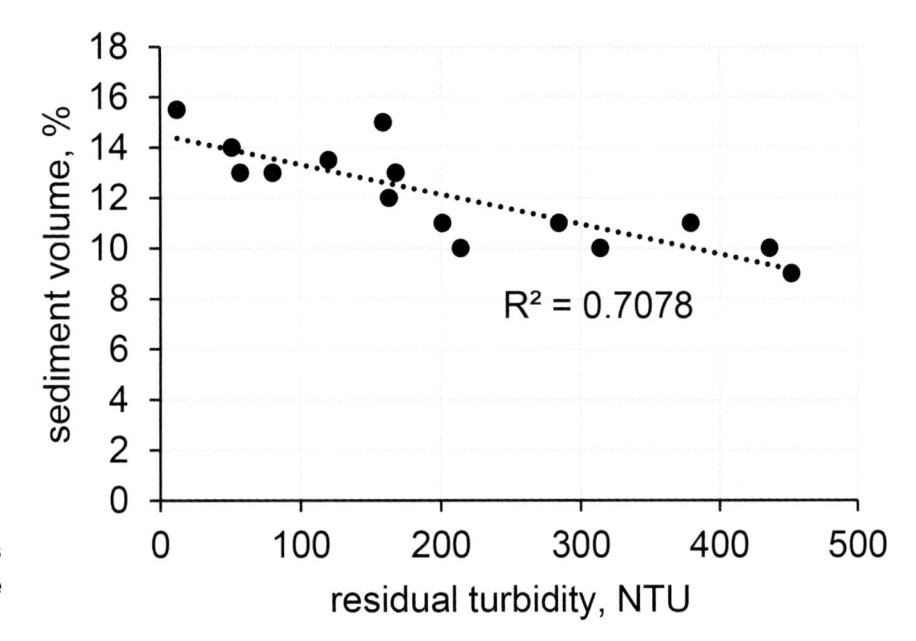

Figure 2.15: Sediment volume after a 15 hours' settling period of a white juice with diverse clarification adjuvants as affected by residual juice turbidity.

bottoms. At best, however, all these do is reduce residual turbidity. The volume of sediment depends primarily on the amount of solids brought to sedimentation. The more juice solids settle and the clearer the supernatant juice, expressed as NTU, the greater the bottoms' volume. An example is given in Figure 2.15. Only a longer cold settling period in conjunction with appropriate storage and cooling capacity can reduce the bottoms' volume somewhat. The level of juice clarification required for contemporary white wines therefore justifies the use of a lees filter prior to fermentation.

There is much practical interest in processing the bottoms before fermentation starts. This way, the juice obtained can be blended back into the clarified juice without losses of quality. However, if bottoms remain after the onset of fermentation, a wide array of undesirable compounds contained in the solids start dissolving in the alcohol-containing medium. Wines obtained from fermented bottoms suffer heavy quality losses that require supplementary treatments, frequently with charcoal, before they can be used for blending into low-tier brands.

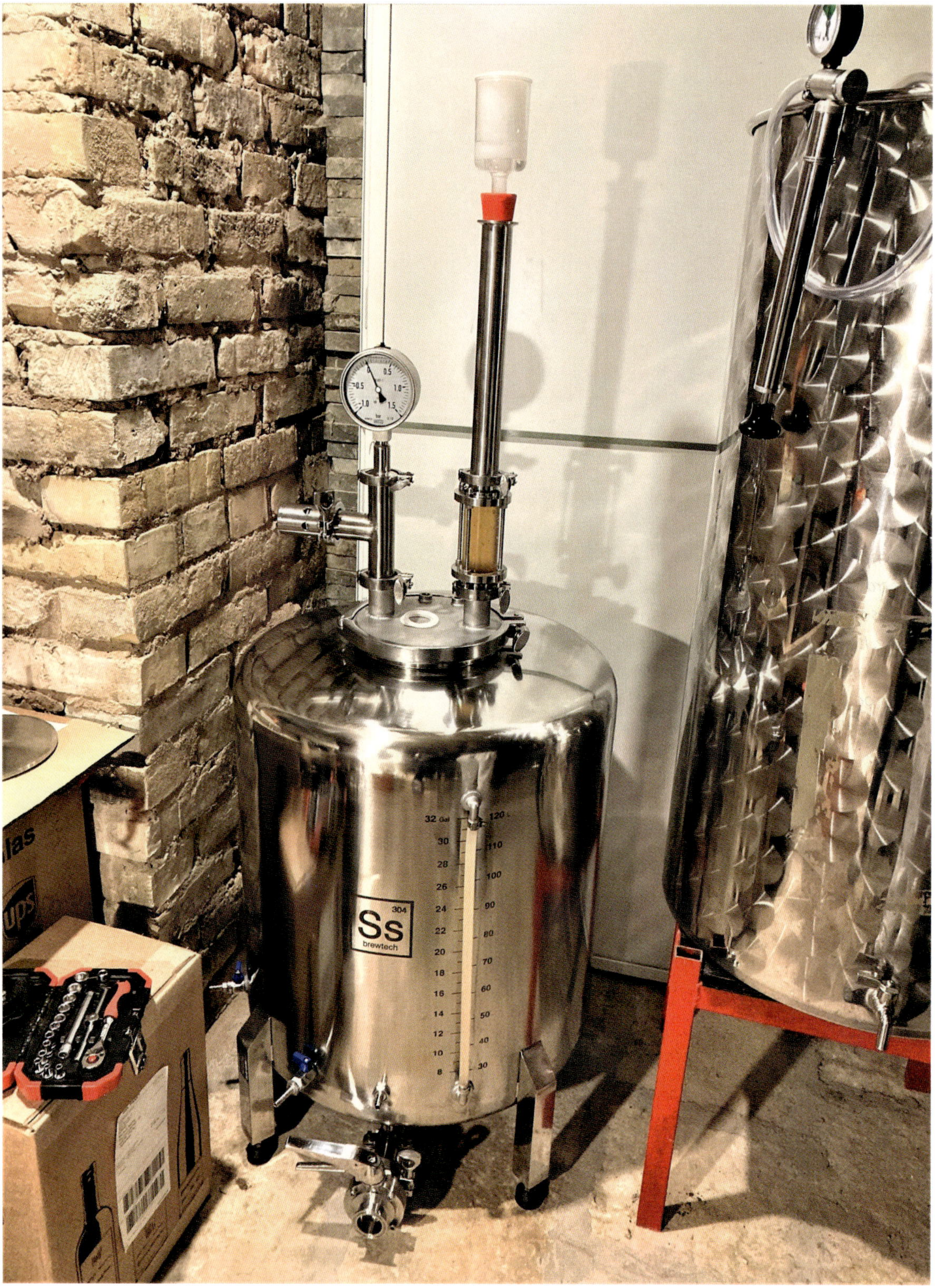
Ss
304
brewtech

CHAPTER 3

FERMENTATION STRATEGIES

Before the introduction of selected dry yeast strains in the 1970s, spontaneous fermentation was the standard. It is still possible today and sometimes yields amazingly complex wines, although little is said about the wayward examples. Due to changes in consumer expectations, climate and winemaking conditions, its implementation now requires more stringent measures. Fermentation using selected dry yeast strains is now common practice. Their diversity prevents any dreaded uniformity of wines, but does not solve all fermentation problems. Sluggish or stuck fermentation and the formation of reductive taints are the most common of them. To prevent them, parameters such as fermentation temperature, nutrient supply, survival factors, and the specific requirements of the individual strain must be considered. In times of global climate change, yeast-assimilable nitrogen has become one of the most important analytical features of juice. Its adjustment by providing nitrogen-containing yeast nutrients is explained here, as well as the 'emergency procedure' of restarting of stuck fermentations, which is comparable to the start of the second fermentation in sparkling wine production. Too low a temperature is one of the most common causes of stuck fermentations. Such low temperatures are useless for maximising fermentation aroma if they cannot be preserved during subsequent wine storage.

3.1 Optimising Fermentation Conditions

Since their introduction in the 1970s, selected active dry yeasts (ADY) have rapidly displaced spontaneous fermentation and become an industry standard even in small-sized wineries. They have made many things easier and most wines better. Nevertheless, fermentation problems frequently occur despite the large number of commercially available ADY strains with varying properties, because the general conditions in white winemaking have considerably changed over the last decades due to consumer expectations and climate change. The optimisation of fermentation conditions has as much or even more influence on wine quality as the selected yeast strain.

Preparation of Starter Cultures

When rehydrated ADY is used, the manufacturer's instructions should be observed with respect to both the medium and the temperature used for rehydration. For the majority of strains, the temperature of rehydration should be between 35 and 40°C. Higher temperatures will cause a lethal temperature shock to the yeast, while lower temperatures decrease its viability.

The rehydration medium is usually water, but many strains perform better when roughly 10 per cent of fresh grape juice or an equivalent amount of

OPPOSITE: **Fermentor for micro-vinification trials with simultaneous control of temperature, oxygen supply and pressure.**

sugar (20g/L) is added to the water. Sometimes the addition of micronutrients in the form of inactivated dry yeast preparations is also advocated. However, diammonium phosphate (DAP), commonly added to fermenting juice as an inexpensive yeast nutrient, should not be added to the rehydration medium as it risks seriously damaging the yeast cells. The same applies to SO_2, which would kill the yeast immediately if mixed together in the inoculum. Likewise, the use of wine is only recommended for yeast strains used under specific conditions for secondary fermentation of sparkling wine, as this easily leads to losses of viability due to the alcohol shock.

The yeast should be added slowly during vigorous stirring to avoid formation of clumps. It should not sit longer than roughly 20 minutes in water before being added to the juice. During that period, it cools down. When it is added to the juice, the temperature difference should not exceed 10°C. When the juice is too cold, it is preferable to start the yeast in a fraction of pre-warmed juice and use that juice as the inoculum once the yeast has started fermenting. For practical reasons, addition to the bottom of the tank prior to filling with the clarified juice facilitates its dispersion in the whole volume. When fermenting must is used as an inoculum, its fermentation should not have progressed too far to make sure that its ABV is not higher than 7 per cent. Otherwise the yeast would be subjected to an osmotic shock upon contact with the fresh must and prevented from further propagation.

Hazards Associated with Sluggish Fermentations

Problem fermentations can be divided into two broad categories: issues with the fermentation rate, resulting in sluggish or stuck fermentations; and off-character formation, such as elevated levels of volatile acidity or reductive taints caused by stinky volatile sulphur compounds. Both are difficult to predict and only recognised once they have arisen.

Reductive taints can be removed at almost every stage, while undesirable residual sugar levels after stuck fermentations can be dealt with by blending them down or trying to restart fermentation. However, much more serious consequences of sluggish or stuck fermentations can arise if a spontaneous malolactic fermentation (MLF) starts. Spontaneous MLF, whilst not necessarily negative as such, carries the danger of producing increased volatile acidity (VA) levels in the presence of residual sugar.

Under cool-climate conditions, the vast majority of VA problems are indeed the direct consequence of fermentation troubles. Turbid young wines without any free SO_2 but with unfermented sugar (>4g/L), which slowly ferment for weeks and months, are an ideal culture medium for indigenous malolactic bacteria (MLB), some of which can develop astonishingly cold-resistant populations. Whether these actually lead to the formation of VA from sugar depends strongly on the individual bacterial strain that proliferates and less strongly on pH. Indeed, increased VA produced by indigenous MLB has already been observed in wines with pH 3.1 that were left to uncontrolled alcoholic fermentation at 9°C for many weeks. When such a problem is observed for the first time in a winery, disinfection is not enough to avoid the problem in the future – sterilisation of all cellar equipment before next harvest is essential.

The basic problem of VA formation by MLB during sluggish fermentations is that its detection threshold is quite high in fermenting juices, frequently above 1.0g/L as compared to 0.6g/L VA easily detectable in filtered white wines. This is due to masking effects by

Microscopic image of budding yeast cells. Yeasts reproduce by budding, wherein a mother cell creates a smaller daughter cell that is first attached to the mother cell before it grows and eventually separates. A budding percentage of at least 10 per cent during the early stages of fermentation indicates a good yeast vitality.

Screening Organic Acids to Reveal Fermentation Problems

Monitoring alcoholic fermentation can require more than just daily checks of SG and temperature. In some cases, it is reasonable to complement such checks by measuring organic acid levels. More than 0.3g/L lactic acid indicates that MLF has already started, less than 0.2g/L malic acid means that MLF is finished, and more than 0.6g/L VA informs that a fault will be perceived at a more advanced stage of wine development.

sugar and yeast biomass. Furthermore, it consists of pure acetic acid, which is hardly detectable by smell, as it is not accompanied by the more odoriferous ethyl acetate, which is formed simultaneously when VA is produced by *Acetobacter* under careless aerobic storage conditions.

The addition of lysozyme (20–50g/hL) is an effective means of suppressing MLF for approximately two months even in the absence of SO_2 and at high pH. As an unstable protein, it has to be removed with bentonite before bottling (section 8.1). Since it is considered in most legislations as an allergen whose application must be indicated on the label, its use has considerably decreased. In some cases it is replaced by chitosan, which is not an equivalent alternative. Belated removal of VA requires high-tech processing involving reverse osmosis and anion exchange, which is usually not available. For all these reasons, it is advisable to stop a problem fermentation in good time by SO_2 and filtration when the acid profile indicates that it is threatening to run out of control.

Overcoming Critical Factors Contributing to Fermentation Problems

The sugar consumption profile can help the winemaker diagnose the cause of fermentation issues to some extent. For example, when a fermentation is only sluggish at the beginning and then becomes normal, the cause may be a deficient yeast population, which can occur with spontaneous fermentations, too low a temperature, a lack of yeast assimilable nitrogen (YAN), or the presence of a yeast toxin. However, in most problem fermentations, the sugar consumption rate is normal at the beginning and then becomes sluggish. This behaviour indicates a deficiency in survival factors or too low a temperature. In many cases, several causes act simultaneously and overlap, so that the primary cause cannot be adequately determined.

When a fermentation starts to become sluggish, there are steps that can be taken to restore yeast vitality. However, when a fermentation has already become stuck, its reactivation in most cases requires a second inoculation by means of a carefully prepared starter, similar to that in sparkling wine production. This demands a great deal of time and patience and is not always successful. We can now consider the conditions that must be fulfilled for a smooth fermentation and how they can be improved in order to get a sluggish fermentation back on its feet.

Yeast Strain

Active dry yeast strains differ from each other in their:

- Fermentation rate, and in particular their ability to ferment completely
- Cold resistance
- Resistance to high sugar and alcohol levels
- Nutrient requirements
- Tendency to form reductive taints
- Formation of fruity-floral aromas and their sensory expression

With more than 200 yeast strains on the market, some of them commercialised under different brand names, the range is confusing. There is a superficial distinction between strains of the genus *Saccharomyces cerevisiae* and those of the genus *Saccharomyces bayanus*. The latter are preferred as starters for sparkling wine due to their supposedly low nutrient requirements and their resistance to initial alcohol levels, but the differences between the two genera are not systematic and are sometimes less than the differences between strains within the same genus.

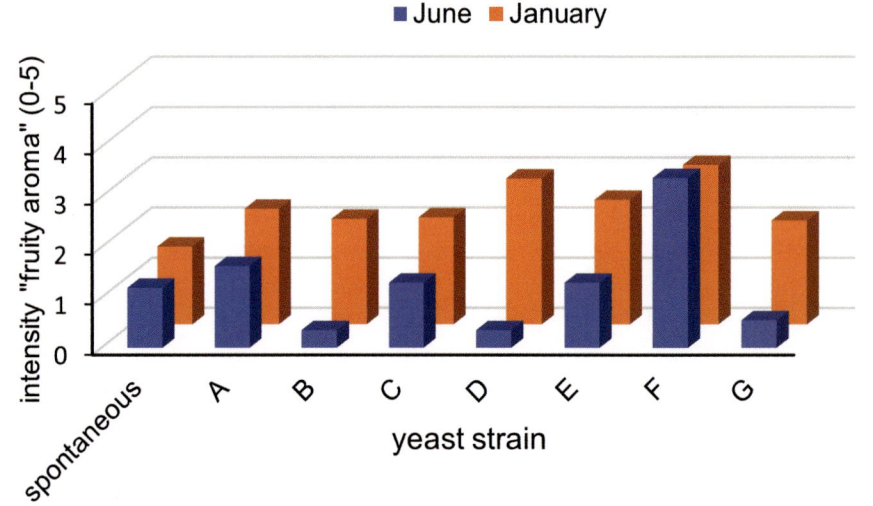

Figure 3.1: Intensity (0–5) rating of fruity aroma perceived by smell as a function of ageing and yeast strain of a Pinot blanc wine fermented with eight different yeast strains under identical fermentation and storage conditions. Sensory evaluation two (January) and seven (June) months after primary fermentation. Means of twelve panellists.

For primary fermentation, yeasts are often chosen based upon the sensory attributes touted in advertising. Usually, the more flowery the aromatic properties described, the worse the fermentation characteristics are. There are no all-rounders. Additionally, the impact of wine ageing and the time point of sensory evaluation is rarely considered. Yeast-derived aroma compounds can rapidly fade away during wine ageing. Figure 3.1 shows that this variable should not be underestimated. The best possible preservation of flavour is as important as its generation, as Chapter 7 will show.

It makes little sense to use a specific yeast strain for each grape variety. Even wineries with a wide range of varieties can do well with two or three strains adapted to the styles of wine they want to produce. Those who have had good experience with their strains should not replace them recklessly. However, it is important to use very specific strains with appropriate enzymatic characteristics for fermenting Sauvignon and similar varieties whose aroma is based on aromatic thiols. These aroma compounds, also known as varietal thiols, are responsible for aroma attributes such as the passionfruit and blackcurrants typical of Sauvignon wines obtained from ripe grapes. For such varieties, strains are required that release these aroma compounds from their odourless precursors, otherwise the varietal aroma will hardly appear. Apart from Sauvignon, other varieties that display this trait include Scheurebe and Petite Arvine along with, to a limited extent, Bacchus. Highly aromatic varieties such as Traminer and Schönburger do not display it, since their aroma consists primarily of terpenols. The latter are a group of aromatics that are partially bound to glucose in an odourless form, from which they can be split off by intervention of a ß-glycosidase enzyme (section 2.5).

Temperature

During fermentation, yeasts produce esters of fatty acids and acetates of higher alcohols, which strongly contribute to fruity and floral aroma attributes. They are fairly volatile due to their low boiling points. Hence, low fermentation temperatures help retain them by reducing losses due to evaporation. With that in mind, it has become fashionable in many wineries to ferment at temperatures much lower than 15°C, where a smooth fermentation is hardly possible. Moreover, additional aromas obtained at fermentation temperatures below 18°C are subject to gradual hydrolysis catalysed by wine pH and storage temperature and, hence, are fairly sensitive, short-lived and hardly able to survive the following summer in an unrefrigerated storage area. Uncontrolled low fermentation temperatures are also one of the most common causes of sluggish fermentation in cool-climate areas. For many wineries, it would make sense

Figure 3.2: Residual sugar at fermentation arrest of juice fermented by ten commercial yeast strains at four different temperatures. Inoculation rate = 10g/hL.

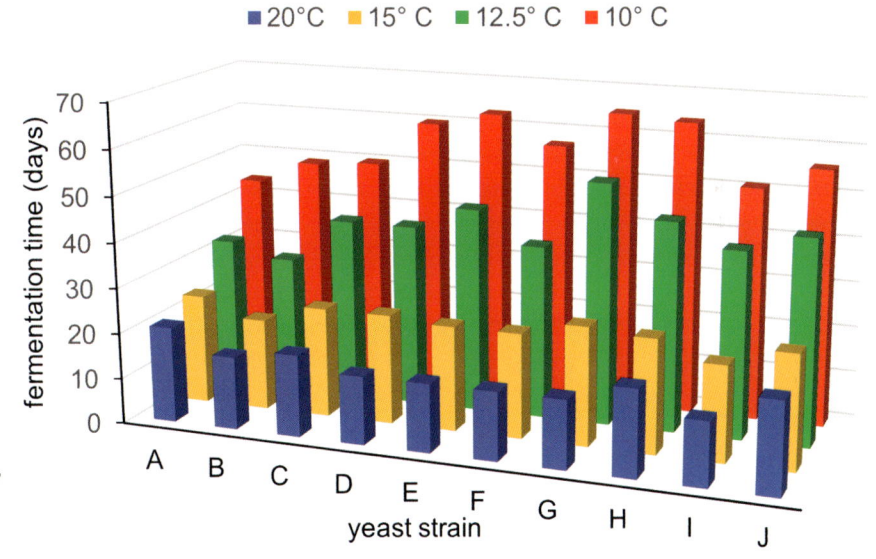

Figure 3.3: Fermentation time of ten commercial yeast strains until fermentation arrest at four different temperatures. Inoculation rate = 10g/hL.

to invest more in cooling the bottle storage area than the juice during fermentation.

Figure 3.2 shows that most yeast strains can ferment to dryness at 15°C if the framework conditions are suitable. Lower temperatures challenge this undertaking and require significant oenological input, as temperatures in that range become the most decisive factor for the overwhelming majority of yeast strains. Differences of only 1°C, which are hardly relevant to human sensation, are of considerable importance for yeast metabolism.

Even if a yeast strain is able to ferment to dryness at temperatures below 15°C, it can be assumed that considerably more than one month is required for this purpose. This is illustrated in Figure 3.3, which refers to the strains already shown in Figure 3.2 under identical fermentation conditions. During this long period, a lot can happen in microbiological terms that is not related to fermentation and is mostly undesirable.

Whenever a fermentation gets stuck in a cold cellar, it is reasonable to first take a sample and store it overnight at ambient temperature of about 20°C. If the fermentation is active again the next morning, the cause is identified and the remedy clear. If not, other causes must be sought.

Yeast-Assimilable Nitrogen

In the initial growth phase of fermentation, yeast multiplies many times to eventually achieve eight generations. To build up its biomass and synthesise its enzymes, it needs yeast assimilable nitrogen (YAN), both in the ammonium and in the amino form. The optimal supply of YAN is therefore a key part of fermentation considerations, although it can by no means solve all problems.

A minimum of 150mg/L YAN is required for smooth fermentations with the formation of up to 12% ABV. For every 1% ABV more, one should allow 30mg/L more YAN. After dry summers, in the case of severe rot or restrained nitrogen fertilisation, this minimum is by no means guaranteed. Under the influence of global climate change, average YAN data have decreased considerably, so its measurement has become a standard in most wine-growing areas. Formol titration is a simple and rapid determination of YAN that provides a useful index of the nutritional state of juice. It titrates ammonia together with amino acids (Gump et al. 2002). Based on the results obtained, deficiencies can be supplemented by adding commercial yeast nutrients.

In the absence of YAN data, the addition of diammonium phosphate (DAP) is the minimum measure to ensure yeast viability. An amount of 100g/hL DAP is permitted by law, but in practice it should be limited to 30g/hL, because otherwise the phosphate it contains, together with iron any wine contains, would lead to an iron haze. Therefore, it is sometimes marketed as a mixture with ammonium sulphate or organic yeast nutrients. The composition indicated on the packaging should be studied carefully. In any case, and in contrast to more complex organic nutrients based on yeast derivatives, the addition of DAP provides only pure nitrogen (N) in the inorganic ammonium form that is rapidly metabolised by yeast. Specifically, 1g/L DAP is equivalent to 212mg/L N.

Figure 3.4 shows the impact of a 30g/hL DAP addition on the residual sugar after fermentation of juices fermented with eighteen yeast strains on

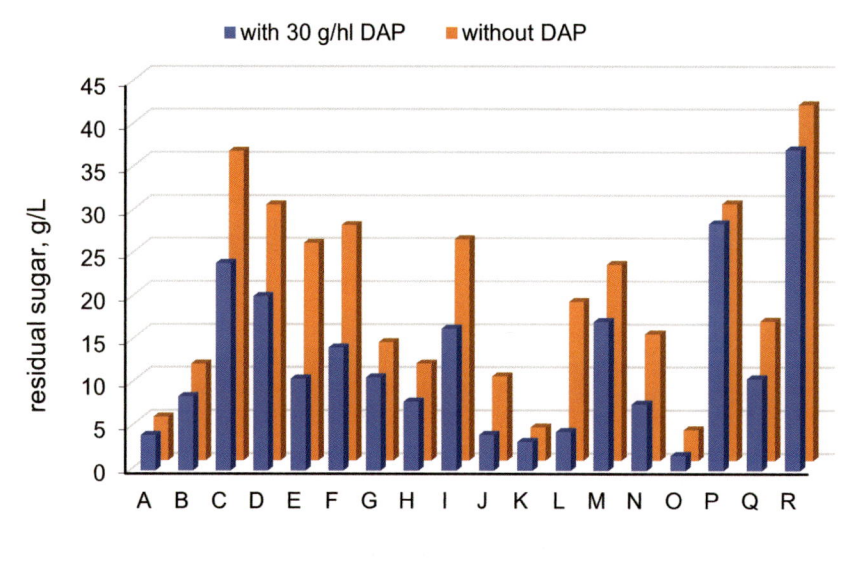

Figure 3.4: Impact of DAP addition (30g/hL) on residual sugar after fermentation arrest of juices fermented with eighteen yeast strains. Means of two juices per variant. Juice turbidity = 30 NTU, YAN = 130mg/L, inoculation rate = 20g/hL, fermentation temperature = 18°C.

Figure 3.5: Impact of DAP addition (30g/hL) on the formation of hydrogen sulphide (H_2S) during the fermentation of juices fermented with eighteen yeast strains. Means of two juices per variant. Juice turbidity = 30 NTU, YAN = 130mg/L, inoculation rate = 20g/hL, fermentation temperature = 18°C.

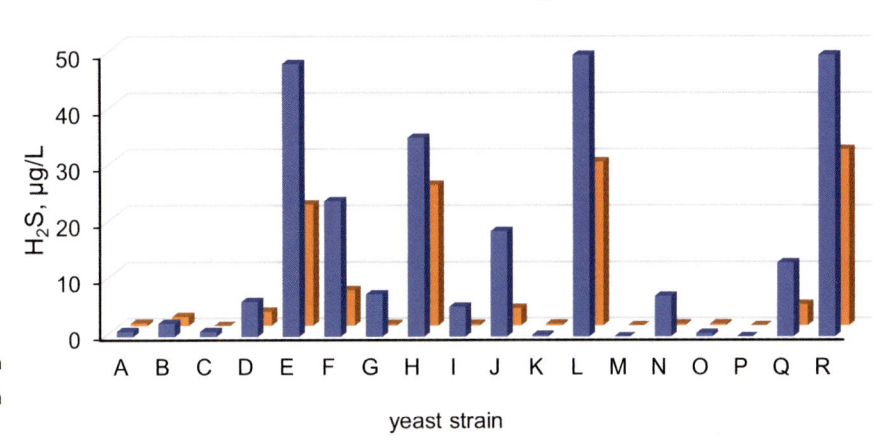

pilot scale. For almost all yeasts, whether good or bad fermenters, DAP significantly improves the fermentability, expressed as residual sugar.

When grape juice is deficient in YAN, yeast is stimulated to produce elevated amounts of malodorous volatile sulphur compounds (VSCs) responsible for the appearance of reductive off-odours during primary fermentation. One of the key compounds is hydrogen sulphide (H_2S), which, due to its reactivity, gives rise to a large array of other VSCs during consequential reactions even long after fermentation (Vos and Gray 1979, Kinzurik et al. 2016). Therefore, the quantity produced by yeast during fermentation provides an early clue to the susceptibility of the resulting wine to developing reductive taints.

Within the framework of the experiment presented in Figure 3.4, the formation of H_2S during fermentation was also measured by means of specific gas detection tubes used as fermentation locks. Figure 3.5 displays the results. The addition of 30g/hL of DAP reduced H_2S production by 39 per cent on average, but with a clear dependence on the yeast strain. Strong H_2S producers respond more strongly to DAP than strains that produce only low amounts of H_2S. Furthermore, some of these strains appear unsuitable for winemaking per se due to their high H_2S formation.

These results make clear that the amount of H_2S produced during primary fermentation depends basically on the specific YAN demand of the yeast strain and its YAN supply. Hence the choice of the yeast strain and an adequate YAN supply is a crucial step to mitigate problems with reductive taints appearing pre- and post-bottling.

Timing of Nutrient Additions

It stands to reason that yeast consumes most YAN when it is propagating and building its cell biomass. Therefore the first addition of nutrients should be made during its exponential growth phase, that is, when the juice shows visible signs of fermentation and a drop of density by approximately 0.010 SG (10° Oechsle). This applies to both simple DAP and complex organic nutrients. If there are no data about YAN and the specific YAN requirement of the yeast strain, as is often the case in practice, it is reasonable to use the mean recommended dosage of commercial nutrient preparations containing both.

Tackling Reductive Taints During Fermentation

When YAN is completely depleted by the end of the exponential phase, it may become necessary to perform another nutrient addition in the further course of fermentation. This is indicated by the fact that the juice produces H_2S and begins to stink. When this happens, another small amount of approximately 10g/hL DAP should be added and further developments observed. The yeast will now cease H_2S production, the still dissolved H_2S will be entrained by the CO_2 bubbles, and the stink will disappear within a few hours. If it recurs, the process must be repeated, but only as long as the yeast is still fermenting. Dead yeasts can no longer assimilate DAP and leave it behind in the wine. Any reduction flavour appearing post-fermentation must be removed with copper fining (section 8.2).

Copper salts, in particular copper sulphate, are known as the most important oenological tool to remove or prevent reductive taints in wine by complexing H_2S and other VSCs. Some still believe that copper also protects against reduction flavour during fermentation, for example, when it arrives with the grapes from the vineyard after a copper spraying. Unfortunately, exactly the opposite is true. This is illustrated in Figure 3.6, showing H_2S formation during fermentation of a juice provided with increasing amounts of copper ions in the form of copper sulphate. In this context, it must be appreciated that copper sulphate ($CuSO_4 \cdot 5\,H_2O$) contains 25 per cent pure copper.

This counterintuitive result was already found and explained in the early 1970s (Eschenbruch 1971), but awareness of it has fallen into oblivion. There is no doubt that copper ions remove H_2S during fermentation provided that they are still dissolved in the liquid. However, they are rapidly absorbed into the yeast cells. This is why young wines do not contain any copper right after fermentation. The copper absorbed by yeast cells then acts as a functional component of their enzymes and influences yeast metabolism in such a way that it produces even more H_2S. Thus the removal of H_2S is more than compensated for by an even higher formation. This point can be summed up in the following axiom: reduction flavour during fermentation is removed by DAP additions, but after fermentation by copper salts additions (section 8.2).

Sterols as Survival Factors

For sugar transport through the cell wall, yeasts make use of multiple membrane-bound transport enzymes whose activity is controlled by sterols. These are considered as survival factors. In the final phase of fermentation, they maintain the permeability of the cell membrane to sugars and alcohol. If they are deficient, the exchange of these compounds between the yeast cell and the surrounding liquid breaks down.

The yeast itself contains sterols and can absorb more from the juice. However, the natural sterols of juice are predominantly bound to insoluble solids, which are greatly reduced during juice clarification (Delfini et al. 1993). As discussed in section 2.5, residual turbidity levels of 80–100 NTU are sufficient to meet the qualitative requirements of contemporary white wines, while those below 20 NTU reduce sterols to a level likely to cause fermentation problems. These can be counteracted by returning part of the

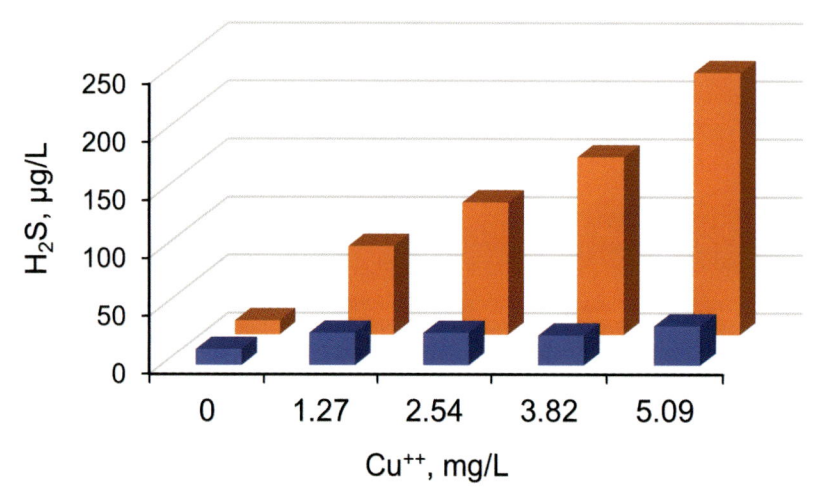

Figure 3.6: Impact of copper (Cu^{++}) in juice on the formation of hydrogen sulphide (H_2S) during fermentation with two yeast strains.

juice bottoms. This shows again how useful simple NTU measurements can be even in the context of fermentation.

Sterols can also be added to juice in the form of yeast hulls (yeast ghosts), which are freeze-dried empty shells of yeast cells. Additionally, these yeast hulls absorb yeast-toxic medium-chain fatty acids produced by yeasts (Muñoz and Ingledew 1990). With a sufficient supply, even filtered juices can be completely fermented with some effort. Last, but not least, yeast is also capable of synthesising sterols itself, provided it is stimulated to do so by the availability of oxygen.

Oxygen

For a long time, fermentation was considered a purely anaerobic process, because it occurs to a certain extent in the absence of oxygen, which is never detectable in the fermenting must. Tradition even suggests that oxygen be kept away with the help of a fermentation lock. However, allowing a passive oxygenation of the fermenting must results in a more rapid fermentation and, above all, a much higher probability of it proceeding to dryness. This is the reason that fermentation is smoother in wooden barrels than in stainless steel tanks, due to their characteristic oxygen uptake (section 6.2). Moreover, in identical tanks, fermentation proceeds better when it takes place in the open vessel with headspace rather than without. The presence of a fermentation lock plays an additional role. These effects are displayed in Figure 3.7. They are particularly noticeable in small volumes with a large juice surface or those that are common in home winemaking. They prove that in the headspace of a fermenting juice, despite the release of carbon dioxide, tiny amounts of oxygen are still present, part of which is supplied to the yeast via the juice surface and is constantly replenished by the ingress of air when the fermentation lock is present.

Brewers take advantage of oxygen through the classic aeration of their wort, thereby facilitating the aforementioned oxygen-induced synthesis of sterols by yeasts. Furthermore, the yeast propagates better and reaches higher cell counts.

Under commercial winemaking conditions, oxygen requirements of yeasts have been reported in the range of 5–10mg/L O_2, depending on the strain. When the oxygen is added at the beginning of the stationary phase, that is at the halfway point of the fermentation

Figure 3.7: Impact of atmospheric oxygen access, differentiated by headspace and fermentation lock, on fermentation kinetics and residual sugar in vertical steel tanks of 200L. Juice turbidity = 18 NTU, YAN = 195mg/L, inoculation rate = 10g/hL, fermentation temperature = 14°C.

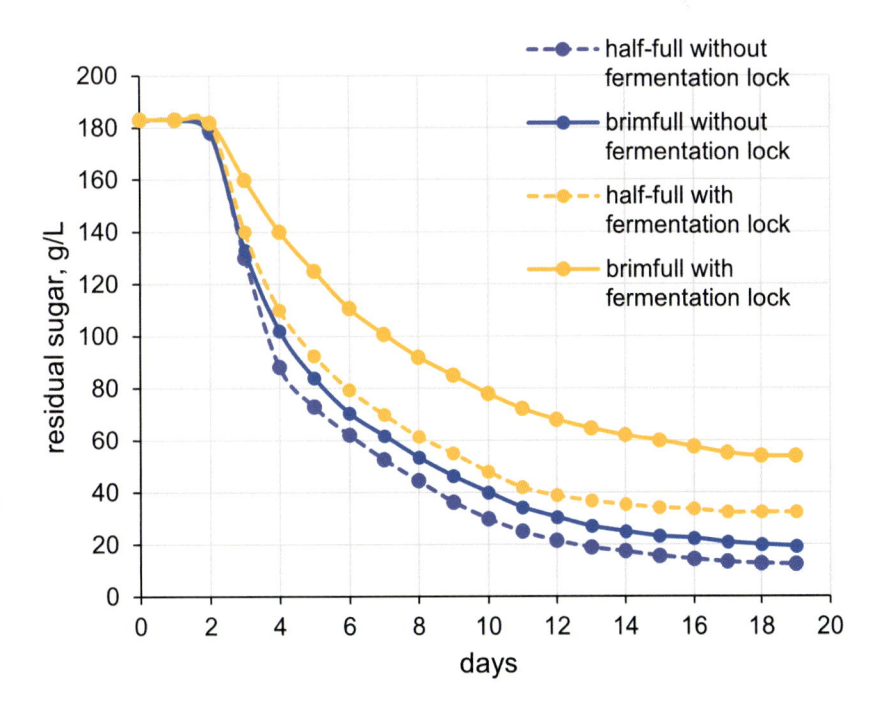

Chart data (Figure 3.8):

Condition	residual sugar, g/L	yeast cell counts (mill./mL)
oxygenation in the 4th quarter of fermentation	~22	~68
oxygenation in the 3rd quarter of fermentation	~12	~82
oxygenation in the 2nd quarter of fermentation	~8	~92
oxygenation in the 1st quarter of fermentation	~10	~98
inert conditions	~45	~62

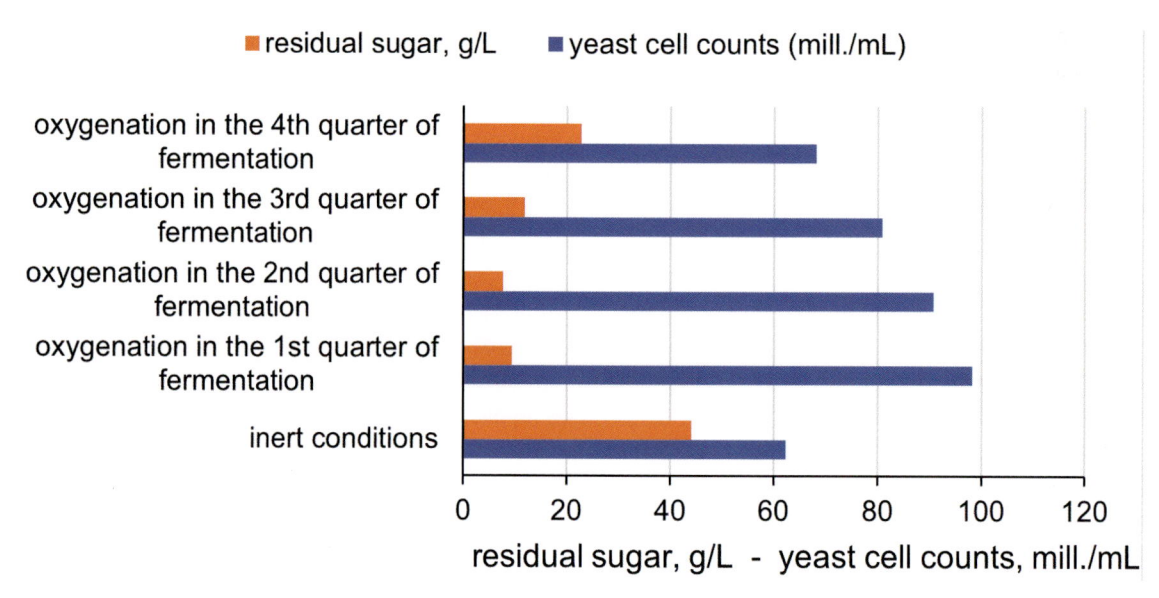

Figure 3.8: Impact of oxygen addition at different fermentation phases on yeast growth and residual sugar of a 24 Brix juice fermented at 15°C after 40 days of fermentation. Oxygenation performed by two successive pump-overs of the entire juice volume.

process, and combined with a concurrent addition of DAP (30g/hL), it is a powerful means of preventing stuck fermentations even in high SG juices (Ingledew and Kunkee 1985, Sablayrolles and Barre 1986, Sablayrolles et al. 1996, Julien et al. 2000, Blateyron and Sablayrolles 2001). Figure 3.8 shows the effect of oxygen additions at different time points as compared to inert fermentation conditions. However, when a fermentation is already stuck, the yeast will be too weakened to be able to react to such stimuli.

Deliberate oxygen additions in the wine industry are typically performed by different pump-over modes or oxygen injection through sintered materials. However, during fermentation, a variable but in any case largest part of the oxygen added in this way is immediately stripped out by the carbon dioxide before it can even dissolve. Although this approach does have some effect, the actual oxygen uptake and dissolution is hardly predictable. Using red wine micro-oxygenation equipment is a better approach to provide quantifiable amounts of oxygen to the yeast (Moenne et al. 2013).

It is important for practitioners to understand that oxygen added during fermentation is in no way related to reactions of oxidation, since it is immediately and entirely consumed by yeast cells if it is not driven out by CO_2. Therefore, it is hardly possible analytically to detect dissolved oxygen during oxygenation at this stage. The oxygen consumption by yeasts continues at a lower rate even after fermentation (section 5.5).

Complex Yeast Nutrients to Replace Oxygen

If sufficient oxygen has been supplied to the fermenting juice, yeast cells will be able to synthesise sterols required to complete fermentation even under adverse conditions. If not, then the sterols will need to be provided by other means. Indeed, they can be found in more complex commercial yeast nutrients based on inactive yeast, yeast extracts and yeast hulls. Ultimately, these preparations are a substitute for a deficient oxygen supply to yeast. Since the supply industry is inventive, care should be taken to carefully read the product description and watch out for undesirable components that are not related to yeast nutrition.

Furthermore, it must be remembered that oxygen deliberately supplied to must before fermentation is no longer available for yeast, since it is immediately bound to phenols due to the action of PPO (section 2.2).

Inert Solids

By acting as bubble nucleation sites, insoluble solids are helpful in the release of carbon dioxide, which hampers yeast metabolism at excessively high concentrations, as can occur in tall tanks fermenting at low temperature. Hence, in some cases of problem fermentations, the addition of inert solids such as bentonite, perlite or cellulose fibres can stimulate fermentation mechanically by facilitating the release of CO_2 and by acting as 'carriers' of yeast cells. Thus they contribute better to keep the yeast floating and more evenly distributed in the juice (Groat and Ough 1978). Figure 3.9 gives an example of the effects when such steps are taken at the mid-point of a sluggish fermentation.

This effect is another reason why bentonite, added to juice for protein stabilisation, does not necessarily have to be removed by juice clarification (section 2.5). Note that diatomaceous earth, although largely comparable to perlite when used as a filter aid in precoat filtrations, is unsuitable for this purpose because its greater weight causes its rapid settling along with part of the yeast.

pH

A high ratio of H^+ ions to K^+ ions – that is, a low pH in combination with a low potassium concentration – can lead to fermentation problems due to acidification of the yeast cells (Kudo et al. 1998). In cool-climate areas

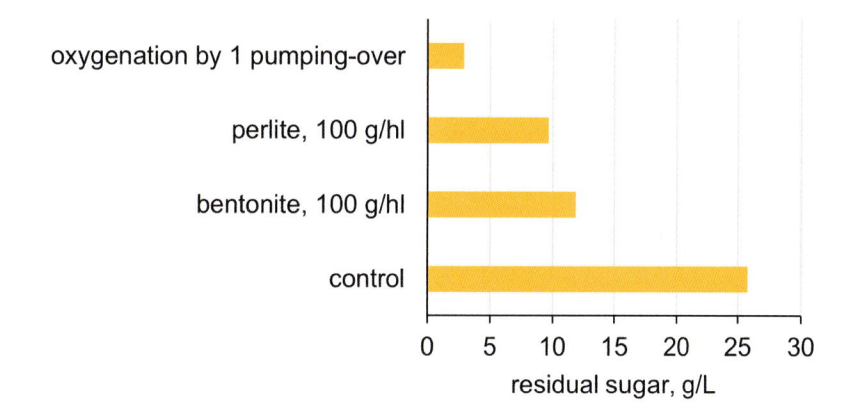

Figure 3.9: Effect of bentonite, perlite and oxygen additions at halfway point of a sluggish fermentation on residual sugar.

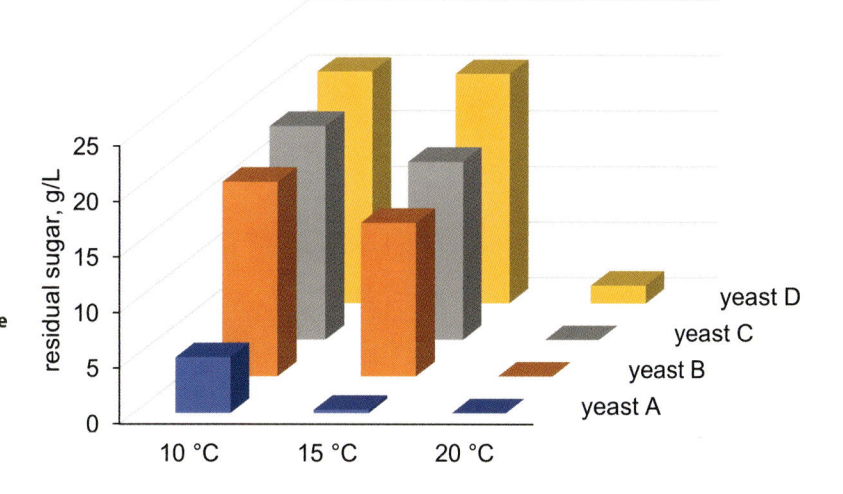

Figure 3.10: Impact of temperature on residual sugar after restarting a stuck fermentation with a pied de cuve using four different yeast strains (50g/hL).

with abundant rainfall, this only affects musts that have been excessively acidified with tartaric acid.

Restarting Stuck Fermentations

If a daily drop of less than 4g/L sugar (~2° Oechsle or 0.002 SG) is observed during what should be an active fermentation, the fermentation is sluggish and likely to become stuck. At this stage, the yeast is no longer able to physiologically respond to stimuli in the form of nutrients or survival factors because irreversible damage to its metabolic pathways has occurred. When a fermentation has definitively become stuck, and a too-low temperature is not the cause, it can only be reactivated by inoculation with new yeast after racking from the old yeast bottoms. There are two ways to implement this.

Inoculation using fresh yeast lees These should come from another wine that has fermented smoothly and without any bacterial activity (<0.2g/L lactic acid, <0.4g/L VA) shortly before. This procedure has the advantage that the yeast is already adapted to the alcohol and, at the same time, the inoculation is performed with a high cell count. Additionally, the whole volume should be supplied with yeast hulls to absorb toxic fatty acids that might have inhibited the completion of fermentation.

Inoculation using new yeast If no fresh yeast lees are available, then the wine has to be inoculated with a new yeast, forgoing the use of the initial choice of yeast and opting for what is called a booster yeast specially known for restarting stuck fermentations. This approach requires the implementation of an elaborated restart protocol to overcome the adverse fermentation conditions. First, the booster yeast must be used at a high dosage of 50g/hL and carefully prepared as a pied de cuve. For that purpose, the yeast is dissolved in ten times its amount of a mixture (1:1) of water and the stuck wine at a temperature of about 30°C. This mixture is supplied with 30g/L sugar (saccharose or glucose) and complex organic nutrients plus yeast hulls in amounts according to product instructions, usually 30g/hL (based on total volume of the wine when inoculated), and forgoing any DAP additions. This starter culture is left at 20–25°C and stirred occasionally until it starts fermenting, generally after two or three days. Then the volume is doubled by adding more of the stuck wine and adjusting sugar to approximately 1.005 SG if necessary. This procedure is repeated two to three more times until finally a fermenting batch of 10–20 per cent of the total volume is obtained to be mixed with the stuck wine. In principle, this procedure also applies to the inoculation for the secondary fermentation in the production of sparkling wine, although here the base wine must be sterile filtered and the use of other yeast strains may be recommended.

Temperature is a critical variable at the end of any fermentation, and this applies even more after a second inoculation of stuck juices or of sparking base wines. Figure 3.10 illustrates that the temperature factor can become more important than the strain factor when a temperature of close to 20°C is maintained in such a situation. Especially under cool-climate conditions, many stuck fermentations could be avoided if the temperature was raised to 18–20°C towards the end of fermentation.

Stopping an Active Fermentation

Marketing strategies sometimes require a fermentation to be stopped at a desired residual sugar level to produce an off-dry or sweeter style of wine. Historically, this goal was achieved by a blind addition of some 100mg/L SO_2 to obtain an approximate level of 50–60mg/L free SO_2. Of course, this approach only works when the fermentation is already sluggish in the cold and there is a low pH. Otherwise, if SO_2 is added to a fully active fermentation, it may slow down and temporarily stop, but it would then eventually recover at a slower pace. When this happens, it will leave behind excessive amounts of acetaldehyde binding to equivalent amounts of SO_2, so that there is the risk of exceeding the legal limit for total SO_2 until free SO_2 is present in the future wine. Furthermore, there are no minimum levels of molecular SO_2 that could be recommended as being effective in such a situation. In short, SO_2 must be used in conjunction with cooling and/or filtration.

In practice, when the desired residual sugar is reached, 100mg/L SO_2 is added and the wine is immediately cooled to 4–5°C; the lower the temperature, the better. Since the wine in this phase cannot be stirred without foaming over, the SO_2 must be added in gaseous form from a cylinder by one fast blow through the wide-open valve on its dosing unit. This is the only way to ensure its dispersal throughout the entire wine volume in a short time. Racking does not help to stop fermentation, since the bottoms removed by racking consist only of dead yeasts, while the fermenting yeasts are still in suspension. Before the wine warms up again, it should be filtered from the bottoms to a fine grade to remove as many yeast cells as possible. The case for sterile bottling is compelling when wines contain more than 2g/L residual sugar.

Conserving Unfermented Juice to Sweeten Later

Off-dry wines obtained from stopped fermentations have varying levels of residual sugar, primarily fructose, which provides much more sweetness than glucose or saccharose. These wines are characterised not only by residual sugar, but when properly handled post-fermentation (section 7.3), they also display a strong and vibrant aroma enhanced by fermentation-derived esters. However, when only small amounts of residual sugar are required for fine-tuning of dry wines or for the secondary fermentation of sparkling wine, storing some unfermented juice is clearly the better solution. Details are outlined in section 2.5.

3.2 Spontaneous Fermentations

By definition, spontaneous fermentations rely on the activity of a broad and variable array of 'wild' *Saccharomyces* and non-*Saccharomyces* yeast strains stemming from the vineyard or the winery. The alcohol-sensitive non-*Saccharomyces* species start fermentation and stop it at about 6–7% ABV, having by that ABV produced volatile aroma compounds considered to enhance aroma complexity. Then, as they die off, *Saccharomyces* strains will have colonised the medium to such numbers that by the end of some days their population dominates the juice and completes fermentation to dryness.

Since inoculation with commercially available active dry yeasts (ADYs) has become the industry standard, an increasing number of winemakers consider a return to spontaneous fermentation as a viable alternative. Indeed, any winery above a certain brand reputational standing can hardly afford not to refer to it in its marketing strategy. The reasons are many and varied, some of them rational and others emotional. The ethical argument for a return to natural or near-natural processes in winemaking is one of these reasons, especially as ADYs have a somewhat artificial image. Many opinion leaders designate them as synthetic yeasts, deliberately ignoring the fact that ADYs are entirely natural yeasts that have been isolated from spontaneously fermenting musts on the basis of their positive properties, propagated, and made available to the user in constant quality. Hence the distinction between wild, natural yeasts as opposed to synthetic or artificial yeast is not applicable. There is no such thing as artificial or fabricated yeast. The difference is whether the fermentation is performed by wild or inoculated yeasts.

Another reason for using spontaneous fermentations is their association with vineyard-derived yeasts, which are supposed to reflect vineyard biology and transfer the sensory characteristics of terroir, vineyard or soil to the wine. This theory is highly debatable; a possible connection between spontaneous fermentation and the expression of terroir is scientifically untenable and sensorially not traceable. The decisive point, however, is whether the wild yeasts from the vineyard are able to complete a fermentation at all and produce the alcohol associated with it, since they are known to consist of less than 1 per cent of the *Saccharomyces* species able to run a fermentation to dryness.

In one trial, grapes of various cultivars and growing areas were cut by scissors and collected in sterile bags without hand contact. After manual crushing of the immediately sealed bags, the must thus obtained was transferred into fermentation vessels previously sterilised in an autoclave and sealed with similarly sterilised fermentation locks. Thus, by skipping the whole winery processing chain, potential sources of contamination within a winery were eliminated. After fermentation at 20°C, only 14 per cent of the musts had fermented to dryness, 36 per cent had ceased fermentation at 29–61g/L residual sugar, and the remaining half had fermented less than one-third of their initial sugar content. The lag phase was up to one month.

These results show that the indigenous yeasts coming in from the vineyard, if not augmented by winery-derived yeast, are rarely capable of fermenting must into wine. Rather, resident winery microflora surviving typical cleaning methods are picked up from winemaking equipment and take over spontaneous fermentation. They are a complex mix of escaped cells from ADYs used in previous years plus non-*Saccharomyces* yeasts brought from outside. Due to the absence of a resident cellar flora, spontaneous fermentation in a newly established winery is hardly possible in accordance with contemporary quality concepts (Mortimer 1995, Martini et al. 1996, Constanti et al. 1997). This relativises the role of spontaneous fermentation as a means to help express terroir.

Spontaneous fermentation can indeed result in great wines reputed for their complexity, but no rule can be derived from this. The reason is that they are unique, neither defined nor reproducible, and can never be compared with each other even when juices are from the same vineyard and fermented side by side. As a consequence, it is pointless to deepen the discussion about their value. Instead, it makes more sense to address the following suggestions for those who wish to perform it.

Juice clarification Depending on the initial bioload of *Saccharomyces* cells and the presence of SO_2, spontaneous fermentation can lag for a week or longer. Additionally, it can require several weeks and frequently come to a premature arrest, because indigenous yeasts rarely reach the cell counts known from inoculated fermentations. To make fermentation conditions easier, residual turbidity after juice clarification should not be below 100 NTU. Where necessary, a part of the juice bottoms should be returned to adjust NTU levels.

SO_2 Less than 1 per cent of the microorganisms present in freshly pressed juices belong to the *Saccharomyces* species, which is the only one capable of producing more than 6% ABV and completing fermentation. However, prior to that point, at the beginning of spontaneous fermentation, the microbial spectrum is dominated by bacteria and non-*Saccharomyces* species able to produce significant amounts of VA and ethyl acetate. Hence the addition of some 50mg/L SO_2 is advisable to keep this fraction of the juice flora more or less under control and to give the *Saccharomyces* genus the time to dominate.

Topping before fermentation start During the long lag phase until the start of fermentation, moulds can easily grow on the juice surface unless the vessel is topped to the brim without any liquid surface. In the absence of this, mould metabolites would stunt yeast activity and impart strong off-flavours. SO_2 additions are not sufficient to impede the growth of mould. Only when fermentation has visibly started should appropriate headspace be created by removing a small juice volume.

Yeast nutrients Since there is no information about the yeast strains involved in spontaneous fermentations, we are inevitably ignorant of their nutrient requirements. In practice, spontaneous fermentations are often left to themselves without even thinking about their nutrition status. This is one of the reasons they often lead to a premature arrest with residual sugar. A simple addition of at least DAP after the lag phase should be considered.

Temperature Spontaneous fermentations tend to drag on for weeks and months or hang on to the last few grams of residual sugar. They respond even more sensitively to low temperatures and temperature fluctuations than inoculated fermentations. Therefore maintenance of a relatively constant temperature of 16–20°C throughout the fermentation process is recommended, for example with the use of thermostatically controlled heaters. Uncontrolled low temperatures are by far the most common cause of problems with spontaneous fermentations in cool-climate areas.

Monitoring VA Generally, spontaneous fermentations produce 0.2g/L more VA than an inoculated fermentation of the same juice. This is not a problem as long as the absolute level does not exceed 0.6g/L VA. Higher values, however, compromise further fermentation, as VA is toxic to yeasts. When they are noticed, arresting fermentation by an adequate SO_2 addition in conjunction with cooling is the best solution. This explains why fermentation control should also include VA measurements when a spontaneous fermentation runs sluggish.

Variations of Spontaneous Fermentation

The difficulties and risks associated with spontaneous fermentation have led to different variations with smooth transitions. They can be classified according to the following scheme:

Traditional spontaneous fermentation The juice starts fermentation by itself; the fermentation is not influenced and hardly predictable. In the event that the fermentation goes wrong, blending with sound wine obtained from inoculated fermentation is required so that all is not lost.

Pied de cuve The juice awaiting fermentation is inoculated with a portion of wine that has already undergone spontaneous fermentation without problems. Alternatively, some wineries pick a small portion of their grapes a week before harvest, press them and get the juice fermenting on its own. When it ferments vigorously after several days, it is used as a starter culture to inoculate subsequent juices. The advantage is a faster start of fermentation by the active *Saccharomyces* population already built up in the fermenting portion.

Partial spontaneous fermentation The start of fermentation is spontaneous with the possibility of the desired aromatic characteristics being formed. After a third of the sugar has fermented, many winemakers choose to inoculate with a *S. cerevisia*e strain to ensure complete fermentation. The inoculation makes use of strains known as strong fermenters and goes along with a nutrient addition.

Controlled spontaneous fermentation The juice is inoculated with commercial yeasts isolated from spontaneous fermentations. Such yeast preparations contain both *Saccharomyces* and *non-Saccharomyces* strains. Inoculation occurs simultaneously if both are present in one package. Alternatively, sequential inoculation is performed with the non-*Saccharomyce*s strain first and a few days later with the *Saccharomyces* strain meant for completing fermentation. Such mixed cultures have been experimentally optimised to avoid killer effects between the two yeast strains. They represent the transition from spontaneous fermentation to inoculated fermentation in an attempt to combine the advantages of both.

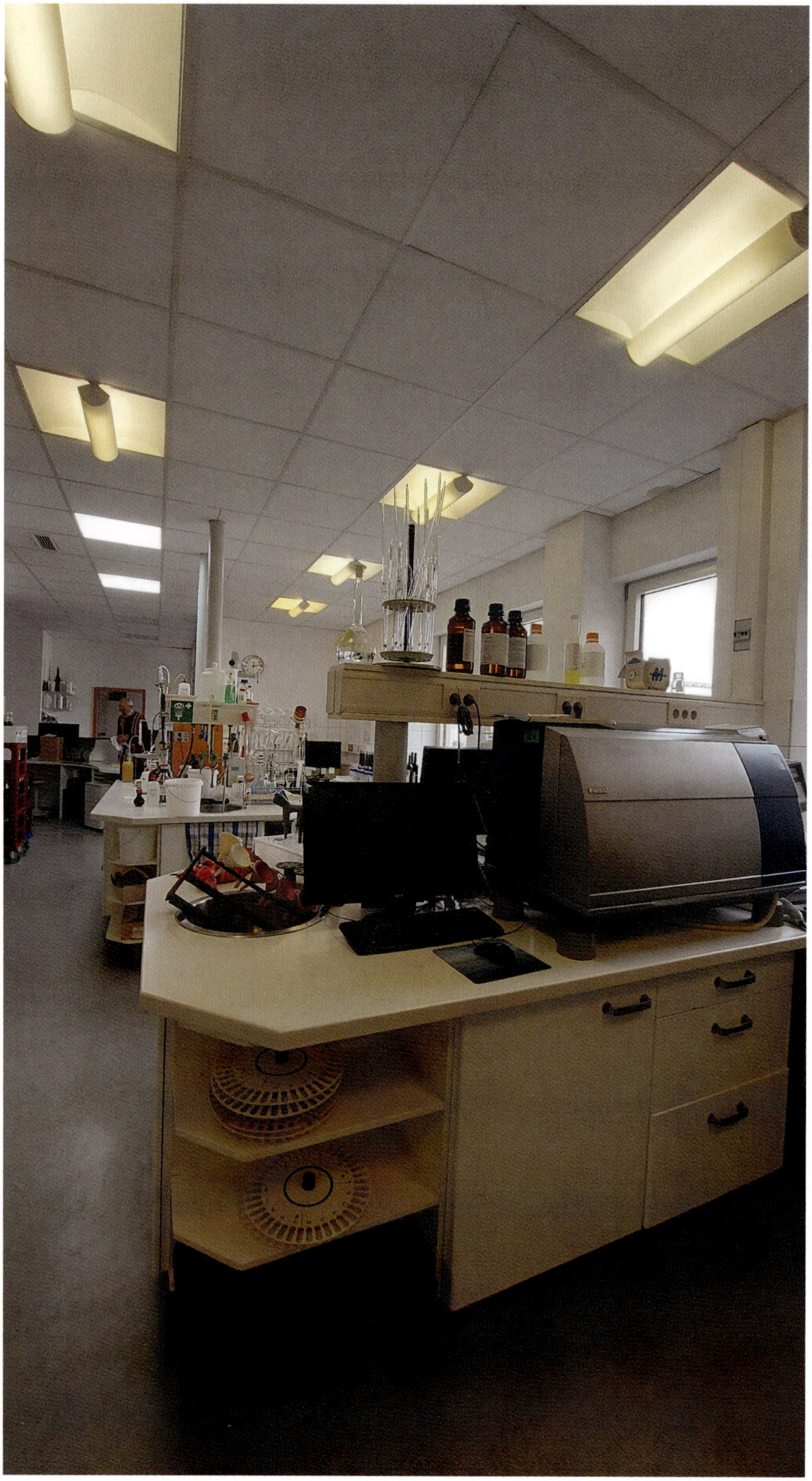

CHAPTER 4

ACIDITY CORRECTIONS

Under cool-climate conditions, acidity corrections upwards are easy to perform but rarely necessary. Rather, deacidification is at the forefront, and even becomes a major challenge in some years. Thanks to the introduction of efficient selected strains of malolactic bacteria, malolactic fermentation is preferred for this purpose. In this process, malic acid is degraded to the softer lactic acid, accompanied by a loss of total acidity. The most important prerequisites for success are a temperature of approximately 18–20°C and very low levels of sulphur dioxide. Depending on the bacteria strain, its inoculation can be performed simultaneously with yeast inoculation or sequentially after alcoholic fermentation. In some cases, the varietal aroma can be affected, but this chapter will explain how this can be avoided.

In bad years, chemical deacidification may also be necessary. Despite its bad reputation, it works very well if a number of chemical basics are observed. It is primarily based on the precipitation of tartaric acid by means of potassium carbonates or calcium carbonate, so the precise level of tartaric acid currently present must be measured beforehand. If there is not enough of it, residues of calcium or potassium will remain in the wine, affecting taste and crystal stability negatively. Case studies are given to facilitate understanding of the chemical reactions and the calculations required. However, it should be noted that the use of some of these procedures may be subject to legal restrictions at a national or regional level that must be respected.

4.1 Biological Deacidification by Malolactic Fermentation

Deacidification, rather than acidification, is a primary issue in cool-climate growing areas when fruit acidity is not sufficiently reduced during grape ripening. Biological deacidification by malolactic fermentation (MLF) is one way to deliberately reduce total acidity (TA). The other way to achieve this objective is chemical deacidification (section 4.3). Both have their pros and cons. An absolutely inappropriate way to tackle excessive levels of sourness is to try to convince consumers that high TA is a desirable feature or blandish it with impressive terms such as terroir, minerality, bright and taut acidity and so on. This strategy only works as long as local competitors are weak. In the long term, it does not even work with sparkling wines, which allegedly must have higher TA. It is not without reason that many of the sparkling base wines of all prestigious sparkling producing regions are subjected to MLF as carbon dioxide intensifies the perception of sourness.

OPPOSITE: **Up-to-date laboratory equipment is indispensable for professional acidity management.**

During MLF, malolactic bacteria (MLB) convert the diprotic and relatively sour malic acid into the less sour lactic acid and CO_2. While this process can be induced by indigenous MLB, inoculation with selected bacteria strains is preferred. These freeze-dried bacteria cultures consist predominantly of strains of *Oenococcus oeni*, previously also known as *Leuconostoc oenos*. In more recent times, the array of suitable strains has been completed by some of the *Lactobacillus plantarum* genus. While MLF was in the past limited primarily to red wines, progress in bacteria selection has also long since opened the way for it to deacidify white wines.

Spontaneous Malolactic Fermentation

Before MLB starter cultures were available, MLF was induced by contamination with the microbial populations that originated in the winery. All that was required was to wait long enough for the ubiquitous bacteria to become active before the first post-fermentation SO_2 addition. This uninoculated MLF by 'wild' MLB is still used without any problems by some wineries, but its outcome is highly winery-dependent and cannot be generalised: it all depends on which strain of MLB has come to contaminate the winery. One of its major risks is the early onset of activity of the strains involved. Many of them are relatively resistant to low pH and low temperatures, can become active very quickly, and are able to convert residual sugars to acetic acid under anaerobic conditions (section 3.1).

Another drawback of spontaneous MLF is the formation of elevated levels of biogenic amines, to which some people experience allergic reactions. The use of starter cultures helps to minimise this risk. For the quantification of biogenic amines, histamine is usually used as the key amine. Figure 4.1 shows how spontaneous MLF affects histamine levels as compared to wines with inoculated MLF and without MLF in a total of 44 randomly selected samples.

Inoculation Strategies

When selected bacteria strains are used, the winemaker can choose between three inoculation strategies:

- Sequential inoculation with yeast first, whilst *Oenococcus oeni* is inoculated only at the end of alcoholic fermentation, generally after complete sugar depletion.
- Co-inoculation, whereby MLB starters are inoculated simultaneously or shortly after the beginning of alcoholic fermentation. Potential advantages of this approach, as compared to the more traditional sequential inoculation, are the reduction of the overall time required for both alcoholic and malolactic fermentation, thus enabling the winemaker to protect the wine with

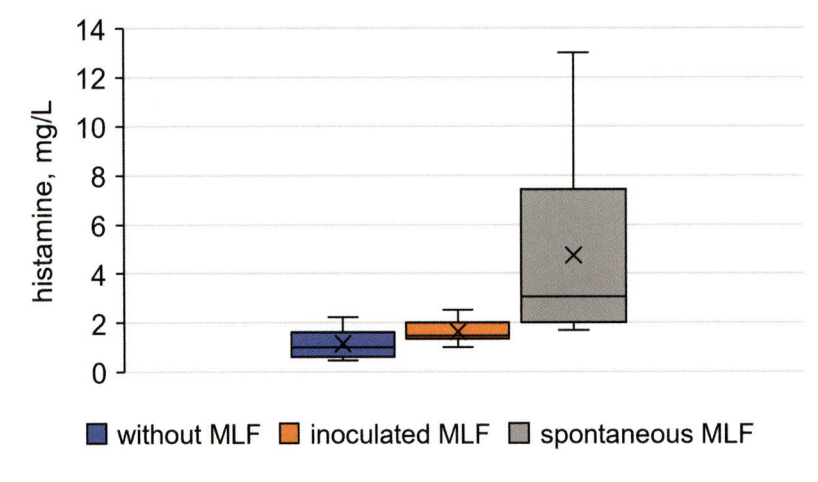

Figure 4.1: Histamine content of 44 white wines having undergone spontaneous or inoculated malolactic fermentation. X = average, – = median, T = extremes, □ = lower and upper quartiles in which 50 per cent of the data is found.

earlier SO$_2$ additions and to reduce the risk of spoilage microorganisms.

- Sequential inoculation with MLB first, followed by inoculation with a yeast starter a few days later. This technique is less common and based on the use of *Lactobacillus plantarum* strains. Preparations comprising mixtures of *L. plantarum* and *O. oeni* are also commercially available. Since all these strains are extremely sensitive to SO$_2$, it is important that SO$_2$ additions to must are very moderate. For the same reason, the bacterial cultures are usually added only some days after the yeast. In this way, the yeast can degrade any free SO$_2$ that may still be present, and thus the bacteria are no longer inhibited.

The performance of MLB starter cultures is related to the specific species, the environmental and nutritional conditions, and to microbial interactions with yeasts. Due to its relatively high tolerance for low pH, high ethanol concentrations and scarcity of nutrients, *O. oeni* is the best known and the most used species of the *Oenococcus* genus. However, strains of *L. plantarum* are also registering increasing interest because of their fast consumption of malic acid, the suppression of the activity of spontaneous MLB populations, and their inability to produce volatile acidity in the presence of residual sugar.

Required Environmental Conditions

MLB are hardly able to start MLF in the presence of any free SO$_2$. Therefore, MLF can only be conducted as long as the wine has not yet been subject to SO$_2$ additions after alcoholic fermentation. Additionally, in contrast to yeasts, MLB are also sensitive to bound SO$_2$, which should not exceed approximately 20mg/L. This requires judicious handling of pre-fermentation SO$_2$ additions, taking into account that about half of the SO$_2$ added to musts is found in bound form after alcoholic fermentation, while the other half is eliminated from the system by oxidation to sulphate.

Regardless of bound SO$_2$, which is not related to pH, pH is still a critical parameter. A pH of 3.2 is commonly considered the lower limit above which the start of MLF is possible. Some special MLB strains can still initiate MLF at lower pH values if they are carefully adapted to them. However, it is easier to add 1g/L potassium bicarbonate (section 4.3) to slightly raise pH when necessary.

When sequential inoculation is used with the yeast starter added first, care must be taken to ensure that the yeast strain is compatible with MLF. This is not the case with all yeasts, which either produce too much SO$_2$ or consume too many nutrients, which are then no longer available for MLB. Most yeast strains produce between 15 and 30mg/L SO$_2$; strains producing less than 10mg/L SO$_2$ are very rare. Figure 4.2 gives an idea

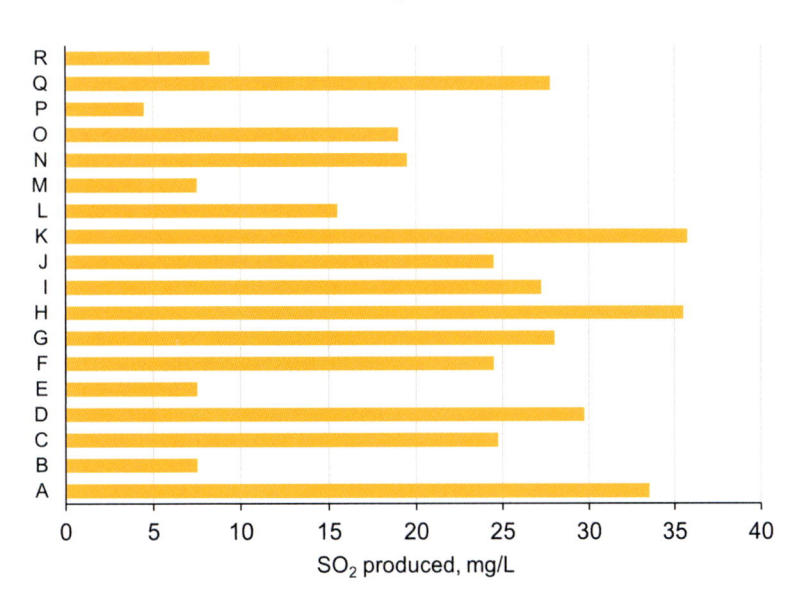

Figure 4.2: SO$_2$ production (mg/L) by eighteen randomly selected yeast strains (A–R) during fermentation. Means of four juices.

of the amounts of SO_2 produced by yeast strains during primary fermentation.

Nutrient requirements of MLB are more complex than those of yeasts. The measurement of yeast-assimilable nitrogen, so valuable for assessing the nutrient status of yeasts, says little or nothing about the nutrient availability to MLB. Special MLB nutrients are commercially available and they are useful when sluggish MLF occurs. In such cases, the addition of complex yeast nutrients has also proven helpful. However, diammonium phosphate (DAP) is not metabolised by MLB and is therefore useless.

Most MLB strains require a minimum temperature of 18°C, but 20°C is more advantageous. This becomes relevant when in cool-climate areas the MLB are inoculated sequentially after completion of alcoholic fermentation. Under these conditions, temperature control of the container is usually required.

All in all, there are several limiting factors impacting commencement and completion of MLF. Their inhibiting effect can be potentiated by their synergistic action. On the other hand, MLF may run smoothly if one of the conditions is not met, but all the other factors are perfectly fulfilled instead.

Impact on Acidity

During MLF, 1.0g of malic acid is converted into 0.67g of lactic acid in stoichiometric terms. This corresponds to a loss of 0.56g TA expressed in tartaric acid. However, microbiological processes rarely respect stoichiometric rules, and that is why this equation is usually simplified as the breakdown of 1.0g/L malic acid lowers TA by 0.5g/L.

If a deacidification did not comprise more than simply a reduction of TA to a given extent, there would be no qualitative differences between methods of deacidification. But as shown in detail in section 4.2, all methods of chemical deacidification affect the mineral cation balance in one way or another. As a result, their sensory effects involve more than a mere removal of TA. One of the most fascinating features of MLF is that in contrast to chemical deacidification, it does not leave behind any residual calcium or potassium, which might detract from sensory quality and require subsequent measures of crystal stabilisation.

Monitoring MLF

The progress and end of MLF is monitored by measuring malic acid. This is usually done by enzymatic analysis, HPLC (high-pressure liquid chromatography) or with lower accuracy by paper chromatography. MLF can be considered finished when no more than 0.2g/L malic acid remains. Determination of TA or pH does not provide reliable information as to whether MLF has been completed. A crackling noise heard at the bunghole may indicate bacterial activity, but may also be due to a trivial release of surplus CO_2.

In the event of a spontaneous MLF, volatile acidity (VA) should also be monitored when more than 3g/L fermentable sugars are still present. However, most strains of *O. oeni* can also produce VA via sugar metabolism after depletion of malic acid. This is where the risk of co-inoculation with *O. oeni* lies, especially if alcoholic fermentation gets stuck for some reason.

Impact of MLF on Aroma

Apart from the conversion of malic acid into the less sour lactic acid, MLF comprises much more than just a lowering of acidity and an increase of body and volume resulting therefrom. It also has an impact on aroma quality in a subtle, manifold and complex way. The reason for this is the myriad of side-products of bacterial metabolism that are not always perceived as positive, depending on the intended style of wine. Therefore, a closer look at the impact of MLF on wine's olfactory qualities and the oenological practices that influence it is justified.

Unfortunately, the influence of MLF on the aroma profile can hardly be generalised and varies from wine to wine. In the worst case scenario, it is described as a decrease of the fruity aroma characteristics typical of the variety, and the presence of a lactic, buttery aroma component reminiscent of whey, milk or butter that is caused by diacetyl produced by MLB. For this reason, there is a tendency to limit the use of MLF in white wines to those obtained from more neutral varieties in which there is less distinct varietal aroma to be lost. Under such circumstances, a modest aroma can even be enriched in a positive way by additional components resulting from MLB metabolism.

The decrease of fruity varietal aroma attributes can be explained in four possible ways:

- The concentration of the underlying aroma compounds remains unchanged, but the intensity of their perception is reduced by the sensory masking effect of diacetyl.
- Fruit aromas are metabolised by the secondary metabolism of the bacteria involved.
- Fruit aromas are destroyed chemically by the prolonged oxidative phase associated with MLF at ambient temperature and in the absence of SO_2.
- Fruit aromas are reduced in concentration by the purely physical process of mass transfer across the wine surface (evaporation) if the container is not completely topped during MLF (section 7.2).

The Critical Role of Diacetyl

Diacetyl with its lactic odour is already formed by yeasts during alcoholic fermentation and may even be involved in the aroma of wines that have not undergone MLF via sensory synergisms (Martineau and Henick-Kling 1995). However, concentrations with olfactory significance can only be found after MLF.

The conditions under which diacetyl accumulates during MLF are largely known. It is formed by the bacterial degradation of citric acid and, to a lesser extent, of pyruvate. Citric acid is only degraded towards the end of MLF, when malic acid is depleted. Unfavourable metabolic conditions, such as low pH and low temperature, enhance the synthesis of diacetyl (Revel et al. 1989), as does insufficient bacterial biomass (Martineau et al. 1995). Yeasts reduce it enzymatically to acetoin and further to 2,3-butanediol, which are sensorially inactive. Therefore, it is recommended for MLF to be carried out in the presence of the whole biomass of suspended post-fermentation yeast lees and before any measures of clarification take place. The more suspended yeast lees are present, the lower the accumulation of diacetyl tends to be. SO_2 additions and filtration stop the breakdown of diacetyl at least temporarily. However, it is possible to further reduce the diacetyl level by subsequent addition of yeast lees from other wines. MLB are also capable of metabolising the diacetyl they have produced at a later stage as long as no free SO_2 is present. In all respects, premature clarification of wines post-MLF is contrary to the desire to reduce diacetyl and the buttery odour it might impart.

Furthermore, anecdotal evidence indicates a slow decrease of excessive buttery aroma notes in filtered wines stored under anoxic conditions in stainless steel. With increasing age, wines lose the specific odour profile of MLF and become similar to that of the control that has not been subject to MLF. These observations indicate that, in addition to the described microbial degradation, a purely chemical degradation of diacetyl is also possible.

The instantaneous net concentration resulting from synthesis and concomitant degradation of diacetyl is closely related to the intensity of its flavour. Odour threshold data for diacetyl vary in a wide concentration range from 0.2 to 5mg/L and depend considerably on the wine matrix and personal sensitivity. At concentrations below 1mg/L, it can contribute to aroma complexity with attributes of fresh bread, caramel and hazelnuts, while the well-known one-dimensional lactic 'buttery' aroma attribute only appears at concentrations above 2mg/L (Davis et al. 1985, Dubois 1994, Martineau et al. 1995, Sauvageot and Vivier 1997, de Revel et al. 1999). Free SO_2 reduces the odour intensity of diacetyl, which can be restored when posterior SO_2 losses occur during ageing (Bartowsky et al. 2008). Eventually, the impact of MLF on aroma profile and intensity of white wines can only be definitively assessed when free SO_2 has been adjusted post-MLF.

More recently, commercial MLB strains have appeared that produce significantly less diacetyl because they lack the metabolic pathway that can degrade citric acid to diacetyl. These are referred to as citrate-negative. Nevertheless, they can still produce diacetyl from pyruvate that originates from alcoholic fermentation. Ultimately, the content of diacetyl found in wine is strongly dependent on the MLB species used as a starter for MLF (Bartowsky and Henschke 2004), though the introduction of citrate-negative strains has been a great progress.

MLF starter cultures are undergoing a very dynamic process of continuous improvement. Currently, they have reached a stage of development that, in contrast to former times, does not necessarily affect varietal aromatics. Thanks to this evolution, MLF is finding increasing acceptance for deacidification of fruity white wines from cool-climate growing regions and characterised by very specific varietal aromatics, thus replacing the traditional chemical deacidification in these areas. Its positive image as a biological procedure accelerates this trend, particularly in the light of growing interest in minimal or non-interventionist winemaking approaches. Another reason is that many winemakers feel insecure about chemical deacidification or have difficulty mastering it (section 4.2).

Potential Aroma Losses from Storage Deficiencies During MLF

Losses of varietal aroma attributable to oxidation or to evaporation through the wine surface occur when MLF is conducted in partially filled vessels instead of completely topped stainless steel containers. Such losses are basically controlled by the ratio of surface area to liquid volume, expressed as cm^2/L. In this context, the height or volume of the headspace is not important. Hence, it is a good idea to top containers immediately after alcoholic fermentation. Details will be discussed in section 7.2. Regardless of their topping, fruity white wines are also sensitive to heat, so the minimum temperature of 18–20°C required for MLF should only be maintained until MLF is finished.

MLF Cannot Always Replace Chemical Deacidification

Despite the increasing prevalence of MLF in white wines from growing areas where such a measure was not common in the past, it also has natural limitations: extremely high TA levels such as those resulting from unripe fruit in bad years or some borderline cool-climate sites make it difficult to use MLF as the sole means of deacidification. The reasons for this are two-fold:

- High TA inevitably includes high malic acid levels, which, though they are the direct substrate for MLF bacteria, are susceptible of hampering bacterial activity when they exceed a certain concentration threshold. As a result, MLF proceeds rather slowly in those wines, thus making it necessary to hold them at the required temperature level of around 20°C over weeks and months without SO_2 able to prevent oxidation.
- Low cellar temperatures and limited warming capacities frequently set practical limits on the use of MLF on a broad scale in many cool-climate wineries. For this reason, chemical deacidification will continue to be of importance in those areas, particularly in years affected by poor ripeness. The basic question relates only to the extent of this deacidification. It can mean a strong TA reduction that has to be performed on juice or young wine, and the appropriate procedures are discussed in the following section. However, it can also mean a minor TA correction that can be performed when the wine has reached a more advanced stage or even shortly before bottling. In the latter case, it is based on the sensory evaluation of bench trials, as covered in section 8.2.

4.2 Spontaneous Acidity Losses by Potassium Bitartrate Precipitation

In wine, tartaric acid is the only acid that can produce insoluble salts. During and after alcoholic fermentation, the deposit of a crystalline mass on the walls and on the bottom of the container can be observed. These crystals of various size consist of potassium bitartrate, also known as potassium hydrogen tartrate (KHT). This is an acidic salt of tartaric acid, in which only one of its two acid groups is neutralised by potassium (K^+). In stoichiometric terms, with each g/L of tartaric acid dropping out in this process, 262mg/L of potassium are removed. Simultaneously, titratable acidity (TA), measured as tartaric acid, decreases by 0.5g/L. In summary, this results in the following quantitative relationships for potassium bitartrate precipitation:

- 1.0g/L tartaric acid precipitates with 262mg/L potassium as 1.262g/L KHT, resulting in a loss of 0.5g/L TA.

- A 1.0g/L decrease of TA caused by KHT precipitation involves a loss of 2.0g/L of tartaric acid and of 524mg/L of potassium.
- The precipitation of 1.0g/L of KHT reduces tartaric acid by 0.8g/L, TA by 0.4g/L, and potassium by 207mg/L, respectively.

During spontaneous KHT precipitation after alcoholic fermentation of white wines, a decrease of titratable acidity by 1.0–2.5g/L can usually be observed. These losses are reinforced when measures of cold stabilisation are taken to remove additional amounts of unstable KHT. Their exact extent depends on temperature and wine chemistry, more precisely on potassium content, tartaric acid content and pH. In borderline cases of slightly increased TA, such a spontaneous type of deacidification may be sufficient to achieve balance. However, it should not be expected to replace specific deacidification measures in wines made from underripe grapes.

An example for clarification: analysis of a white grape juice obtained under cool-climate conditions yields 6.0g/L tartaric acid and 11.0g/L TA. After spontaneous KHT precipitation in the young wine, TA has been reduced by 2.0g/L, leaving only 9.0g/L TA. The difference indicates that tartaric acid has been reduced by 2.0 × 2 = 4.0g/L and potassium by 4 × 262 = 1,048mg/L K^+. Therefore 2.0g/L of tartaric acid remains.

In reality, losses of titratable acidity by KHT crystallisation are partially overlapped by the synthesis of organic acids by yeasts during alcoholic fermentation. These acids comprise essentially succinic acid, citric acid and acetic acid. Figure 4.3 shows the extent to which the formation of these acids can increase the total acidity during fermentation when precipitation of KHT is inhibited. However, only when the initial juice TA is very low and when little KHT drops out can the formation of these yeast-derived acids result in an increase in TA during alcoholic fermentation.

Besides the general losses in TA that KHT precipitation causes, the change in associated analytical parameters is of comparable interest. As a general rule, it can be stated that young white wines contain approximately half of the tartaric acid and half of the potassium content of their respective juices. However, this estimate is not valid when juice has been subjected to measures of acidification or deacidification.

The losses of tartaric acid are of major importance when wines have to be subjected to chemical deacidification (section 4.3). On the other hand, potassium fulfils a sensory function that has been underestimated for many years, but there is an emerging appreciation of its role in the gustative perception of wine. Besides its property of lowering TA by neutralisation of acids as outlined in section 4.3, potassium and its salts also provide a particular mouthfeel sensation, which is able to partially mask perceived sourness.

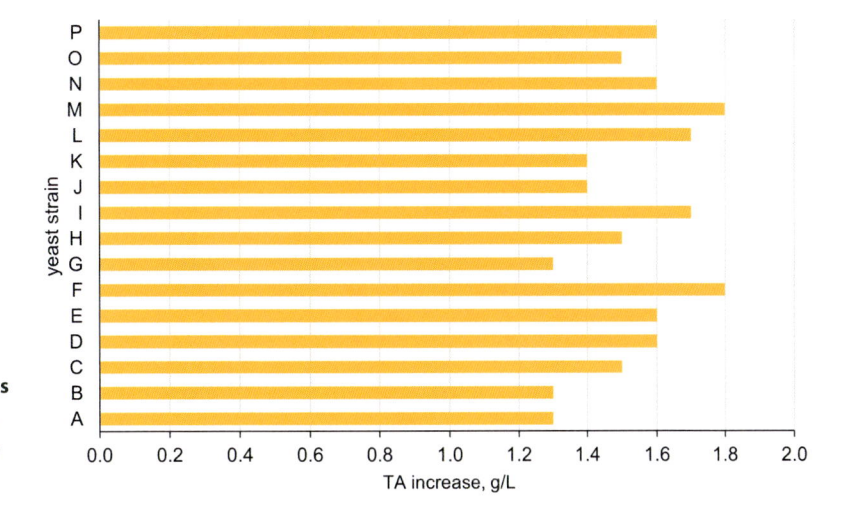

Figure 4.3: Increase of titratable acidity (g/L) during fermentation with sixteen different yeast strains (A–P) in the absence of potassium bitartrate precipitation. Means of four juices.

The Taste of Potassium

The sensory properties of potassium on the palate can be studied by spiking a wine with increasing amounts of potassium without modifying its TA. For that purpose, potassium is added in the form of one of its neutral salts, for example potassium malate. Alternatively, potassium bicarbonate can be added in conjunction with an equivalent amount of malic acid. Under these conditions of comparable TA, the difference threshold of potassium is approximately 200mg/L in both white and red wines. This kind of experimental approach mimics the same conditions occurring in wines with naturally elevated potassium contents: they are held in solution by malic acid and other soluble acids.

From a sensory perspective, high levels of potassium salts enhance the perception of gustatory parameters such as body, weight, volume and fatness. They contribute much more to these sensory perceptions than the legal additives such as mannoproteins, tannins or gum arabic usually recommended for that purpose. In some way, they are also comparable to those elicited by high (~ 20g/L) glycerol contents. However, when potassium exceeds a certain concentration, the wines are described as soapy, bitter, salty, fat or oily, while the untreated standard is considered as more filigree, crispy, delicate, subtle but also more meagre. Conducting the sensory exercise outlined here will demonstrate this dependency.

Apparently, every single wine has a subjectively optimal potassium content, at which it is considered typical by hedonic conventions. In a broader sense, when the focus is on the production of varietal wines, an optimum potassium content can be ascribed to each variety. Clearly, potassium is an underestimated gustatory element in oenology.

Taking such experiments further, it becomes clear that increasing potassium content by 500mg/L K^+ at identical TA lowers the intensity of perceived sourness to an extent that corresponds to 0.5g/L TA. This amount of potassium is removed from solution when 1.9g/L tartaric acid or 0.95g/L TA precipitate as potassium bitartrate during spontaneous KHT crystallisation or by cold stabilisation.

Impact of Increasing Concentration of Potassium on the In-Mouth Sensations

The table below gives measurements for gradually increasing the concentration of potassium (K^+) in a sample of standard white wine (< 700mg/L K^+) at identical TA to see how it affects mouthfeel. Potassium is added as potassium bicarbonate ($KHCO_3$) and neutralised by addition of equivalent amounts of malic acid. Before tasting, use vigorous shaking to remove the carbon dioxide produced.

Sample	Preparation / additions
White wine (reference) + 0mg/L K^+	–
White wine + 300mg/L K^+	+ 0.77g/L $KHCO_3$, + 0.517g/L malic acid
White wine + 600mg/L K^+	+ 1.54g/L $KHCO_3$, + 1.034g/L malic acid
White wine + 900mg/L K^+	+ 2.31g/L $KHCO_3$, + 1.551g/L malic acid
White wine + 1,200mg/L K^+	+ 3.08g/L $KHCO_3$, + 2.068g/L malic acid

Note:
• In this exercise, 1.0g/L $KHCO_3$ can be replaced by 0.69g/L K_2CO_3 (potassium carbonate), and 1.0g/L malic acid can be replaced by the equivalent amount of 0.995g/L citric acid.

Differentiation of Potassium by Viticultural Variables

Potassium uptake by the roots and its accumulation in grapes and must is affected by several viticultural variables, among which rootstock and the availability of soil moisture are the most crucial. High precipitation rates during the ripening period boost potassium content. In contrast, untreated wines from grapes harvested from dry soils or in dry years are characterised by considerably lower levels of potassium (Mpelasoka et al. 2003). Heavy, moist soils lead to higher potassium uptake and storage in the grapes than light or stony soils. These interactions partly explain why wines grown in humid climates tend to have more volume on the palate than those from hot, dry areas. However, when potassium levels exceed an optimum, these wines can become soapy and their acidity can lose its crispness.

Differentiation of Potassium During Vinification

The transfer of grape potassium into must and wine is influenced by winemaking procedures. Free-run juices contain significantly less potassium than their respective pressings. Figure 2.13 gives an example. Increasing mechanical load on the must during consecutive pressings and pressure increases the potassium extraction, which, in turn, raises pH and lowers TA to a non-negligible extent. A similar potassium uptake occurs during skin contact periods. In contrast, when musts or wines from hot growing conditions have tartaric acid added for whatever reason, 1g/L of tartaric acid will reduce potassium by approximately 262mg/L. However, under cool-climate conditions, chemical deacidification is more likely to be required. The following section will show how it affects potassium levels in a sensorially significant way.

4.3 Chemical Deacidification

MLF is not always feasible or compatible with the desired wine style. Hence chemical deacidification remains relevant for white musts and wines from cool-climate growing areas, cool seasons and some high-TA varieties, even including some red varieties. It is fruitless to wait for the problem of too high a TA to miraculously solve itself. As stated in the previous section, TA reduction by natural bitartrate precipitation is limited and largely completed soon after alcoholic fermentation.

However, despite its importance, chemical deacidification appears difficult to master in many wineries. One of the problems to solve is the choice of the deacidification agent. The answer depends on a large array of analytical features and the sensory outcome that is desired. Another problem is that it is necessary to know the exact content of tartaric acid, since this is the only acid that can be removed by precipitation. If, as is so often the case, deacidification is performed in ignorance of the current tartaric acid content and some chemistry basics, the results are disastrous and explain why this way of deacidification has fallen into unjustified disrepute.

Basic Principles

Chemical deacidification makes use of three carbonates, comprising potassium carbonate (K_2CO_3), potassium bicarbonate ($KHCO_3$) and calcium carbonate ($CaCO_3$). The effect of the first two is based on reactions of the potassium ions they donate, while calcium carbonate works through its calcium. The carbonate content of these agents indicates that they are salts of carbonic acid. As they dissolve in the acidic medium, they ionise into potassium/calcium and carbonate ions, for example:

$$K_2CO_3 \rightarrow 2\ K^+ + CO_3^{2-} \text{ or}$$
$$CaCO_3 \rightarrow Ca^{2+} + CO_3^{2-}$$

Next, the carbonate reacts with H^+ ions to yield water and carbon dioxide:

$$CO_3^{2-} + 2\ H^+ \rightarrow H_2O + CO_2$$

The CO_2 escapes through the wine surface without any significant effect on the deacidification process.

Calcium carbonate can be used in three different ways:

- As standard deacidification removing only tartaric acid.
- As simple double-salt deacidification removing tartaric plus malic acid, the latter in a proportion limited by the tartaric acid concentration.

- As extended double-salt deacidification by adding tartaric acid, supplementing that of the wine to facilitate removing unlimited amounts of malic acid in addition to the added tartaric acid.

Unlike calcium carbonate, the potassium ions provided by potassium carbonate or bicarbonate are monovalent and as such not able to generate a double salt consisting of tartrate and malate.

Any chemical deacidification proceeds in two phases:

1. The neutralisation of acids to their corresponding potassium or calcium salts after addition of the deacidification agent. This reaction takes place immediately.
2. The precipitation of the generated salts by means of crystallisation. This proceeds slowly and is responsible for the long waiting times frequently required after chemical deacidification.

When potassium carbonate or bicarbonate is used, the salt that precipitates is potassium bitartrate (KHT), the ordinary cream of tartar. When calcium carbonate is used, the salt precipitating is calcium tartrate in the case of standard calcium deacidification, or calcium tartrate malate in the case of double-salt deacidifications. Some commercially available proprietary blends containing unspecified proportions of both calcium and potassium carbonates promise easy deacidification regardless of the individual wine composition and style. Their careless use can result in disastrous consequences and is highly discouraged.

The Importance of Tartaric Acid Content

Tartaric acid is the only acid in musts and wines able to generate insoluble salts with both calcium and potassium ions provided by the deacidification agents, so it determines the maximum extent of chemical deacidification. Even when a double-salt deacidification is performed, malic acid can only be removed in conjunction with tartaric acid. Therefore, the removal of malic acid and the maximum deacidification span provided by a double-salt deacidification are limited by the concentration of tartaric acid.

Moreover, only a part of the tartaric acid is available for deacidification. This portion is the amount exceeding 1g/L when calcium carbonate is used regardless of the way it is applied, that is, as standard or double-salt deacidification. This means that at least 1g/L of residual tartaric acid should remain in the wine. The less residual tartaric acid remains, the higher the concentration of residual calcium, which can cause serious problems with crystal stability and aftertaste perceptions. In contrast, when potassium carbonates are used, a residual tartaric acid of 1.5 ± 0.3g/L should be allowed for. This threshold is empirical and derived from the average of thousands of unfiltered dry white wines at a cellar storage temperature of 8–15°C. The amount exceeding this threshold is referred to as precipitable tartaric acid. In practical terms, this means that when a wine has only 1.5g/L of tartaric acid, we can assume that almost none of the potassium we add will drop out.

It is important to note in this context that when tartaric acid is measured, this measurement determines the acid anion regardless of whether it exists as free tartaric acid, partially neutralised (potassium bitartrate) or completely neutralised (dipotassium tartrate) salt. In the pH range of wine,

Two types of crystals that can be formed during chemical deacidification and afterwards. The amber fused crystals are made of potassium bitartrate, and the small white ones consist of calcium tartrate.

Tartaric and Malic Acid During Grape Ripening

Using some simplification that is admissible for technical considerations, one can state that the titratable acidity of musts obtained from sound fruit comprises only tartaric and malic acid. The relative amount of these acids sometimes leads to conclusions about grape ripeness. This approach is partially justified by the different behaviour of these acids during grape ripening.

Tartaric acid is almost biologically inert. Compared to malic acid, it undergoes much less degradation during ripening. After crushing or pressing, its content is poorly related to grape ripeness and varies between 4 and 8g/L at best. In contrast, malic acid is easily depleted in the fruit by respiration. Therefore, juices obtained from ripe grapes show markedly lower levels of malic acid than those from unripe fruit.

Varying amounts of malic acid are primarily responsible for the considerable fluctuations of titratable acidity, while tartaric acid remains relatively constant. When malic acid level is high, TA also tends to be high. In this case, the percentage share of tartaric acid is obviously lower.

the major portion of tartaric acid actually exists in the form of its salts, which are partially soluble. For that reason, wines always display some tartaric acid even after strong deacidifications.

Many winemakers in cool-climate areas in need of chemical deacidification tend to assess tartaric acid content as a percentage of titratable acidity. This approach can be disastrous when it is used to calculate the amount of tartaric acid available for chemical deacidification. In reality, tartaric acid content is not closely related to TA. Annual weather conditions and differences between growing areas, microclimates and even vineyard blocks make the actual tartaric acid level hardly predictable. Hence, when juices are to be deacidified by more than 2g/L TA, the choice of the deacidification method should be based on the tartaric acid concentration measured previously.

For wine deacidification, knowledge of the instantaneous tartaric acid concentration is even more important. Even though there might be some weak relationship between TA and tartaric acid in juices, it is without any foundation in wines. The reason for this lies in the heavy and variable losses of tartaric acid caused by KHT precipitation during and after fermentation, meaning the tartaric acid content in wine is absolutely unpredictable. Since quite often too little attention is paid to this detail, many wines end up entirely different than expected after deacidification.

Timing of Chemical Deacidification – Juice vs Wine – and its Impact on Potassium

Minor chemical deacidifications are possible at any stage during production and storage of wine. They are frequently useful even in the realm of sensory fine tuning when the wines move into their final phase. A typical example is the addition of some 0.5 or 0.7g/L of potassium bicarbonate, followed by addition of metatartaric acid or CMC for crystal stabilisation just before bottling. When such minor acidity corrections are based on careful bench testing (section 8.2), they are not associated with side effects detrimental to overall wine quality. On the contrary, they can make a tremendous contribution to in-mouth quality.

However, the question of timing chemical deacidification is different in bad years for cool-climate growing areas with juices displaying 10 or 12g/L TA, which need to be transformed into white wines with 6.0 or 7.0g/L TA. More precisely, should extensive chemical deacidification by several g/L TA be better performed on juice or on wine? As already explained, considerable amounts of tartaric acid drop out as KHT during and after alcoholic fermentation. With some variation, these precipitations halve the initial contents of tartaric acid and potassium in most wines (section 4.2).

In contrast, when deacidification is performed on juice, tartaric acid is removed to a large extent and is no longer available for the precipitation of potassium. Each g/L of tartaric acid that is removed by juice deacidification stabilises an additional 262mg/L of potassium in solution. Deacidifications removing several g/L of TA from juices are not unusual for certain varieties grown in cool-climate areas. Under these conditions, tartaric acid is reduced to an extent that prevents any further KHT precipitation and stabilises potassium at its initial high juice level. Postponing deacidification until after fermentation allows for a natural decrease of potassium.

Based on a comparable final TA, the basic difference between juice and wine deacidification lies in the potassium content of the finished wine. The gustatory differences resulting from this are far reaching and directly impact the way the wine is perceived on the palate. They explain why wines deacidified prior to fermentation show up as more full-bodied and less sour than could be explained by their TA: they contain more potassium, which masks sourness. How this effect is rated in terms of quality depends on the individual wine and consumer preferences. For sparkling wines, base wines with low potassium levels are preferred.

Damp growing conditions during grape ripening mobilise soil potassium, promoting its uptake and storage in the grapes (section 4.2). Such weather conditions also tend to yield underripe fruit with high acidity. When juice deacidification is performed under these circumstances, wines can be flawed by surplus potassium. In analytical terms, they display relatively high pH figures in relation to TA. As shown in Figure 4.4, potassium strongly boosts pH. High pH figures affect microbial safety during fermentation and facilitate the occurrence of spontaneous MLF afterwards. In order to prevent an uncontrolled, additional loss of TA in this way, measures should be taken to ensure smooth alcoholic fermentation (section 2.3) and provide at least 30mg/L free SO_2 soon after.

Ultimately, sensory goals play a major role. When the intention is to emphasise weight and volume on the palate, one might tend to deacidify the juice and preserve natural potassium. On the other hand, when natural potassium levels are known to be high and when more vibrant and filigree white wines are to be obtained, one might opt for potassium depletion during primary fermentation and deacidifying the wine. Thus there is no definitive answer to whether deacidification should be carried out on the juice or the wine. Both options have benefits and drawbacks that must be evaluated on a case-by-case basis.

Timing of Chemical Deacidification – Juice vs Wine – and its Impact on Workload

While juice can often be deacidified by standard procedures using potassium or calcium carbonate, extensive deacidification of wine frequently requires

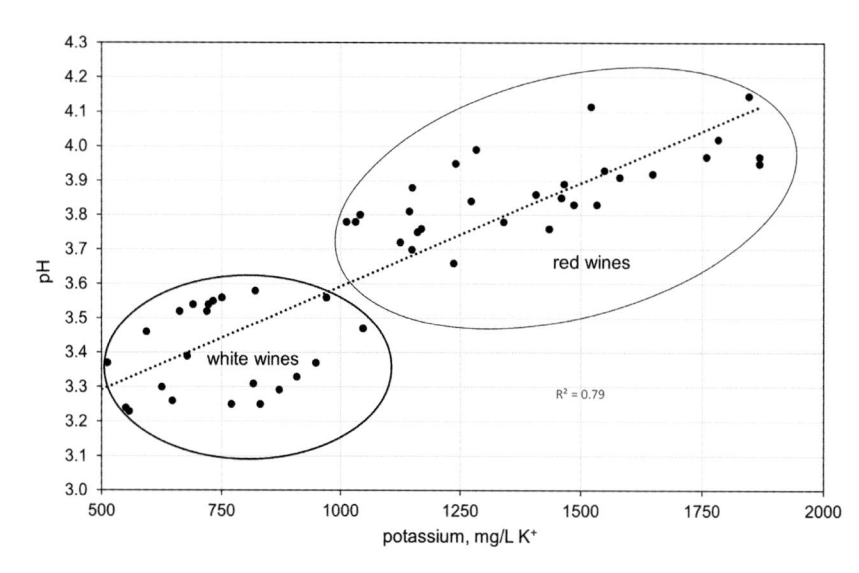

Figure 4.4: Potassium content of wines related to pH.

the more cumbersome double-salt procedure. The reason for this is the heavy loss of tartaric acid during fermentation already discussed, which means that it is no longer available for simple standard procedures of deacidification. Ultimately, the currently available tartaric acid content and the extent of deacidification are the deciding factors for the deacidification procedure to be applied.

When deacidification of young wine requires the use of calcium carbonate in one way or another, measures must be taken to reduce residual surplus calcium and stabilise the wine against post-bottling calcium precipitations. Adequate procedures for doing so are time-consuming. Accordingly, early deacidification of juice allows more time for natural calcium stabilisation until bottling.

Chemical Deacidification with Potassium Carbonates

Whenever chemical deacidification is required, the use of potassium carbonates is preferred to calcium carbonate, because the precipitation of the potassium bitartrate (KHT) generated proceeds faster than that of calcium tartrate. In general, it takes some two to three weeks when it occurs spontaneously in young white wines stored at typical cellar temperatures. After this period, the relative degree of KHT stability or instability existing before deacidification is restored. Absolute crystal stability required for bottling can easily and quickly be achieved (section 7.3), so potassium carbonates can also be suitable for deacidification shortly before bottling. Furthermore, an increase of wines' natural potassium content is not necessarily detrimental to quality in cases where the potassium provided does not completely precipitate. In contrast, elevated calcium residues must always be removed.

Efficiency Depends on Tartaric Acid Content

When practitioners deacidify with potassium carbonates, they expect the potassium ions to completely drop out with tartaric acid as potassium bitartrate. Thus, according to stoichiometry of basic chemistry, they also expect to need 0.67g/L of $KHCO_3$ or 0.46g/L of K_2CO_3 to remove 1.0g/L TA. This is the popular formula found in most textbooks. Under practical conditions, however, additions of these amounts of $KHCO_3$ or K_2CO_3 need some time to give the final TA as calculated by this simplified stoichiometry. Indeed, the final TA is sometimes never attained even after longer waiting periods. This means that higher amounts of $KHCO_3$ or K_2CO_3 are required than expected.

The assumption that deacidification by 1.0g/L TA requires 0.67g/L of $KHCO_3$ or 0.46g/L of K_2CO_3 certainly only applies to a very limited extent. Reactions are much more complex than a simple precipitation of tartaric acid. The explanation lies in what is understood by 'precipitable' or 'technically usable' tartaric acid, which complicates calculations. The following explanations will illustrate why the efficiency of $KHCO_3$ and K_2CO_3 depend considerably on the individual wine and particularly on its tartaric acid content.

Potassium carbonate and bicarbonate work similarly, but with a different stoichiometry since they differ in terms of potassium content. Thus, they are interchangeable according to the conversion factor:

$$1.0\text{g/L KHCO}_3 \triangleq 0.69\text{g/L K}_2\text{CO}_3$$

In the following examples, equations are only given for $KHCO_3$. However, these can easily be converted into K_2CO_3 if required.

When $KHCO_3$ is added to wine, the acidic environment makes it dissociate into potassium cations and carbon dioxide according to the formula:

$$KHCO_3 \rightarrow K^+ + HCO_3^-$$
$$HCO_3^- + H^+ \rightarrow H_2CO_3 \rightarrow H_2O + CO_2$$

In a first step, the potassium cations neutralise an equivalent amount of titratable acidity. Since TA is expressed as tartaric acid, the following general reaction and mass equation applies:

$2 \cdot KHCO_3$ + tartaric acid equivalents → potassium salts
$2 \cdot 100.1 + 150.1$
$1.334\text{g/L} \triangleq 1.0\text{g/L}$

Where 100.1 and 150.1 are the molecular weights of $KHCO_3$ and tartaric acid respectively.

This means that the addition of 1.334g/L of $KHCO_3$ leads to the neutralisation of 1.0g/L TA. The reduction of TA thus generated is immediate. There will be no additional losses of TA as long as the potassium ions added remain stable in solution. This is the case when there is no tartaric acid available to precipitate them as KHT or when that precipitation is inhibited by wine constituents.

In the presence of tartaric acid able to precipitate potassium ions, the whole picture will change. Section 4.2 showed that KHT is an acidic salt, in which only one of the two acid groups of tartaric acid is neutralised. It also showed that when 1g/L of tartaric acid precipitates in the form of KHT, this inevitably causes a decrease of TA by 0.5g/L.

Now imagine that the wine contains enough tartaric acid and a chemical makeup that allows the potassium ions added to entirely precipitate as KHT. Then the TA neutralisation as the first step is followed by a reduction of TA to an identical extent, so the addition of 1.334g/L of $KHCO_3$ now leads to a decrease of TA by 2.0g/L in total. As a result, we arrive with the quite popular formula stipulating the need of 0.67g/L $KHCO_3$ to reduce TA by 1.0g/L. This formula takes into account the loss of TA that would occur when the added potassium (K^+) drops out completely as KHT. In other words, there is a two-step reaction:

1. Addition of 0.67g/L $KHCO_3$ → immediate reduction of TA by 0.5g/L.
2. Precipitation of K^+ as KHT → further reduction of TA by another 0.5g/L.

The cumulative effect is 0.67g/L $KHCO_3$ → reduction of TA by 1.0g/L.

It cannot be overemphasised that the cumulative effect of 0.67g/L $KHCO_3$ per 1.0g/L TA only occurs when the added potassium entirely drops out. Only then is the final TA striven for attained in analytical and sensory terms. This process requires both enough tartaric acid and some time for crystallisation.

This kind of two-step sequence does not occur when calcium carbonate is used. In this case, calculated final TA is attained right after addition of the $CaCO_3$ regardless of any precipitation of calcium tartrate. As a neutral salt, its precipitation does not affect titratable acidity.

Recap: Efficiency Factors of $KHCO_3$

In conclusion, deacidification with $KHCO_3$ can follow three different scenarios:

1. Deacidification by 1.0g/L TA requires 0.67g/L of $KHCO_3$ when the wine contains enough tartaric acid that can actually be precipitated as potassium bitartrate.
2. When potassium added as $KHCO_3$ is prevented from precipitating due to inhibition of crystallisation or lack of precipitable tartaric acid, the reduction of TA by 1.0g/L requires the addition of 1.34g/L $KCHO_3$.
3. Only a portion of the added potassium drops out, while the rest remains in solution. In such a wine, the reduction of TA by 1.0g/L requires the addition of $KHCO_3$ somewhere in the range of 0.67 to 1.34g/L. In other words, 0.67g/L of $KHCO_3$ causes a reduction of TA by 0.5 to 1.0g/L according to the particular wine.

Let's summarise once more to clarify: to reduce TA by 1.0g/L, the amount of $KHCO_3$ required is 0.67–1.34g/L. The exact amount depends on whether, and to what extent, the added potassium will precipitate tartaric acid. However, this precipitation does not occur or is incomplete when:

- The tartaric acid level currently available is too low to allow precipitation.
- Wines already contain metatartaric acid or CMC (section 7.5) inhibiting potassium bitartrate precipitation. A similar behaviour can be observed in red wines, in which tannins and anthocyanins hamper potassium bitartrate precipitation.

In case studies 2 and 3, the specific taste of potassium (section 4.2) will emerge to a greater or lesser extent. Concurrently, there will be a significant increase of pH, which might affect microbiological stability if the wine is stored at too high a temperature and not filtered.

$KHCO_3$ can be used for deacidifying by several g/L of TA, always bearing in mind the level of tartaric acid

Case Studies

The three scenarios mentioned in the text can be clarified by the following real-world white wine case studies.

Case Study 1
TA = 7.0g/L
Tartaric acid = 2.5g/L
Final TA desired = 6.0g/L
→ deacidification range = 1.0g/L TA
Residual tartaric acid = 1.5g/L
→ 1.0g/L tartaric acid available for precipitation with potassium

Calculation:
2.5g/L tartaric acid − 1.5g/L residual tartaric acid
= 1.0g/L precipitable tartaric acid × 0.67 = 0.67g/L $KHCO_3$

Case Study 2
TA = 7.0g/L
Tartaric acid = 1.5g/L
Final TA desired = 6.0g/L
→ deacidification range = 1.0g/L
Residual tartaric acid = 1.5g/L
→ almost no tartaric acid precipitable with potassium

Calculation:
Deacidification without precipitation of tartaric acid using 1.34g/L $KHCO_3$. The added potassium will remain in solution and act on the palate regardless of the deacidification achieved.

Case Study 3
TA = 8.0g/L
Tartaric acid = 2.5g/L
Final TA desired = 6.0g/L
→ deacidification range = 2.0g/L
Residual tartaric acid = 1.5g/L
→ tartaric acid partially available for precipitation with potassium

Calculation:
1. Precipitation of 1.0g/L of tartaric acid with 0.67g/L $KHCO_3$
2. Neutralization of another 1.0g/L of TA with 1.34g/L $KHCO_3$ without precipitation

This deacidification requires a total of 0.67 + 1.34 = 2.01g/L $KHCO_3$. The added potassium remains partially in solution and acts on the palate regardless of the deacidification achieved.

---

that is currently available for precipitation. In contrast to calcium carbonate ($CaCO_3$), its use represents a gentler treatment of wine since potassium is a natural wine constituent and has a positive effect on the palate over a large concentration range. Furthermore, it facilitates crystal stabilisation. Based on these benefits, deacidification with $KHCO_3$ is preferable to using $CaCO_3$ as long as the analytical and sensory features of the wine permit doing so. However, there are situations when $KHCO_3$ must be replaced by $CaCO_3$ or other means of deacidification. These are when:

- Initial TA is very high or the deacidification range striven for is high.
- Tartaric acid level is low.
- pH is already relatively high in relation to TA, thus indicating a naturally elevated potassium content (section 4.2) that should not be increased further.

Practical Application of Potassium Carbonates
Potassium carbonates react regardless of the way they are applied. However, some commercial brands tend to form clumps that dissolve poorly, so it is advisable to crush any clumps before use to ensure their complete dissolution.

Despite their ease of use, potassium carbonates should not be directly added to the whole wine volume. The carbon dioxide produced can cause overflow when no headspace is available in the container. Its release strips out appreciable amounts of volatile aromatics from sensitive white wines, particularly when they are deacidified at higher storage temperatures. A good way to avoid these side-effects is the initial dissolution and neutralisation of the potassium carbonates in a fraction of the total wine volume. Upon blending back the overdeacidified fraction, no more CO_2 is produced in the original lot. The volume of the fraction used to dissolve the potassium carbonates must be large enough to provide sufficient acidity for its complete neutralisation and the release of all carbon dioxide.

For example, say 5,000L of wine with 8.0g/L TA should be deacidified using 1.5g/L of $KHCO_3$, corresponding to a total amount of 7.5kg $KHCO_3$. Complete neutralisation of 1.5g $KHCO_3$ requires 1.5÷1.34 = 1.12g TA (as tartaric acid). This results in 5,600g TA for 7,500g $KHCO_3$. In order to make this amount of TA available, the fraction must contain at least 5,600÷8.0 = 700 L.

A modification of this procedure is to put the solid potassium bicarbonate, free of clumps, into a tank and to add the wine slowly making sure the tank is filled from the bottom. This can be done when racking, blending, or filtration require a transfer from one tank to another. After transfer of some 20 per cent of the total volume, the wine flow is interrupted for some minutes. Formation and release of surplus CO_2 takes place in the first subsets of wine flowing into the tank. The transfer replaces vigorous stirring, which would otherwise become necessary to mix the wine after deacidification. This way of first dissolving potassium carbonates in a partial volume before adding the rest of the wine has the additional advantage of accelerating the precipitation of KHT produced and improving crystal stability. Previous cooling of the wine to a temperature of less than 10°C additionally promotes the crystallisation rate.

Chemical Deacidification with Calcium Carbonate

The simplest way to use calcium carbonate ($CaCO_3$) is simply to combine it with the total amount of juice or wine to be deacidified. In doing so, the wine is slowly pumped to the $CaCO_3$ previously dissolved in a small volume of the wine to prepare a paste. The objective is to precipitate tartaric acid as calcium tartrate within the limits of available tartaric acid minus 1g/L. This means, for example, that when the tartaric acid level is 3.5g/L, only 2.5g/L can be removed and 1.0g/L should remain. Thus, TA is lowered by 2.5g/L. If less residual tartaric acid is left by adding too high amounts of $CaCO_3$, the levels of residual calcium will increase dramatically and complicate crystal stabilisation.

The precipitation of 1.0g/L tartaric acid requires 0.67g/L of $CaCO_3$. This amount derives from the underlying reaction and mass equation:

Tartaric acid	+	$CaCO_3$	→	Ca-tartrate	
150.1	+	100.1	→	180.2	(formula 1)
1.0g/L	≙	0.67g/L			

In practice, a rounding up to 0.7g/L $CaCO_3$ per 1g/L TA is usual and justified, as the lime sometimes does not entirely dissolve. The calculated TA reduction occurs instantaneously because the calcium tartrate formed is a neutral salt whose precipitation does not cause any additional reduction in TA.

The calcium tartrate formed shows a different and delayed crystallisation from the potassium bitartrate formed after deacidification with potassium carbonates. This makes crystal stabilisation extremely complex, as will be shown later. Therefore, for this purpose, the calcium carbonate is usually replaced by potassium carbonates.

Double-Salt Deacidification with Calcium Carbonate

The use of calcium carbonate is only of interest when there is not enough tartaric acid that can be precipitated to achieve the desired final TA. This happens essentially in high-acidity juices and wines that contain much more malic acid than tartaric acid. Addition of calcium carbonate by the standard method previously described would then exhaust tartaric acid and leave elevated calcium levels, causing a chalky aftertaste and a strong calcium crystal instability. In such cases, if MLF (section 4.1) is not possible or desirable, the use of calcium carbonate in the form of the so-called double-salt deacidification will become indispensable. It is the only way of chemical

$$+ \text{ 2 CaCO}_3$$

COOH-CHOH-CHOH-COOH   COOH-CHOH-CH$_2$-COOH
tartaric acid   malic acid

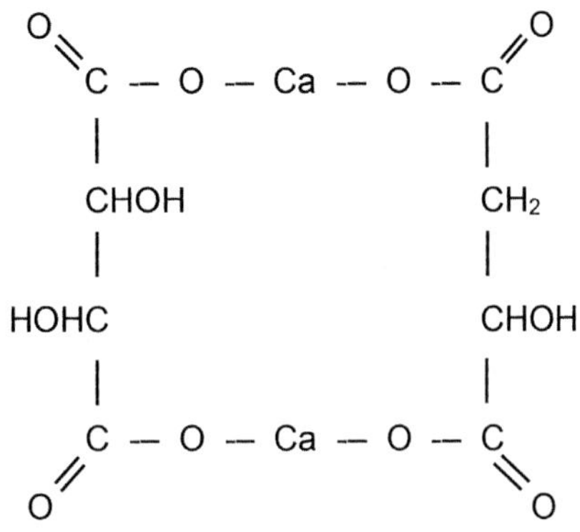

Figure 4.5: Chemical structure of calcium tartrate malate (double salt).

deacidification that also addresses malic acid, thus enhancing the maximum deacidification range. When tartaric and malic acid precipitate simultaneously with calcium ions, a double salt is generated which is called 'calcium tartrate malate' or 'calcium tartro-malate'. In this process, two moles of acid react with two moles of CaCO$_3$. Therefore, a 1:1 relationship applies. As a result, to reduce TA by 1.0g/L, 0.67g/L CaCO$_3$ is required just as for the standard use of CaCO$_3$.

Theoretically, the double salt contains equal molar amounts of tartaric and malic acid, but this only happens when malic acid has twice the tartaric acid concentration. Otherwise there will be a preferential removal of tartaric acid. Frequently the malic acid percentage of the crystal mass obtained is only 25–40 per cent (Steele and Kunkee 1978). When the double-salt procedure fails for technical reasons, the malic acid percentage is even less, while the predominant portion of the precipitated crystal material is tartaric acid in the form of calcium tartrate as single salt.

Although the double-salt procedure does not require more CaCO$_3$ than the standard deacidification with CaCO$_3$, its technical implementation is substantially different. Since malic acid is a weaker acid, it cannot bind to calcium ions to form a precipitate at wine pH. Hence the pH needs to be raised to at least 4.5 to allow calcium to also bind to malic acid and thus enable double salt precipitation. For that purpose, double-salting is only performed on a partial volume of the original lot. This fraction is separated and overdeacidified with the CaCO$_3$ calculated for the entire must/wine volume, filtered, and blended back with the untreated residual volume. The fraction (F) is calculated as:

$$F = \frac{DR \bullet 100}{TA - 2} \quad \text{(formula 2)}$$

for musts and as:

$$F = \frac{DR \bullet 100}{TA - 3} \quad \text{(formula 3)}$$

for wines.

In the following formulas, F = fraction in per cent of the total volume to deacidify, TA = titratable acidity in g/L, and DR = deacidification range in g/L TA.

The terms -2 and -3 are applied as empirical correction factors. Their purpose is to ensure that there is enough tartaric acid in the calculated fraction, and to limit carry-over of dissolved, residual calcium from the fraction into the untreated volume. Therefore, the fraction of wine should be somewhat larger than the fraction of juice.

The maximum deacidification range DR_{max} is calculated for musts as:

$$DR_{max} = \frac{(TH_2 - 1) \bullet (TA - 2)}{(TA - 2) - TH_2} \quad \text{(formula 4)}$$

and for wines as:

$$DR_{max} = \frac{(TH_2 - 1) \bullet (TA - 3)}{(TA - 3) - TH_2} \quad \text{(formula 5)}$$

Here, TH_2 = tartaric acid in g/L and 1 = the residual tartaric acid that has to remain in g/L. Alternatively, 1.0g/L for residual tartaric acid can be replaced by different values ranging from 1.0 to 2.0g/L.

Example: a must has 12.5g/L TA and 3.2g/L tartaric acid. According to formula 4, the maximum possible deacidification range DR_{max} is:

$$DR_{max} = \frac{(3.2 - 1) \bullet (12.5 - 2)}{(12.5 - 2) - 3.2} = 3.16 \text{g/L}$$

For lack of tartaric acid this must can only be deacidified by 12.5 − 3.16 = 9.34g/L final TA. In this case, the fraction F is calculated according to formula 2:

$$F = \frac{3.16 \bullet 100}{12.5 - 2} = 30.1\%$$

and the amount of $CaCO_3$ required amounts to 3.16 • 0.7 = 2.2g per litre total volume (formula 1).

Mathematics for calculating must and $CaCO_3$ additions under harvest stress can be tricky, but spreadsheet applications to streamline calculations are available online. However, many of them do not show the correction factors. As a result, less malic acid is removed and more calcium remains in the wine.

Double Salting – Step by Step

1. Measure the wine/must volume.
2. Calculate the exact amounts of $CaCO_3$ and fraction needed. As a general rule, too small a fraction volume is less detrimental for the double salt formation than too large a fraction.
3. Dissolve the $CaCO_3$ lime in some three times its volume of wine/must to prepare a paste. The lime should be fresh and reactive. If it does not produce foam in a tasting glass containing some wine, it is too slow to react and can only be used for standard deacidification. Pour the $CaCO_3$ paste into a deacidification vessel equipped with a strong propeller mixer and with headspace large enough to prevent foaming over.
4. Add the fraction slowly and without interruption into the deacidification vessel that contains the lime paste over at least 30 minutes under constant and vigorous stirring using the mixer. Add it onto the blade of the mixer. The purpose of stirring is to ensure proper reaction conditions and persistently drive out the carbon dioxide produced, which would otherwise lower the pH and impede the formation of the double salt. A low, stable wine flowrate and strong stirring ensure that reaction conditions and proper pH adjust by themselves. During the process, pH must not drop below 4.5 and should be controlled with a portable pH meter if the winemaker does not feel secure or lacks experience. If the process threatens to finish in less than 30 minutes, reduce the wine inflow rate.
5. Continue stirring for another 10 minutes after the addition of the fraction to the $CaCO_3$ is finished. The reaction is completed when no more CO_2 is released.
6. The double salt slurry is quite voluminous. The bulky structure of its hedgehog-like crystals impedes their compaction to a solid sediment, so it makes up almost half of the fraction volume at the end.
7. Performing the double-salt method does not necessarily ensure the formation of the double salt. When the procedure fails, the wine will behave as if it has been overdeacidified by the standard procedure, exhausting the tartaric acid content. The TA reduction looked for will be achieved anyway, but fairly high residual calcium levels will be an embarrassing outcome. The easiest way to monitor the success of the operation is to sample a glass of the fraction after switching off the mixer. If the crystal lees settle slowly, the process is successful. In contrast, if they settle within 10–15 minutes, the result has been a standard deacidification, meaning that calcium tartrate crystals have been produced instead of double salt crystals.
8. The double-salt is only stable at pH higher than 4.5. It must therefore be entirely removed before the

fraction is recombined with the residual volume, or it would disintegrate into calcium tartrate crystals and cancel the double salting effect. Hence the fraction has to be filtered. The filtrate obtained is immediately added to the untreated residual volume.
9. The filtration should be executed without delay the same day. The high pH makes the filtrate susceptible to oxidation and microbiological degradation.
10. For filtration, diatomaceous earth filters, lees filters or hydropresses (section 2.5) are the best choices. Cross-flow filters should be handled with care since there are anecdotal reports about cartridges damaged by the double-salt crystals. In any case, the filtration could be a coarse one since the crystals are bulky. Removal of the crystal mass by settling and racking is a bad improvisation, causing large wine losses. Furthermore, suspended double-salt crystals would get into the original lot, redissolve, release calcium and shift calcium content to troublesome levels.
11. The following details have to be taken into account for filtration: each 1kg of $CaCO_3$ applied will require a volume of 3 litres in the filter. The double salt slurry contains approximately 50 per cent of wine. Diatomaceous earth filters take up an amount of double salt slurry corresponding to some 2kg of $CaCO_3$ per $1m^2$ of filter surface area. Hence the filter might be emptied and restarted several times when larger volumes are to be processed. On the other hand, the bulky structure of double salt crystals facilitates filtration, as they act as a filter aid.
12. After the double salt lees have been removed by filtration, the filter cannot be used for subsequent filtration of the residual untreated wine volume without cleaning it, or the double salt crystals remaining in the filter would redissolve in the untreated portion passing through. The outcome would be a badly performed standard deacidification.
13. The filtrate is quite clean and should be immediately recombined with the original lot, as its high pH makes it prone to microbial and aroma degradation. The surplus of calcium it still contains will gradually precipitate with the tartaric acid completely preserved in the untreated lot. It is essential to mix well after blending back.
14. It is obvious that all the agitations and pumpings involved in the double-salt process run counter to the philosophy of gentle wine treatment and are detrimental to volatile aromatics of fruity white wines. A fraction of the aromatics evaporates as a result of an agitated wine surface, temperature and stripping out by CO_2 release (section 7.3). When this kind of deacidification is performed on wine, it is therefore recommended to do so at the lowest possible temperature to restrict aroma losses by volatilisation.

Extended Double-Salt Deacidification
In extreme cases, juices or wines can contain a large excess of malic acid compared to only a minimal amount of tartaric acid to such an extent that even the double-salt procedure runs into its limits. It must be remembered that the deacidification range it permits is limited by the tartaric acid level, and that one cannot remove more malic acid than there is tartaric acid available. Enhancing the ratio of tartaric to malic acid allows us to extend the scope of this kind of deacidification.

The addition of tartaric acid to the entire volume of wine is the easiest way to overcome this problem, improve the ratio of tartaric to malic acid, and allow for an unlimited deacidification range regardless of the initial tartaric acid content. When this approach is chosen, care must be taken to perform the double-salt process immediately after the addition of tartaric acid. Otherwise a major part of the tartaric acid added would spontaneously precipitate as potassium bitartrate and no longer be available for double salting. A more economic method involving adding tartaric acid only to the fraction to be overdeacidified is described in the literature (Schneider and Troxel 2022).

Workload and Accurate Data
Double salting is a laborious procedure. For that reason, standard deacidification is preferable as long as there is enough tartaric acid available for achieving the final TA required. However, the correct way to deacidify is never a matter of choice. It is important to remember

that the instantaneous level of tartaric acid determines whether standard, double-salt or extended double-salt deacidification is required. Tartaric acid figures measured several weeks previously may not remain valid since they tend to decrease by KHT precipitation. Inaccurate tartaric acid data are one of the primary reasons for failure of the double-salt process and any other method of chemical deacidification.

Calcium Residues and their Consequences for Crystal Stability

However deacidification with calcium carbonate is performed, it always leaves elevated calcium residues for a considerable time, which can lead to their delayed crystallisation as calcium tartrate after bottling. While untreated juices and wines rarely display more than 100mg/L Ca^{++}, they do not pose a risk of such a

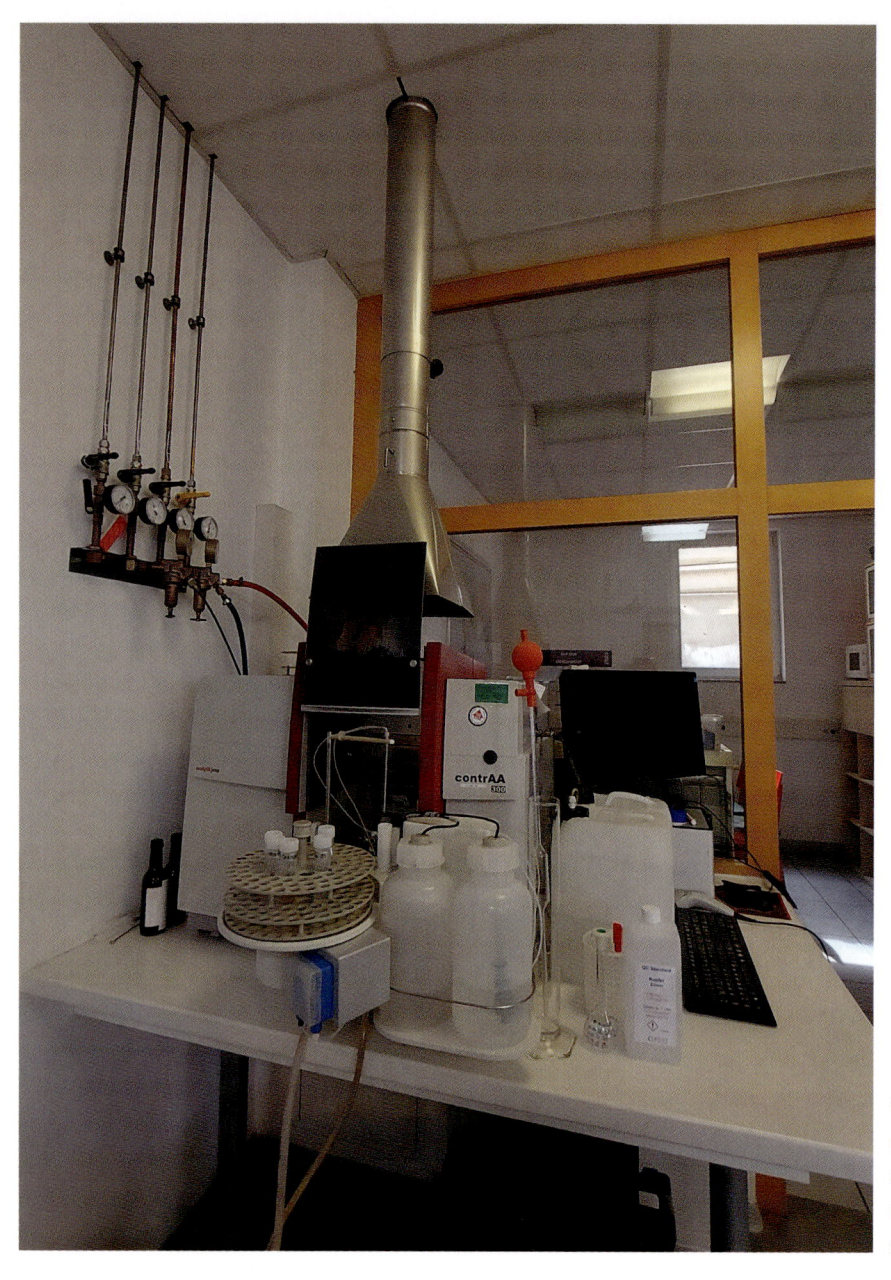

Calcium and numerous other mineral cations are routinely measured using atomic absorption spectroscopy (AAS).

post-bottling crystallisation. In contrast, after most deacidifications with $CaCO_3$, enhanced calcium levels of 150–350mg/L Ca^{++} can remain in the wine for many months even if deacidification has been performed correctly.

When calcium tartrate drops out in the bottles, the corresponding crystals are usually too small to be identified as such by the naked eye – they appear as a rather amorphous deposit or cloudiness. Their identification is relatively easy by adding sulphuric acid 10% or 25%. They do not dissolve in sulphuric acid but are converted into insoluble white crystals of calcium sulphate (gypsum). In contrast, the better-known potassium bitartrate crystals dissolve under the same conditions within a couple of minutes. Analytical measurement of calcium and potassium in the dissolved crystal mass gives additional reliability. However, there is a less sophisticated hands-on test based on tasting: the more common potassium bitartrate crystals give a sour taste on the palate as they represent a sour salt, while calcium tartrate crystals do not have any taste. In some wines, a mix of both of them can be observed.

Unfortunately, additions of so-called protective colloids as metatartaric acid, carboxymethylcellulose or potassium aspartate used to stabilise wines against KHT precipitations (section 8.3) hardly show any effectiveness against calcium tartrate precipitations. Hence there is no other choice than decreasing the calcium concentration. Addition of DL-tartaric acid is the most common treatment to do so. In contrast to naturally occurring L-tartaric acid, this is an equimolar mixture of both optically active forms of tartaric acid. It acts by producing an almost insoluble salt with calcium, which is called calcium DL-tartrate. The solubility of that salt is approximately ten times lower than that of the calcium L-tartrate occurring in unstable wines (Viaux et al. 1996). Based on this low solubility, the calcium DL-tartrate generated in wine can precipitate within one month. Details are described elsewhere (Schneider and Troxell 2022).

The main disadvantage of using DL-tartaric acid is the necessity for strict analytical monitoring of the calcium content. If this is not possible, there should be a delay of at least six months before bottling. This suggests that this type of deacidification should be performed as early as possible, preferably on the must.

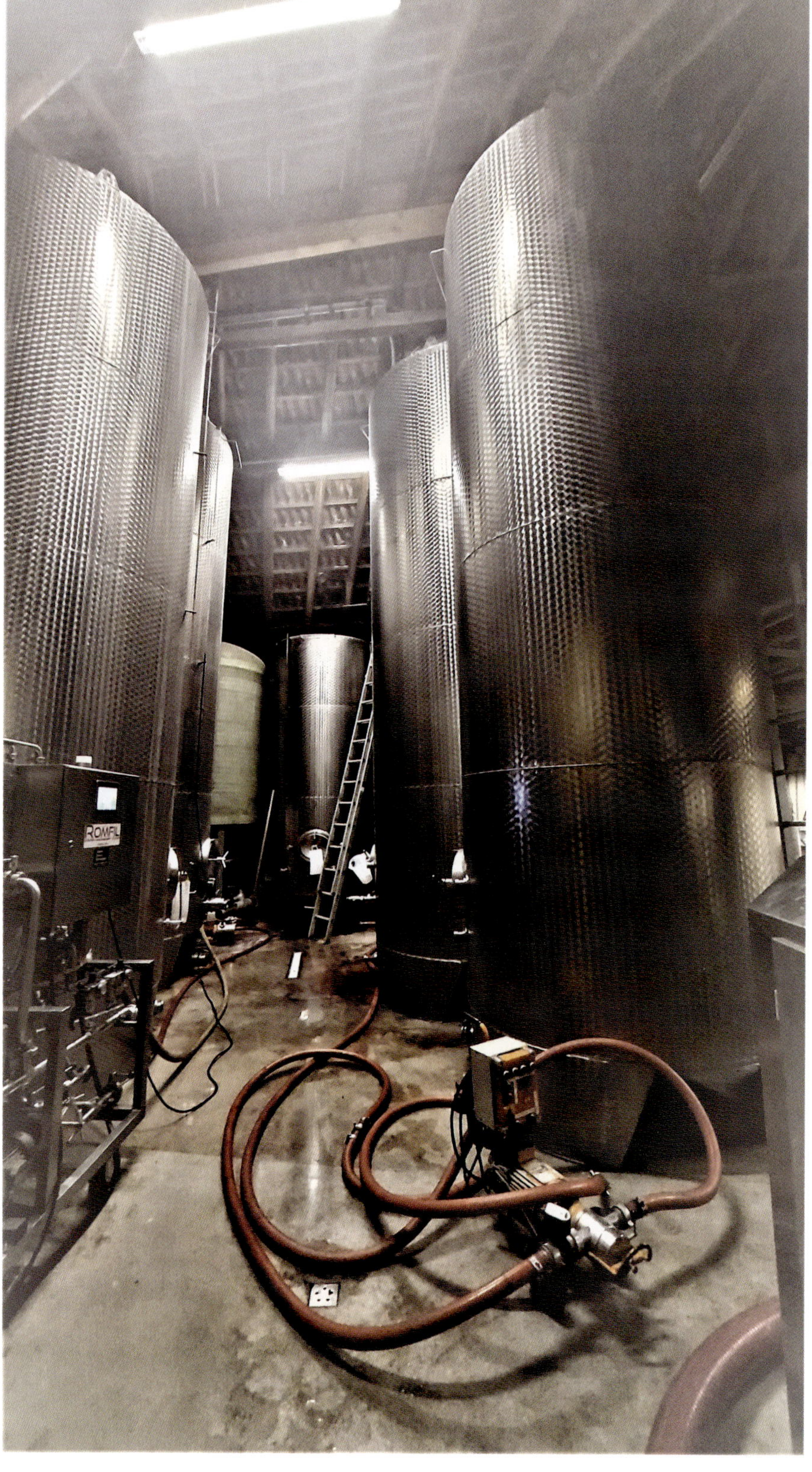
ROMFIL

CHAPTER 5

USE AND EFFECT OF REDUCING AGENTS DURING STORAGE

While oxidation of musts is usually not harmful, oxidation of the wine is always detrimental, even if no browning is observed. It is the result of the often uncontrolled oxygen uptake by wine after fermentation. To mitigate it, sulphite is traditionally added in amounts per litre that are significantly less than the daily production of sulphite by the human body. At the same time, its free form also inhibits undesirable microbiological activities. In this chapter, the timing and quantities of its use are addressed. Its chemical action as a reducing agent is outlined and it is shown that it does not completely prevent the adverse effects of oxygen uptake. The addition of supplementary reducing agents such as ascorbic acid or inactive dry yeast preparations can complement the effect of sulphite to a variable degree. However, the most effective protection against oxidation are yeast lees that remain in suspension after fermentation. They consume a large part of the oxygen directly and thus withdraw it from reactions with wine constituents. Therefore, an unnecessarily early clarification of the wines is counterproductive.

5.1 Sulphur Dioxide

The use of sulphur dioxide (SO_2) in winemaking has three distinctive functions:
- Inhibition of fault-producing spoilage microorganisms.
- Protection against excessive oxidation.
- Binding with free acetaldehyde and other carbonyls and converting them into odourless products.

In aqueous solutions such as wine, sulphur dioxide exists in forms other than only SO_2 dissolved as a gas. First, there is a free and a bound form, with the sum of these two representing total SO_2. Bound SO_2 is basically inactive. Its amount is predetermined by wine composition or, more precisely, by the concentration of its binding partners. Oenological interest regarding wine shelf life is focused upon free SO_2.

Free sulphur dioxide in aqueous solution such as wine exists in three states: molecular (SO_2), bisulphite (HSO_3^-), and sulphite (SO_3^{2-}). These forms are in a dynamic equilibrium with one another according to the formula:

$$SO_2 + H_2O \leftrightarrow H^+ + HSO_3^- \leftrightarrow SO_3^{2-} + H^+$$

Each form has different properties. Molecular SO_2 is dissolved as a volatile gas, has both an antimicrobial and chemical effect and is sensorially active due to its pungent smell. The bisulphite form binds with many

OPPOSITE: **Cellar equipment in a medium-sized winery.**

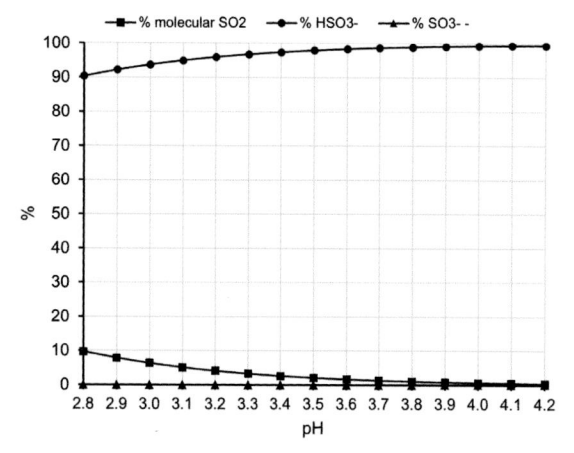

Figure 5.1: Effect of wine pH on the dissociation and relative proportions of forms of free sulphur dioxide.

wine compounds, including acetaldehyde, higher aldehydes, keto acids, glucose, phenols and quinones. These bound products are essentially non-reactive and make up the bound fraction of total SO_2. The sulphite form does not have any oenological interest.

The proportions of these different forms of free sulphur dioxide depend on pH. Their relative proportions in the range of wine pH are shown in Figure 5.1. They explain why pH also has some importance in oxidation control.

This commonly known graph makes clear that:

- The predominant form of free SO_2 in the pH range of wine is the bisulphite ion (HSO_3^-).
- The sulphite ion (SO_3^{2+}) concentration is very small and can essentially be ignored.
- The molecular form (SO_2), although also small at wine pH values, is of crucial importance and becomes increasingly significant with only a small decrease in pH values.

Sulphite (SO_3^{2+}) is the only form of SO_2 able to react directly with oxygen, according to the formula:

$$SO_3^{2+} + O_2 \rightarrow SO_4^{2-} + H_2O$$

However, at wine pH, the concentration of sulphite is so minute that its reaction with oxygen is infinitely slow, so it is not an effective antioxidant in wine. In contrast, the molecular form of SO_2 is quite reactive. For example, it traps hydrogen peroxide (H_2O_2) in accordance with the formula $H_2O_2 + SO_2 \rightarrow H_2SO_4$ in a spontaneous way. This reaction is of outstanding importance and will be examined in detail hereafter.

When, How and How Much Sulphur Dioxide is Added for the First Time

If malolactic fermentation (MLF) is not intended, white wines are usually supplied with 60–80mg/L SO_2 a few days after the end of alcoholic fermentation. If MLF has been performed, the first SO_2 addition should be performed no earlier than two weeks after its completion (section 4.1). However, the indicated amount of SO_2 is only a very rough guideline, because we do not know exactly how much of it remains in the free form and how much is bound. This can be determined beforehand by performing bench trials with increasing amounts. If the added amount is completely bound, additional SO_2 must be added until 20–50mg/L free SO_2 can be measured. This is also the moment, at the latest, when the container should be completely topped.

SO_2 can be added in the form of potassium metabisulphite ($K_2S_2O_5$). This salt theoretically contains 57 per cent SO_2, but much less if the package has been open for a longer time. Its dispersion in the container requires mixing, which easily leads to overflowing due to the CO_2 that escapes. The same applies to liquid forms of SO_2, which are available at a concentration of 5 per cent. For this reason, their use is limited to small containers. For larger volumes, the use of gaseous SO_2 from a cylinder in conjunction with a dosing meter is more appropriate. For this purpose, the outlet valve of the dosing unit is turned wide open so that the gas flows quickly into the liquid, creating some agitation in it. This causes it to disperse throughout the whole wine volume. Even dispersion is achieved after a few days.

If the measurement of free SO_2 is performed correctly and gives at least 1mg/L, the first sensory change will become noticeable. The smell of free acetaldehyde (bruised apples, sherry) resulting from the fermentation metabolism of yeast will have disappeared. This can be explained by the fact that the acetaldehyde has been completely bound to SO_2 with the formation of a sensorially neutral addition product. Free acetaldehyde and free SO_2 cannot coexist, since the reaction equilibrium is entirely on the side of the product.

In this context, how precisely and specifically free SO_2 is measured plays a role. The Ripper method using iodine titration at room temperature is a frequently used, fast and handy method for determining free SO_2 in white wines with the caveat that in such wines it indicates about 6–8mg/L more SO_2 than the wine really has. This error is due to other substances that also react with iodine. In the presence of ascorbic acid (section 5.2), the error becomes much greater and requires a blind titration for correction. It also occurs when iodine titration is performed with one of the numerous test kits offered for this purpose.

Microbial Aspects

The aforementioned target of 20–50mg/L free SO_2 protects the wine from oxidation to a reasonable extent. However, this is not the sole determinant of free SO_2 levels, because free SO_2 is also deemed essential to protect the wine from spoilage organisms. This effect is exerted only by the molecular fraction of free SO_2, which, as shown in Figure 5.1, depends on pH. Therefore, it is an article of faith with many winemakers and consultants to adjust free SO_2 as a function of pH in order to achieve a certain level of molecular SO_2 that is considered safe. Since in oenology, one usually repeats what everyone else is saying, minimum levels of molecular SO_2 are required with monotonous uniformity, especially in the New World wine growing regions, to suppress microbial activity. Typical recommended levels are 0.6 or 0.8mg/L for white wines. However, in the absence of any pertinent published research on this issue, nobody knows exactly under which conditions these figures were determined and are valid. In contrast, what one knows for sure is that they are too low to arrest an active fermentation (section 3.1) or prevent refermentation in the bottles if off-dry wines are not bottled under sterile conditions, thereby questioning their ability to suppress unwanted microbial activity.

The Old World countries largely stayed away from this technocratic approach of relating SO_2 and pH, which focuses solely on prevention and control. While aware that the effectiveness of SO_2 as a microbial inhibitor is greatly diminished at high pH, they put sensory considerations before pH, accept deficient molecular SO_2, forgo absolute safety and adjust free SO_2 instead of molecular SO_2. The viability of this strategy is confirmed worldwide by the many red wines with notoriously high pH figures that allow no other solution at all. The depletion of degradable substrates such as sugar or malic acid, filtration and cool storage play a major role in this approach. Whenever necessary, sterile filtration is implemented as ultimate safety strategy.

Materials and labware for the determination of SO_2 using the Ripper method. As this measurement is frequently performed, it is advisable to keep stocked up with the corresponding reagents.

Oxidation Protection: SO_2 Reacts with Oxidation Products Rather than with Oxygen

Unlike white musts and full-bodied red wines, white wines are fairly sensitive to oxygen. It accelerates their undesirable ageing and the appearance of a typical ageing off-flavour (Figure 2.5). Oxidative ageing in the long term particularly occurs after bottling when the bottle headspace contains oxygen and when the bottle closures allow for oxygen ingress (section 8.4).

To impede oxidation of wine, there are two basic approaches available – adding SO_2 or protecting wine from oxygen pickup. The wine industry relies largely on the first, using SO_2 as the traditional and almost universal antioxidant aiming at keeping oxidation under control. The following section primarily covers the role of SO_2 as a reducing agent and its effectiveness in oxidation control. It is a complex reaction mechanism whose importance justifies going into some detail.

When wine picks up oxygen, phenols are the primary oxygen acceptors that are oxidised. Their oxidation initiates the oxidation of other compounds, including SO_2, in a downstream reaction called coupled oxidation. In a first step, the oxidation of phenols leads to their corresponding quinones with their typical quinoid (=O) groups, which are largely reduced back to the original phenols by SO_2. Concurrently, hydrogen peroxide (H_2O_2) is also generated. In the competitive scenario of wine with the simultaneous presence of sulphites (SO_2) and ubiquitous traces of divalent iron (Fe^{2+}), most of the hydrogen peroxide is scavenged by free SO_2, which, in turn, is oxidised to sulphate. A minor fraction of the peroxide is converted into hydroxyl radicals in a reaction that is also catalysed by heavy metals such as Fe^{++}. These radicals are able to oxidise any kind of wine constituents. This reaction is known as the Fenton reaction. It leads to a nonspecific oxidation of wine components at rates that are proportional to their concentrations, thus oxidising ethanol to acetaldehyde, glycerine to glyceraldehyde, tartaric acid to glyoxylic acid and so on. Figure 5.2 depicts this reaction schema in a simplified way.

In the broadest sense, this reaction is also responsible for the oxidation of higher alcohols to the corresponding higher aldehydes as soon as hydrogen peroxide is generated by oxidation of phenols (Wildenradt and Singleton 1974, Singleton 1987, Waterhouse and Laurie 2006). Thus it explains to a large extent the involvement of higher aldehydes in the aroma profile of aged white wines. In must, the formation of peroxide during oxidation is absent, and innocuous water is formed instead.

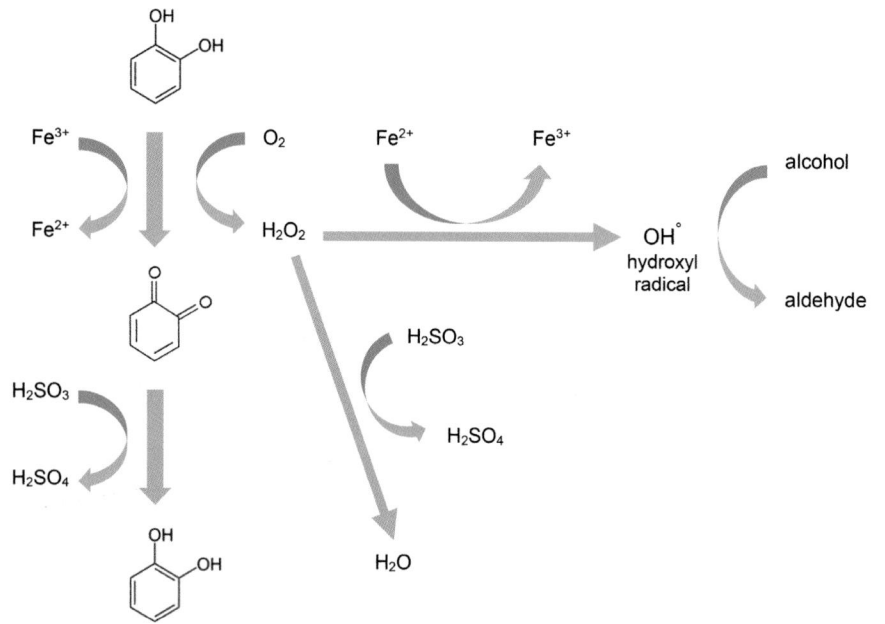

Figure 5.2: Oxidation of phenols, formation of hydrogen peroxide and oxidation of alcohols by the Fenton reaction.

The direct reaction of SO$_2$ with molecular oxygen (O$_2$) is very slow. Free sulphur dioxide protects wine against oxidation only in an indirect way by reducing quinones and trapping intermediate peroxide, thus mitigating the Fenton reaction. Indeed, wanting to protect wine against oxidation means first and foremost controlling the Fenton reaction (Elias and Waterhouse 2010). However, the heavy metals required to catalyse it are present in sufficient concentration in all wines. For that reason, control and limitation of oxygen uptake after alcoholic fermentation (Chapter 7) is of major importance.

Oxidation Products are Only Partially Reduced by SO$_2$

The quinones generated upon phenol oxidation deserve further consideration. As stated, they are partially reduced back by SO$_2$ to the corresponding phenols they stem from. Thus sulphite is oxidised to sulphate (Figure 5.2). However, this reaction is not complete – its extent depends on the initial level of free SO$_2$. In the absence of SO$_2$, it does not occur at all. The incompleteness of this reaction is one of the reasons why a part of the oxygen remains irreversibly bound to the wine matrix instead of being scavenged by SO$_2$, and why a given amount of dissolved oxygen (DO) in wine oxidises less SO$_2$ than expected by stoichiometric calculations (Waterhouse et al. 2016).

Quinones that are not reduced by SO$_2$ to their corresponding phenols undergo diverse reactions, the most important of which is a process of polymerisation that takes on the task of reducing them (Singleton 1987). When flavonoid phenols are involved in that process, their polymers show a brown colour and increasing astringency. The higher their initial concentration, the faster their polymerisation proceeds (Figure 5.3). However, in contrast to juice, they remain in solution in the alcohol-containing medium that is wine.

It is crucial always to keep in mind that sulphur dioxide does not react with oxygen in a direct way, but with quinones and H$_2$O$_2$ appearing upon consumption of DO. Concurrently, it is oxidised to sulphate. When this happens, free and total SO$_2$ are decreased simultaneously, but not necessarily to the same extent; free SO$_2$ decreases somewhat less than total SO$_2$. The reason for this is that it is partially replaced by 'fresh' SO$_2$ released from the pool of bound SO$_2$ when free SO$_2$

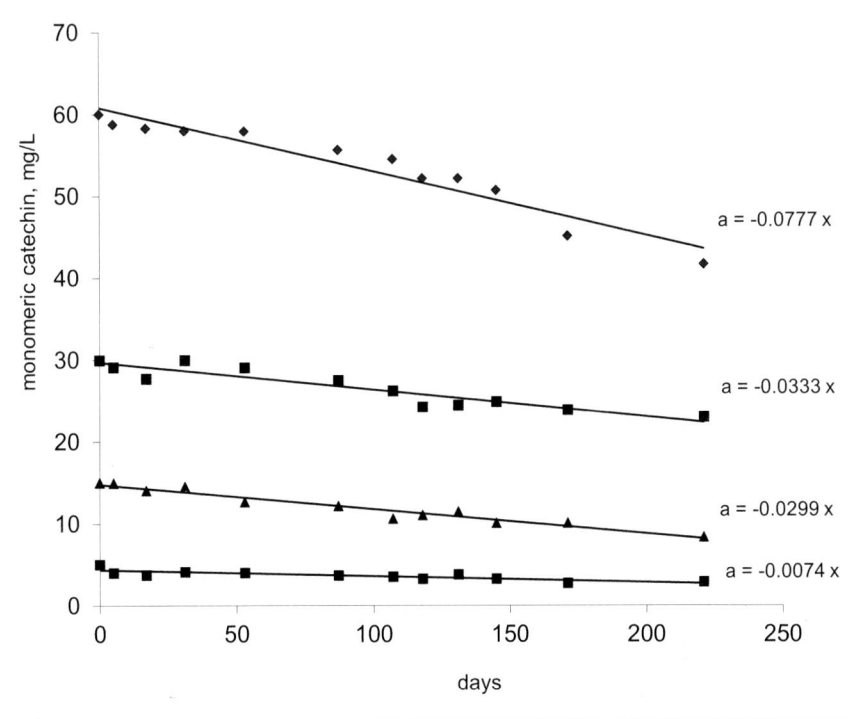

Figure 5.3: Polymerisation of catechin as affected by its initial concentration under conditions of accelerated ageing, measured as the decrease of its monomeric form during exposure to air (12% alcohol, pH 3.6, 21°C).

reaches low concentrations (Waterhouse et al. 2016). Hence, when DO is measured after oxygen uptake and to be related to SO_2 losses, it is essential to measure total SO_2 instead of free SO_2.

The sulphate produced upon SO_2 oxidation is no longer measured as either bound or total SO_2. In a way, this behaviour can be considered as a chemical removal of SO_2. It is well known in the wine industry, for example when wine picks up oxygen during barrel ageing or at bottling (section 8.4).

The $SO_2:O_2$ Ratio

Under ideal conditions, in which SO_2 completely scavenges the peroxide and reduces the quinones produced upon oxygen consumption, the molar ratio of $SO_2:O_2$ is 2:1 (Danilewicz et al. 2008). Expressed as the mass ratio, this means that 4mg SO_2 are oxidised by 1mg O_2, corresponding to a $SO_2:O_2$ mass ratio of 4:1 (Danilewicz 2016). When this happens, the effect of oxygen consumption is entirely reversed by SO_2, and stoichiometric rules would be fulfilled. However, reality in wine is different, and SO_2 does not fully protect against the effects of oxygen consumption.

Otherwise there would be no ageing driven by oxidation.

Under real wine conditions, the $O_2:SO_2$ mass ratio is lower than 4:1, meaning that some DO has irreversibly reacted with other wine compounds than SO_2. Hence the DO measured in the wine at a given moment does not allow for stoichiometrically calculating the decrease of SO_2 to expect. In an attempt to evaluate where the oxygen actually ends up, a total of 7mg/L DO was supplied to twenty sterile filtered white wines containing 40–60mg/L free SO_2, no ascorbic acid, and stored in hermetically sealed white glass vessels without any headspace. The DO decrease was monitored using non-invasive DO measurement through the vessel walls by a fibreoptic meter based on luminescence quenching. When DO was entirely consumed after two months, losses of total SO_2 were measured and related to the initial amount of DO.

The box-whisker plot in Figure 5.4 shows that 1mg/L DO oxidises variable amounts of SO_2, which strongly depend on the individual wine. Instead of 4mg SO_2 per 1mg/L DO ($SO_2:O_2$ ratio = 4:1), the median was only 2.86mg SO_2 per 1mg DO ($SO_2:O_2$ ratio = 2.86:1) or

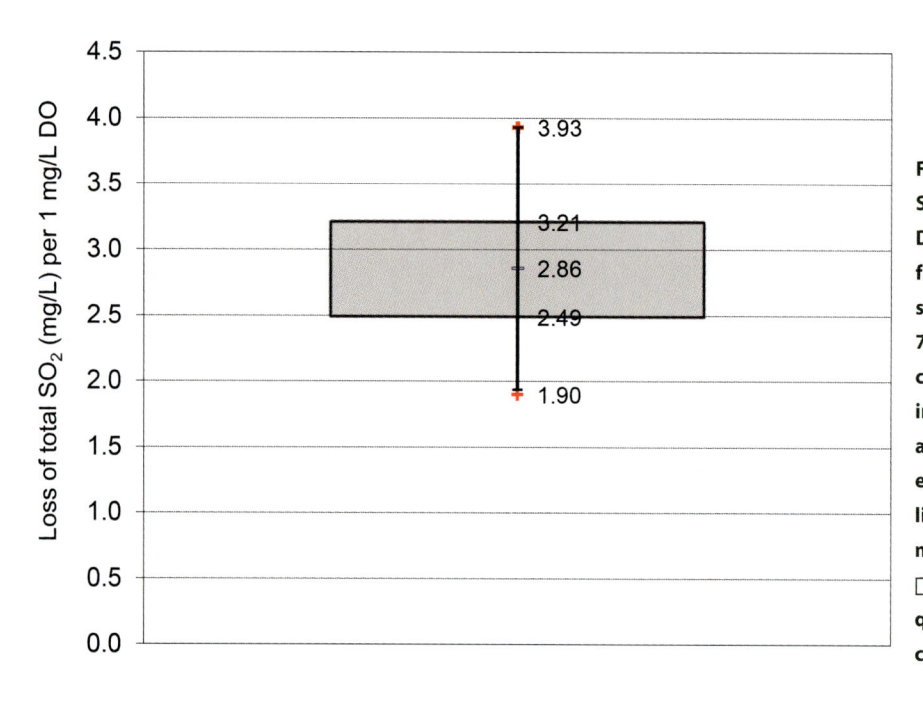

Figure 5.4: Loss of total SO_2 (mg/L) per 1mg/L DO in twenty sterile filtered white wines supplemented with 7mg/L DO. Wines containing 40–60 mg/L initial free SO_2 and no ascorbic acid. – = median, end points of the vertical line = minimum and maximum, respectively, ☐ = upper and lower quartiles, in which 50 per cent of the data is found.

71.5 per cent. The remaining 28.5 per cent of oxygen was not intercepted by SO_2, but available for irreversible oxidation of other wine constituents. Interestingly, 50 per cent of the wines lie within the range of 2.49–3.21mg SO_2 per 1mg DO, and 95 per cent in the range of 1.90–3.93mg SO_2 per 1mg DO.

The results confirm that peroxide and quinones produced upon oxygen uptake are not completely reduced by SO_2. They explain standard observations made in commercial-scale winemaking, which show that free SO_2 is not able to totally protect wine against the adverse effects of oxidation when it picks up oxygen.

The Effect of Initial Free SO_2

The high variability of data shown in Figure 5.4 suggests a closer look at how they are influenced by wine compositional data. For that purpose, a commercial white wine was adjusted to three different pH levels using NaOH or H_2SO_4. Each of the aliquots thus obtained was adjusted to three levels of free SO_2. The resulting nine samples were supplied with oxygen to make up 7mg/L DO, hermetically sealed, and stored in the dark until DO was totally consumed after ten weeks. Then the decrease of total SO_2 was measured in comparison with the non-oxygenated references, and related to the amount of DO consumed. Figure 5.5 demonstrates that both pH and initial free SO_2 have an impact on the $SO_2:O_2$ ratio.

As expected, the higher the initial level of free SO_2, the higher the $SO_2:O_2$ ratio, the more DO is consumed by SO_2, and the less DO oxidises phenols and other wine compounds. From the opposite perspective, in wines with low free SO_2 levels, a larger part of the oxygen reacts with intrinsic wine constituents, thus accelerating the appearance of flavour profiles associated with oxidative ageing. This behaviour appears obvious. Free SO_2 competes with other wine constituents as the ultimate oxygen acceptor. To completely protect white wines against the adverse consequences of oxygen uptake only by means of SO_2 and reach the $SO_2:O_2$ ratio of 4:1, their storage and bottling would require the presence of several 100mg/L free SO_2, which would be extremely disturbing in sensory terms.

From a purely practical perspective, more important than the level of free or molecular SO_2 is its stability over time, which strongly depends on oxygen uptake. A significant acceleration of oxidative ageing of bottled white wines is observed when free SO_2 levels fall below 10mg/L. The typical smell of free acetaldehyde reminiscent of bruised apples or sherry only arises when free SO_2 falls to 0mg/L.

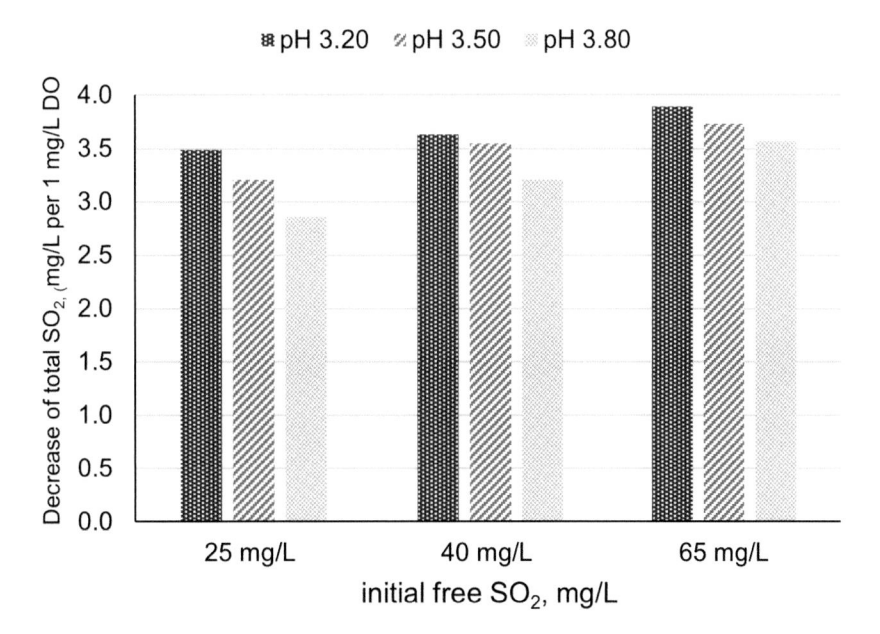

Figure 5.5: Decrease of total SO_2 (mg/L) per 1mg/L DO as a function of pH and initial free SO_2.

The Effect of pH

The higher the pH, the less SO_2 is consumed by 1mg/L DO and the more DO reacts irreversibly with other wine compounds, thus fostering oxidation and ageing. There are two reasons for this. First, the molecular percentage of free SO_2 able to trap H_2O_2 decreases with increasing pH (Figure 5.1). Second, phenols, which are the first oxygen acceptors initiating the oxidation sequence, oxidise more easily the higher the pH. At a high pH for wine, for example 4.0, their oxidation rate is approximately ten times as fast as at pH 3.0 (Singleton 1987). As oxidised phenols tend to undergo polymerisation, some of them are lost before they can be reduced by SO_2. As a result, the oxygen consumed by that portion of oxidised phenols is no longer available for interaction with SO_2.

It follows from the above that the $SO_2:O_2$ ratio has considerable practical importance. Ascertaining it permits identification of wines that become easily oxidised, to assess to what extent free SO_2 protects the wine against oxidation, and to evaluate the percentage of oxygen not scavenged by SO_2 and thus available for oxidative ageing (Waterhouse et al. 2016).

Intermediate Peroxide is not Entirely Trapped by SO_2

Knowing that SO_2 cannot reverse all phenomena of oxidation, it is particularly interesting to understand what happens to the peroxide that is inevitably generated upon the oxidation of phenols. As a strong oxidant, it is known to react spontaneously with free SO_2. Therefore free SO_2 and H_2O_2 cannot occur simultaneously. On the other hand, it is also responsible for the oxidation of alcohols to aldehydes (Figure 5.2), which are known to be strongly involved in the aroma profile of adversely aged white wines.

To track down the fate of intermediate peroxide, fifteen dry white table wines containing 19–99mg/L free SO_2 were supplied with an amount of H_2O_2 previously set to decrease an initial 40mg/L SO_2 in water (pH 3.5 with sulphuric acid) by exactly 20mg/L. After a reaction period of 30 minutes, the decrease of total SO_2 in the wines was measured and related to the decrease in the aqueous solution (100 per cent). Figure 5.6 shows the results.

In the wines, the decrease of SO_2 was only 87.5 per cent on average (74–97%) of that observed in water. The difference of roughly 13 per cent must be attributed to reactions of H_2O_2 with other wine compounds than SO_2 and not contained in the aqueous solution. The weak correlation ($R^2 = 0.32$) between the percentage of H_2O_2 reacting with SO_2 and the initial level of free SO_2 suggests that within the feasible range of free SO_2 in wine, increasing its level, for example from 30 to 60mg/L, is not a reliable means to scavenge more H_2O_2 and better protect wine against oxidation.

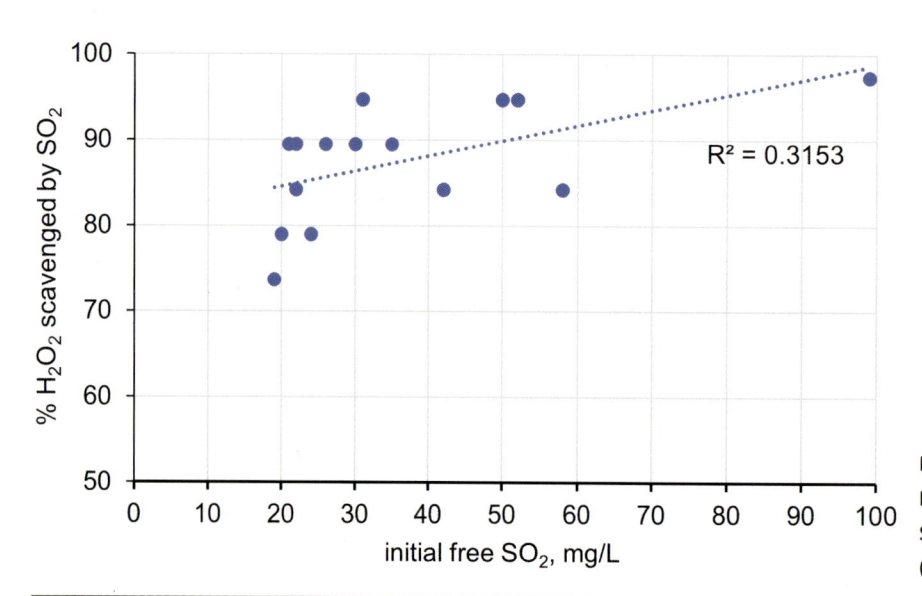

Figure 5.6: Percentage of H_2O_2 scavenged by free SO_2 in fifteen white wines (water = 100 per cent).

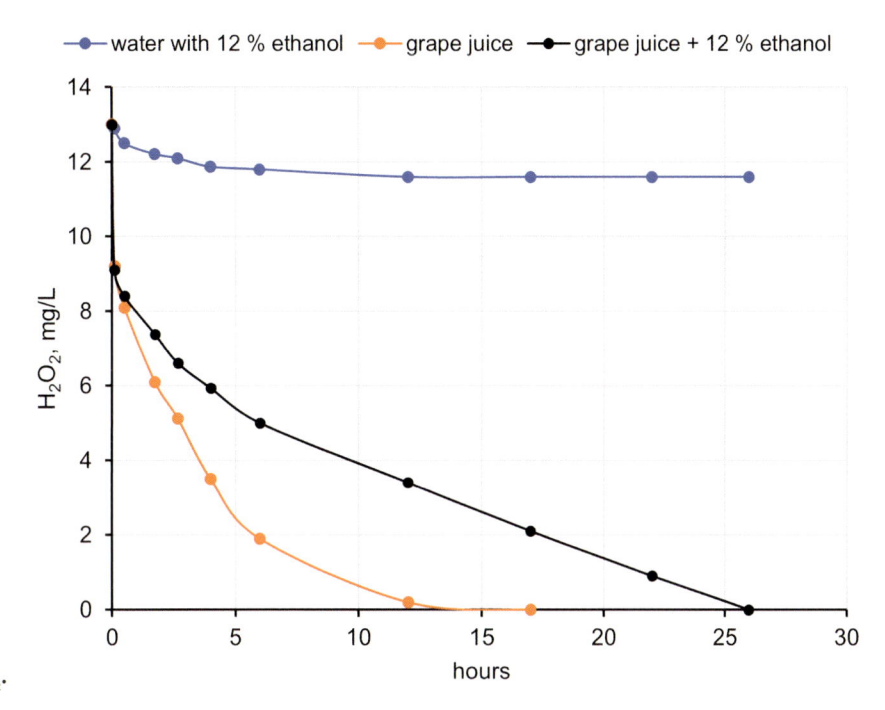

Figure 5.7: Consumption of H_2O_2 (13mg/L) in wine-like model solutions without SO_2.

The additional reactions of H_2O_2 are explained by its behaviour in wines without SO_2. Such wines were modelled using commercial white grape juice with and without addition of 12% ethanol, using water (pH 3.5 with tartaric acid) as a control. After their spiking with 13mg/L H_2O_2, it disappeared in both grape juices within 12 and 16 hours respectively (Figure 5.7). After that, 8mg/L of acetaldehyde were measured in the grape juice spiked with ethanol, while it was 0mg/L in the juice without ethanol as precursor.

Based on the stoichiometric ratio of 1mg H_2O_2 required to produce 1.3mg acetaldehyde by ethanol oxidation, the data show that roughly half of the peroxide not scavenged by SO_2 in wine is actually consumed by oxidation of ethanol to acetaldehyde. The remaining part of H_2O_2 is available for other reactions entailing aromatic changes of the wine, in particular the formation of higher aldehydes. While the acetaldehyde produced is without sensory relevance as long as there is free SO_2 that binds it, higher aldehydes remain sensorially active regardless of the presence of SO_2. Similarly, just as H_2O_2 produced by oxidation is not completely reduced by SO_2, the reduction of oxidised phenols by SO_2 is not complete, and reported to vary between 79 and 96 per cent (Danilewicz and Wallbridge 2010).

5.2 Ascorbic Acid

Ascorbic acid (AA) is reputed to be a strong reducing agent, so it is sometimes added to wine or must to complement the antioxidant effect of SO_2. Its addition in amounts of up to 250mg/L is authorised in most wine-growing countries. In contrast to SO_2, it reacts directly with DO, whereby it is oxidised to dehydroascorbic acid (DAA). In stoichiometric terms, 10.2mg AA binds with 1mg DO. The most striking outcome of this reaction is the production of H_2O_2, which is trapped by SO_2 as long as free SO_2 is present. In short, SO_2 oxidation is coupled with AA autoxidation. A simplified reaction schema is given in Figure 5.8.

As has been shown, stoichiometric relationships only apply on condition that oxygen does not concurrently react with other wine compounds. Thus, in the simultaneous presence of free SO_2, the amount of AA consumed by DO is lower than 10.2mg AA per 1mg DO, with the exact ratio depending on the initial molar ratio of SO_2:AA. On the other hand, AA also lowers SO_2 losses

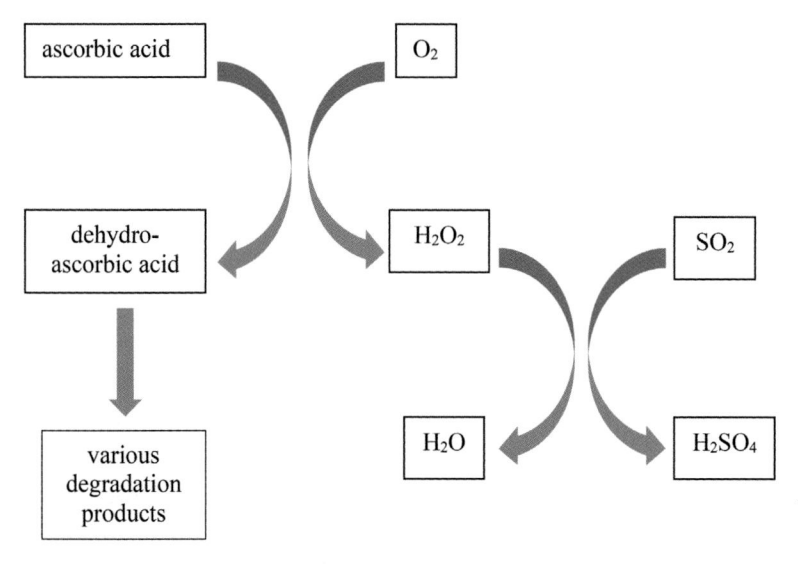

Figure 5.8: Reaction of ascorbic acid with oxygen and basic follow-up reactions.

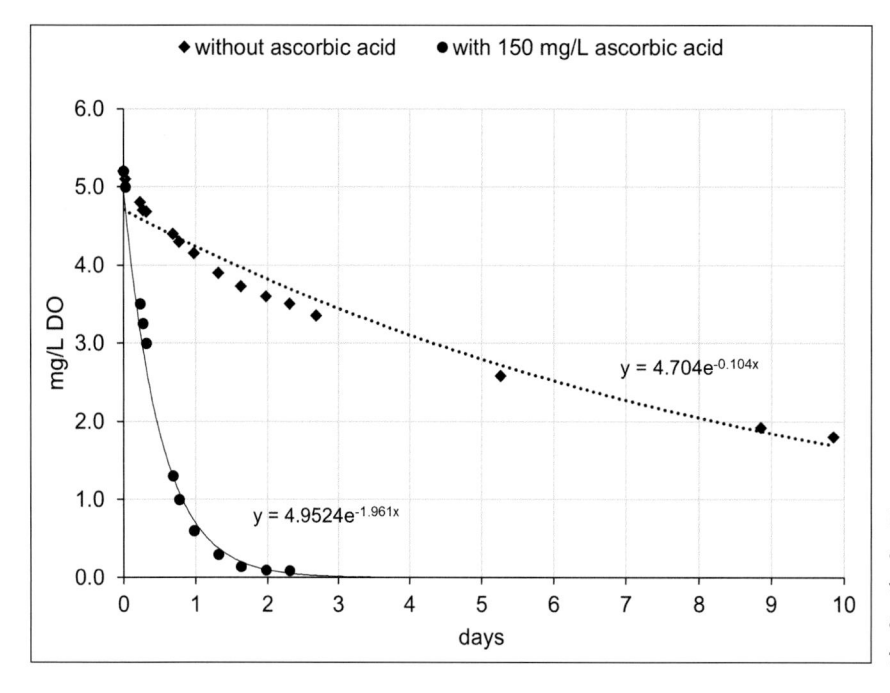

Figure 5.9: Impact of ascorbic acid (150mg/L) on the DO consumption rate in a white wine (40mg/L initial free SO_2).

when DO is consumed under conditions of low oxygen ingress, as occurs in most bottled wines. This is because AA recycles quinones back to the original phenols. Thus no SO_2 is required for the reduction of quinones in the oxidation process, and the $SO_2:O_2$ ratio is decreased by some 50 per cent (Danilewicz 2016). In practical terms, this means that after addition of AA, SO_2 losses per 1mg/L DO are only half of those occurring in the absence of AA.

Due to its high reactivity towards DO, AA leads to DO in wine being consumed many times faster than when compared to the same wine containing only SO_2. This is shown in Figure 5.9 by the example of a standard white wine supplied with oxygen.

Ascorbic Acid Does not Make DO Disappear

As shown in Figure 5.8, hydrogen peroxide is generated when AA consumes oxygen. This is exactly the same by-product that appears when phenols undergo coupled oxidation (Figure 5.2). It must be assumed that it is not completely trapped by SO_2, just as it occurs in the absence of AA.

In wine, AA can only act as a reducing agent in conjunction with sufficiently high levels of free SO_2. When no free SO_2 is available, the intermediate peroxide is entirely consumed by remaining AA and by the Fenton reaction, which leads to an unspecific oxidation of all organic wine compounds (Section 5.1). Consequently, oxidation is even promoted when oxygen is available. Clearly, AA is not a substitute for SO_2, nor is it a means for getting along with lower levels of free SO_2. Moreover, it does not make DO disappear without leaving any traces, but just transfers it in the form of H_2O_2 onto other wine compounds. Thus, DO ends up exactly where it would also get to in the absence of ascorbic acid, only the reaction pathway is different. When both AA and free SO_2 are entirely consumed due to uncontrolled oxygen uptake, the initial antioxidant activity of AA even turns into a pro-oxidant effect (Bradshaw et al. 2003, 2004). Therefore the use of AA during barrel ageing or storage in gas-permeable PE tanks is counterproductive.

Moderate Benefits During Bottle Storage

There are only a few studies on the benefits of AA for protecting wine aroma from the effects of oxidative ageing during bottle storage. In one of them, using sparkling wine, the addition of AA at disgorging gave no additional benefits compared to SO_2 additions alone (Marks and Morris 1993). Similarly, extensive storage trials with Riesling and Chardonnay still wines have shown that the addition of 90mg/L AA at bottling had no impact on aroma during the first six months post bottling. Sensory differences only appeared after three and five years of bottle storage, when fruity aroma was rated higher in the lot with ascorbic acid for one wine but not for the other one (Skouroumounis et al. 2005).

In another trial on Riesling, bottling after addition of 250mg/L AA resulted in higher intensity ratings of fruity aroma and less intensity of oxidised aroma attributes in the young wine. However, these beneficial effects of AA addition were cancelled after six months of bottle storage when an elevated oxygen ingress at bottling and from the bottle headspace took place (Morozova et al. 2015). Further studies (Godden et al. 2001, Skouroumounis et al. 2005, Lopes et al. 2009) indicate that oxygen uptake from the bottle headspace and through the bottle closure (section 8.4) has a comparable or even larger impact on oxidative ageing than the presence or absence of AA.

In some wine-growing areas, the assumption is that AA slows down white wine ageing in general. However, this only applies to a very specific kind of ageing, called atypical ageing, which, in reality, is a wine fault that can occur quite soon after the first post-fermentation SO_2 addition. Corresponding wines are thin with an aroma reminiscent of naphthalene, mothballs, damp cleaning rags and laundry. Causes are viticultural stress factors (Schneider 2014).

Drawbacks of Ascorbic Acid

Under conditions of low oxygen ingress through the bottle closure (section 8.4), AA in bottled wines increases the intensity of post-bottling reductive off-flavour in situations where the wine is prone to develop it (Godden et al. 2001, Skouroumounis et al. 2005, Lopes et al. 2009). This particularly applies to wines sealed with very gas-tight screw caps. Traces of copper may mitigate this effect. On the other hand, AA reduces highly soluble Cu^{2+} to less soluble Cu^+ ions, thus increasing the propensity of wine to develop cloudiness by copper precipitation. Therefore, wines containing AA should not be bottled with more than 0.3mg/L total copper.

Dehydroascorbic acid produced by AA oxidation is not stable but degrades into a variety of products. They comprise furfural, 3-hydroxy-2-pyrone with a caramel-like aroma, xylosone and further unidentified compounds that increase the yellow-brown colour of white wines (Barril et al. 2016). This colour deepening is moderate, commonly accepted by consumers, not accompanied by oxidised flavours, and not related to the kind of browning caused by flavonoid phenols upon oxidative ageing.

It is also worth mentioning that AA does not show any antimicrobial activity, nor does it bind any by-products of wine oxidation, as does SO_2. Furthermore, it interacts with iodine, thus interfering with the SO_2 determination by the Ripper titration and leading to falsely high results. When this method is used for SO_2 measurements, 100mg/L AA simulates 37mg/L SO_2 more than the wine actually contains.

5.3 Hydrolysable Tannins

Hydrolysable tannins comprise gallotannins and ellagitannins, which are not naturally present in grapes but extracted from suitable wood species such as oak, chestnut, quebracho and also gall nuts to be commercialised as wine additives. Their common feature is their astringency and easy oxidisability. Since they consume DO faster than grape-derived phenols in conjunction with a high production of intermediate hydrogen peroxide and acetaldehyde, they are of some interest in the regulation of the maturation process of red wines. As a result of these findings, the addition of ellagitannins to red wines has been intensively promoted by the supply industry.

In the meantime, efforts have also been made to extend their use to white winemaking, invoking their action as a natural antioxidant preventing premature oxidative ageing. However, in contrast to the bulk of research literature covering their effect on red wines, very few studies have been published about their impact on white wines. In one of them on white sparkling wine, the post-disgorging addition of different commercial formulas containing ellagitannins, gallotannins and grape-derived flavonoids were all less effective than SO_2 alone for preventing oxidative ageing over seven months at 15° and 25°C (Fracassetti et al. 2016). Similarly, addition of ellagitannins to white still wines did not extent their shelf life (Panero et al. 2014).

Hydrolysable tannins' main selling point of consuming DO faster than grape-derived phenols does not have any impact on the outcome of the Fenton reaction leading to oxidative ageing perceived by smell (Figure 2.5 and section 5.1). Their ability to cause an increase in the rate of oxygen consumption cannot be used as an indicator of their effectiveness as an antioxidant molecule. Even if these tannins were able to protect white wine against oxidation, their use would cause serious difficulties on the palate since they cause astringency, which is rather unpopular in white wines. Therefore, their addition would invalidate all efforts of gentle grape processing (section 2.4), juice treatments (section 2.5) and phenol removal by fining agents (section 8.2) aiming at minimising phenolic taste and astringency. This holds true despite impressive sensory euphemisms such as roundness, structure, palate weight, and length of finish used for their commercial promotion.

5.4 Inactive Dry Yeast Preparations

Wine contains glutathione (GSH), a peptide consisting of three amino acids: glutamic acid, cysteine and glycine. It occurs naturally in grape juice, but is also released by yeast lees after alcoholic fermentation. Its central cysteine moiety is a sulphur-containing amino acid displaying a free sulphide group (-SH), which is responsible for the anti-oxidative properties of GSH.

The addition of pure GSH to musts and wines has been recommended by OIV, but is not authorised in most legislations. However, apart from its deliberate extraction from post-fermentation yeast lees, it can be legally added in the form of commercially available inactive dry yeast (IDY) preparations obtained from yeast lees by thermal and/or enzymatic procedures. Their effectiveness is frequently evaluated by their content of glutathione in its reduced form.

GSH in the amounts found in wines consumes only little DO. Actually, it hardly reacts directly with DO, but rather protects phenols against oxidation by reducing their oxidised forms back to the original phenols just as SO_2 does (Makhotkina and Kilmartin 2009). In doing so, GSH is oxidised and converted from its

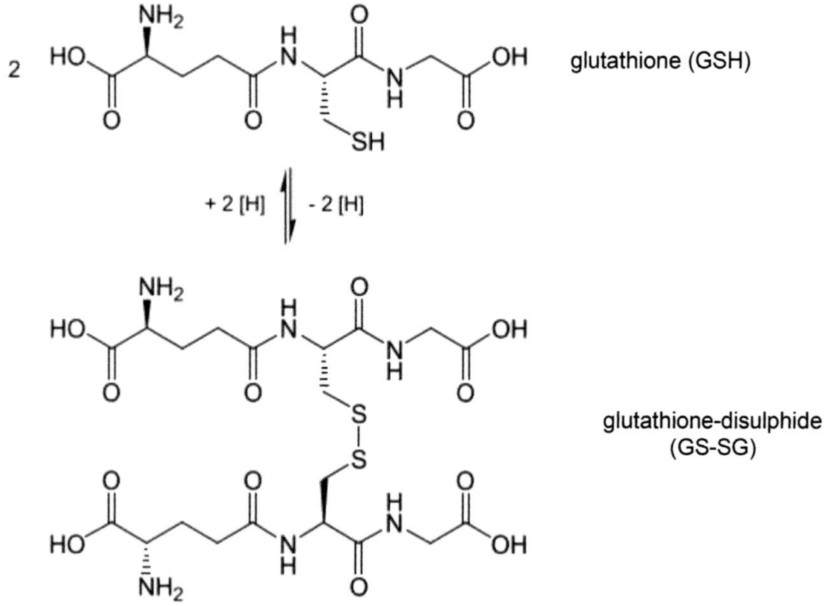

Figure 5.10: Glutathione and its oxidation to glutathione disulphide.

monomeric form via formation of a disulphide bridge into glutathione disulphide (GS-SG), which is inactive (Figure 5.10). These reducing properties are responsible for its global interest for oenology.

GSH occurs naturally in wine in varying concentrations ranging from 0 to 70mg/L (Fracassetti et al. 2011), generally at levels below 10mg/L. GSH-enriched IDY products have been developed with the aim of remedying GSH deficiencies. These developments invoke analytical data reporting an improved stability of fruity varietal aroma compounds during wine storage (Pozo-Bayón et al. 2009, Kritzinger et al. 2013, Andújar-Ortiz et al. 2014, Rodriguez-Bencomo et al. 2014). However, more important than analytical data and absolute GSH concentrations is the question of their actual benefits with regard to oxygen uptake, shelf life and aroma stability.

To answer this question, two sterile filtered white wines were used. One was a standard wine blend consisting of Chardonnay, Riesling, Pinot gris and Pinot blanc, whilst the other wine was a Sauvignon with its characteristic aroma feature of varietal thiols (section 3.1). The wines contained 35 and 47mg/L free SO_2, 2 and 5mg/L GSH, and no ascorbic acid. They were supplied with a commercial IDY (OptiWhite™) in amounts of 250 and 500mg/L each. This addition provided them with 1.5 and 3.0mg/L additional GSH respectively. Subsequently they were supplied with a total of 10mg/L O_2 under controlled conditions, leaving a variant with 0mg/L O_2 for each IDY addition as a reference. When all oxygen was consumed after two months of bottle storage at ambient temperature, oxidative ageing as perceived by smell was scored by a trained panel using a scale ranging from 0 to 5 points. At the time of sensory evaluation, all lots still displayed free SO_2, thus excluding any olfactory interference by the presence of free acetaldehyde (section 5.1). Figure 5.11 gives the results.

Indeed, increasing additions of IDY better protected both wines against the appearance of oxidation-related aroma changes after consumption of 10mg/L O_2. The changes in colour and final SO_2 content they caused were not significant. In the absence of oxygen uptake, the additions caused no significant changes by smell. This positive result is remarkable considering that the relatively high additions of the IDY preparation increased the GSH content by only a modest 1.5 and 3.0mg/L respectively.

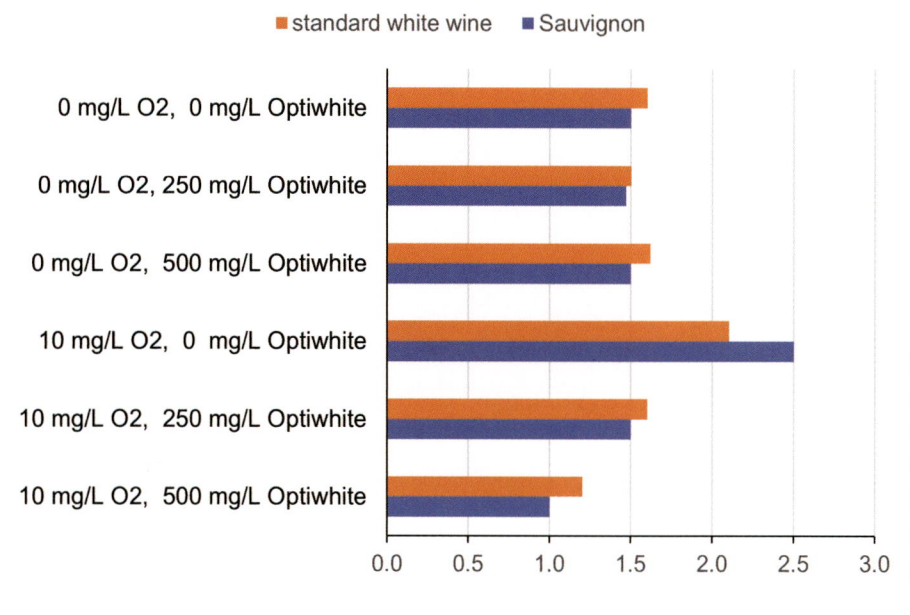

Figure 5.11: Impact of inactive dry yeast (OptiWhite™) added to white wine on the intensity (0–5) of oxidative ageing as perceived by smell.

The Limited Effect of Glutathione

Figure 5.12 shows that replacing the IDY additions by additions of 25 and 50mg/L pure GSH protects only Sauvignon against the sensory effects of oxygen uptake under identical conditions. Increasing amounts of GSH do not do so in standard white wine, in which they rather reinforce the sensory perception of oxidative ageing. Similar results have been obtained for varietal wines elsewhere (Panero et al. 2014, Antoce and Cojocaru 2017). The divergent behaviour observed in Sauvignon can be attributed to the specific aroma chemistry of wines obtained from this variety. GSH blocks the quinones generated by phenols oxidation that would otherwise react with the aroma thiols of Sauvignon and convert them in non-volatile products without odour activity. In fact, practically all experiments reporting positive effects of GSH were carried out on Sauvignon (du Toit 2007, Ugliano et al. 2011, Aguera et al. 2012, Pons et al. 2015).

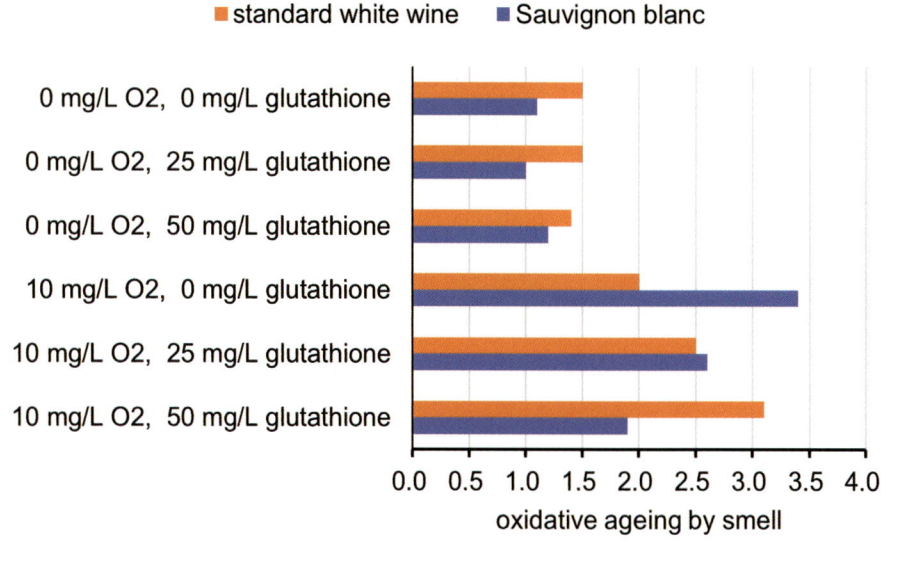

Figure 5.12: Impact of glutathione added to white wine on the intensity (0–5) of oxidative ageing as perceived by smell.

98 USE AND EFFECT OF REDUCING AGENTS DURING STORAGE

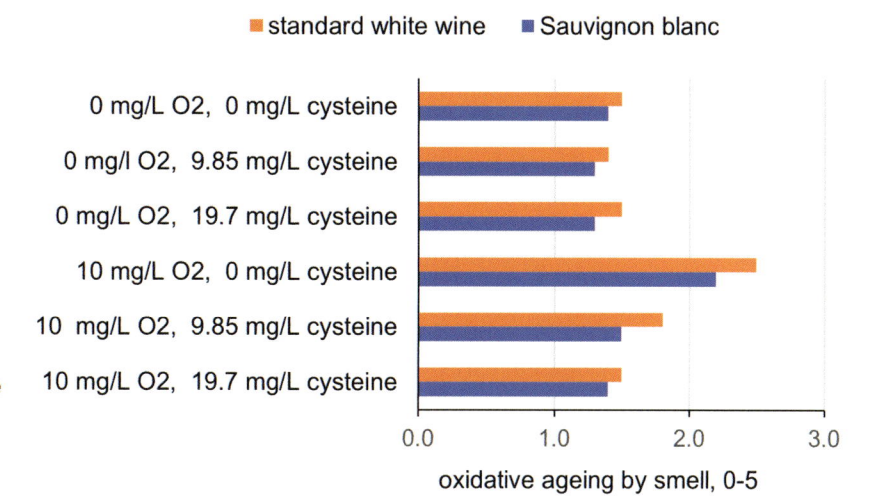

Figure 5.13: Impact of cysteine added to white wine on the intensity (0–5) of oxidative ageing as perceived by smell.

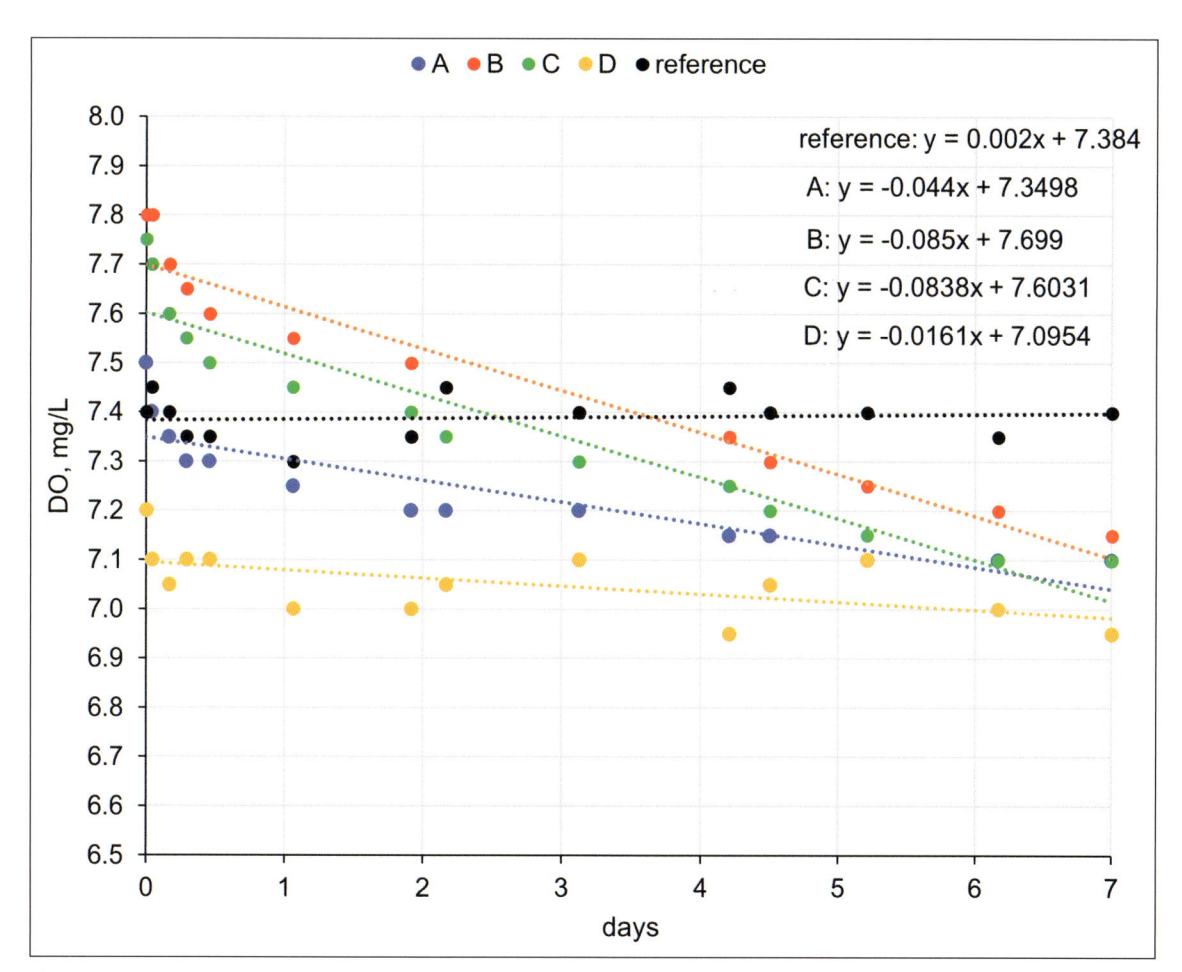

Figure 5.14: DO consumption by inactive dry yeast preparations (A, B, C and D at 40g/hL each) in model wine solution. Alcohol = 13%, pH = 3.5 with tartaric acid, Cu^{++} = 0.25mg/L, Fe^{++} = 1.0mg/L, T = 20°C.

reference: y = 0.002x + 7.384
A: y = -0.044x + 7.3498
B: y = -0.085x + 7.699
C: y = -0.0838x + 7.6031
D: y = -0.0161x + 7.0954

The reason IDY with its low GSH content is effective in all wines, as opposed to pure GSH, is that IDYs contain additional reducing compounds (Bahut et al. 2020). One of these is cysteine, a reducing amino acid that is also a component of the GSH peptide. Figure 5.13 depicts the impact of cysteine additions on oxidative ageing under the experimental conditions specified previously. By analogy with GSH and added in equimolar proportions, increasing cysteine contents protect Sauvignon blanc aroma against oxidation. However, in contrast to GSH, this effect can also be observed in the standard white wine blend.

Apart from cysteine and GSH, IDYs also contain additional compounds that directly and irreversibly consume DO, thus withdrawing it from reacting with intrinsic wine constituents. Figure 5.14 shows the oxygen consumption rate of four IDYs (40g/hL) measured in model solution ethanol (13% ethanol adjusted to pH 3.5). Model solution was preferred to real wine, because the naturally occurring wine phenols would compete with IDYs for DO consumption. After DO supply, its consumption was monitored in a hermetically closed vessel without any headspace by a non-invasive luminescence method. The slope of the curves represents the intensity of the DO consumption.

The IDYs trialled show a clear but low DO consumption, which strongly depends on the preparation and which cannot be explained by the small amounts of GSH the IDYs release (Pons-Mercadé 2021). As will be shown in the following section, an effect two orders of magnitude stronger can be achieved by the wines' own yeast lees that remain after fermentation. As a summary, and in accordance with Figure 5.11, it can be concluded that IDYs can be useful to better protect clarified white wine against oxidation when one is not able to keep oxygen uptake under control. They can complement the effect of free SO_2, but cannot replace it. One of the reasons for this is that they do not remove free acetaldehyde with its unpleasant odour.

5.5 Post-Fermentation Yeast Lees

Yeast lees are able to absorb DO and use it for chemical reactions within the yeast cells. The DO consumed in this way is no longer available for oxidation of wine compounds. This is one of the reasons that ageing on the lees has become an oenological concept for pursuing specific stylistic goals (section 5.6). This concept presupposes that after alcoholic fermentation, lees predominantly consist of yeast cells. During the first couple of weeks after fermentation, the DO they absorb can be consumed by the respiration metabolism of surviving yeast cells. After cell death and throughout the subsequent months and years, it is used for oxidation of lipids and ergosterol localised in the cell membrane (Fornairon et al. 1999, Salmon et al. 2000, Rosenfeld et al. 2002, Fornairon-Bonnefond and Salmon 2003).

In an attempt to quantify the rate and extent to which DO present in wine is consumed by variable amounts of suspended yeast cells as compared to filtered wines, the effect of technological parameters on the rate of this reaction, and its significance under practical winemaking conditions, a specific approach has been developed (Schneider et al. 2016). The oxygen consumption rate (OCR) and yeast cell concentration measured as nephelometric turbidity units (NTU) are the pivotal variables in this context. The OCR informs us how fast yeast lees suspended after primary fermentation consume DO. In wines obtained from thoroughly clarified juices, suspended yeast cell concentrations, expressed as NTU, closely correlate (r = 0.99) with the cell number, with 1 NTU equating to $6.3 \cdot 10^6$ cells/mL. Sedimented yeast lees are not considered because they minimally participate.

Impact of Yeast Concentration

The outstanding effect of yeast concentration on OCR was evaluated in model solution (13% alcohol, pH 3.5) at 20°C, thus circumventing any interfering DO consumption by wine constituents other than yeast. Figure 5.15 shows the results.

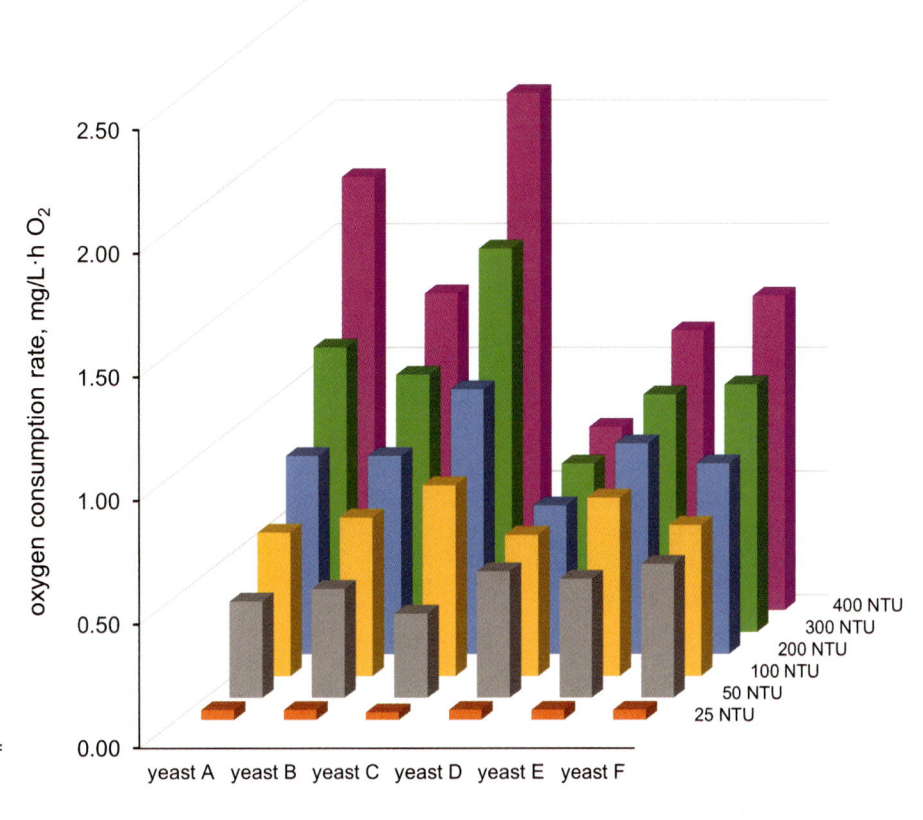

Figure 5.15: Oxygen consumption rate (mg/L·h O_2) of suspended yeast lees of six strains as affected by yeast concentration (NTU). Yeasts harvested and trialled two to four weeks after alcoholic fermentation. Free SO_2 = 0mg/L, T = 20°C).

Although all yeasts were harvested and trialled promptly after fermentation, there were remarkable differences in the OCR among yeast strains at given concentrations. According to logical expectations, OCR increases with increasing yeast concentrations, but not always in a linear way. An OCR deemed useful for oenological purposes requires a minimum concentration of 50 NTU suspended yeast lees. Above that minimum level, OCR ranged from 0.27 to 2.09mg/L·h O_2.

In this context, it is important to correctly interpret turbidity units caused by suspended yeast lees: young white wines display 500–1,000 NTU right after alcoholic fermentation. In the course of settling over several months, turbidity decreases to 50–500 NTU, depending on the height of the storage vessel. After diatomaceous earth filtration, wines usually display only 5–20 NTU. A turbidity of 50 NTU equates to a clearly visible opalescence.

Impact of Oenological Variables

Storage duration on the lees has a minor impact on the OCR of yeast. Figure 5.16 illustrates that there is a slow and irregular decrease of the OCR during the first three months post-fermentation. A residual activity of 11–100 per cent of the initial OCR right after fermentation has been reported (Fornairon et al. 1999).

Wines are stored with variable levels of free SO_2 after fermentation, whose impact on yeast lees OCR is shown in Figure 5.17 for six yeast strains suspended at 200 NTU in model solution (13% alcohol, pH 3.5) spiked with increasing amounts of SO_2. The OCR strongly decreases when free SO_2 increases. At an average wine pH of 3.50, there is a critical limit around 20mg/L free SO_2, above which the OCR of yeast becomes almost insufficient to have any practical effect.

The effect of temperature on the OCR of post-fermentation yeast lees was also studied in model solution and shown to be significant for all yeast strains (Figure 5.18). Under the conditions of cool wine storage, the OCR decreases markedly. At 5°C, it is only 68.5 per cent of that at 20°C.

On the other hand, the oxygen consumption rate in filtered wines, caused by chemical oxidation of wine compounds, also proceeds at a lower rate when the temperature is decreased. Therefore, when yeast lees and oxidisable wine compounds compete for DO in real wines, the yeast percentage contribution to total oxygen consumption is not necessarily affected by temperature.

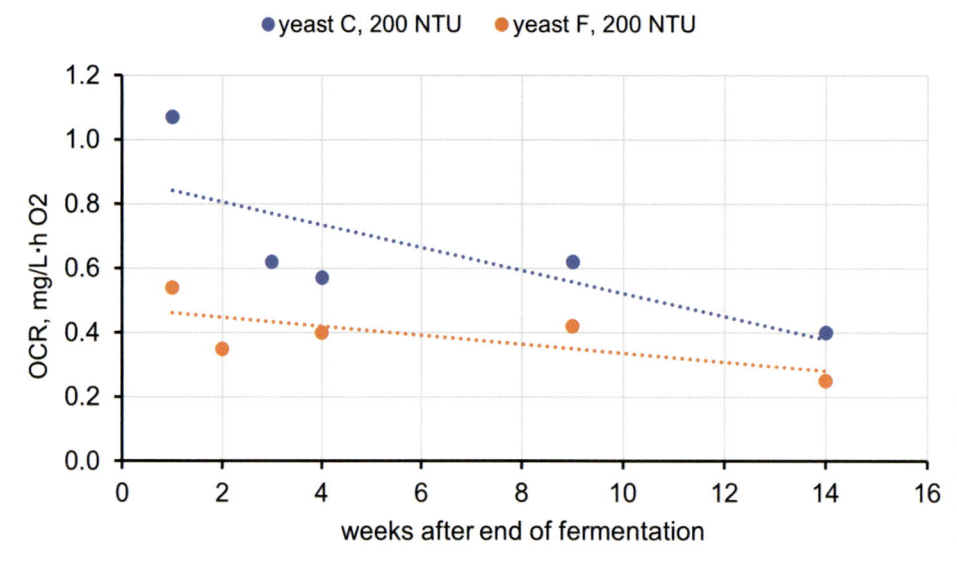

Figure 5.16: Impact of yeast lees' age on their oxygen consumption rate (OCR).

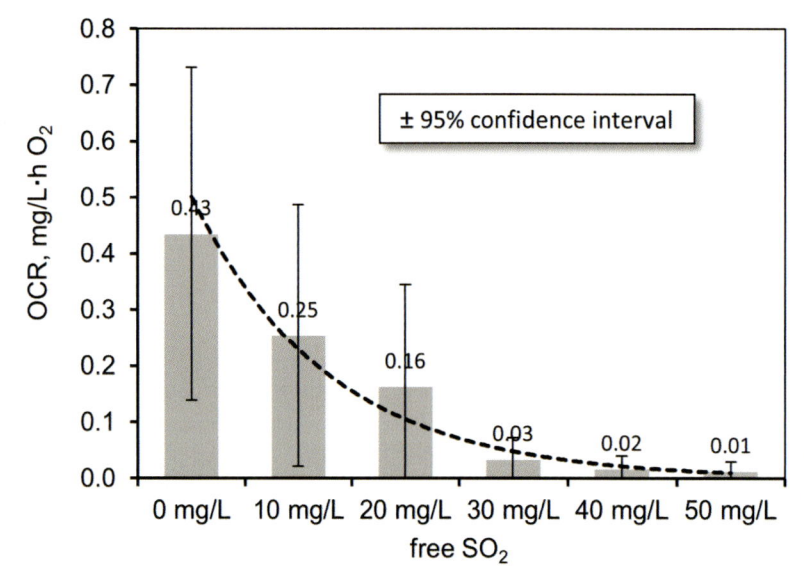

Figure 5.17: Impact of free SO_2 on the oxygen consumption rate (OCR) of yeast lees. Model solution pH 3.5, means of six yeast strains, yeast concentration = 200 NTU.

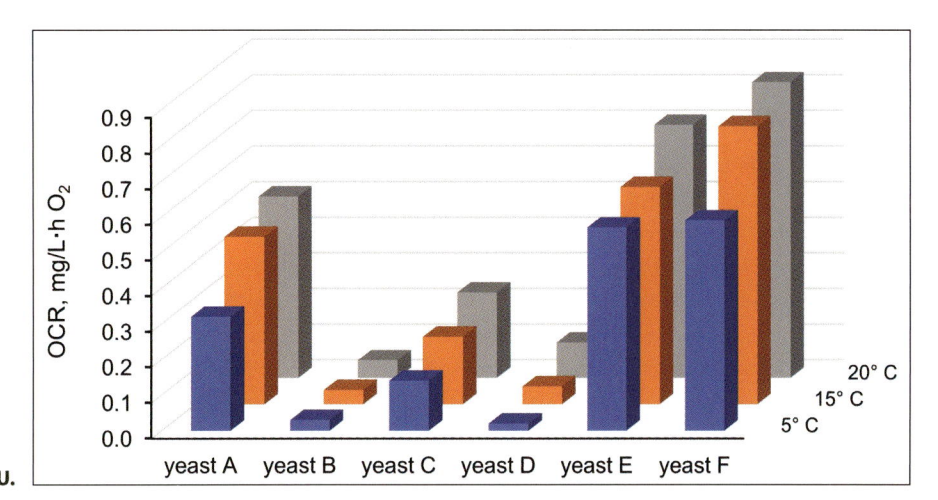

Figure 5.18: Impact of temperature on the oxygen consumption rate (OCR) of yeast lees from six strains. Model solution pH 3.5, free SO_2 = 0mg/L, yeast concentration = 200 NTU.

Total Oxygen Consumption Capacity of Yeast Lees

Knowing the rate of DO consumption by yeast lees and its dependence on oenological variables, another pertinent question relates to the total amount of DO a typical concentration of suspended yeast lees in young wines is able to consume. The total oxygen consumption capacity of yeast suspensions was measured in model solution under conditions of unlimited oxygen supply (Schneider et al. 2016). As shown in Figure 5.19, for three yeast strains at 300 NTU, oxygen consumption of yeast lees keeps to an almost linear pattern at the beginning, followed by a transition to a steady state indicating depletion of the yeast oxygen uptake capacities after 40–60mg/L of DO was consumed. These results show that even minor concentrations of suspended yeast cells, corresponding to approximately 50 NTU visible turbidity as occurring

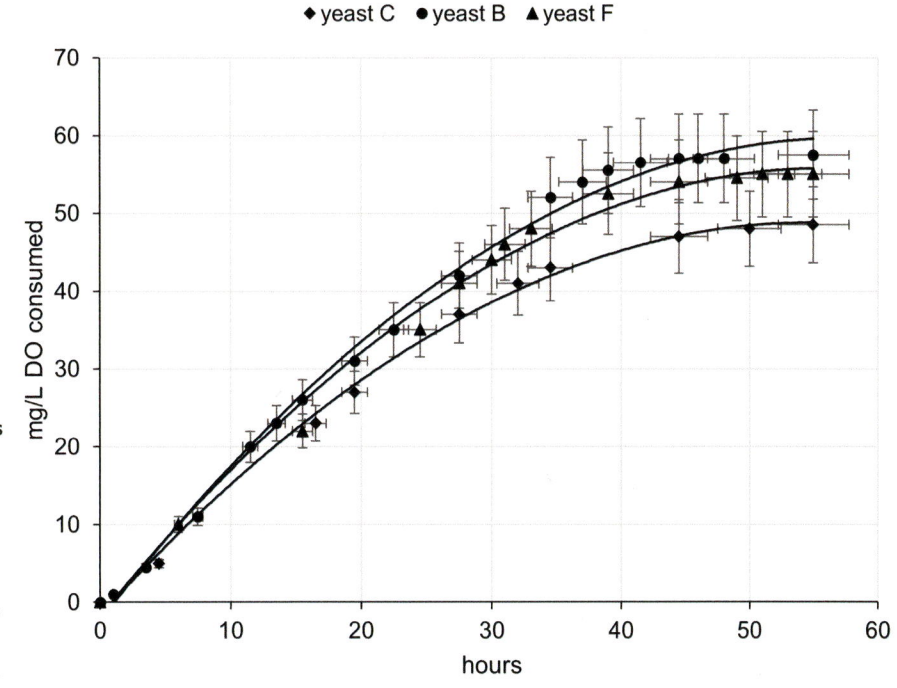

Figure 5.19: Total oxygen consumption capacity and consumption kinetics of suspended yeast cells. Error bars indicate standard deviation of ± 10 per cent. Model solution pH 3.50, free SO_2 = 0mg/L, T = 20°C, yeast concentration = 300 NTU.

in slightly turbid wines would suffice to consume one saturation concentration (8mg/L) of DO. Under industrial winemaking conditions, total oxygen consumption capacity of yeast lees is not a limiting factor to protect wine against oxidation.

However, the ability of yeast lees to consume appreciable amounts of DO should not hide the fact that they need a certain period of time for doing so. During that time, DO is also partially available for oxidation of the wine. Yeast lees and oxidisable wine components compete for DO. Hence yeast lees can never protect wine against oxidation 100 per cent, though they can act as a very effective antioxidant, similar to sulphur dioxide. This is one of the reasons why turbid young white wines devoid of free SO_2 take so much time to brown.

Combined Effects of Lees Concentration, Age and Free SO_2

Real wines have variable amounts of suspended yeast lees of variable age and different levels of free SO_2. The interactions resulting from this complicate the assessment of the oxygen consumption by yeast lees. In a large-scale field trial, samples were taken at different time points from 25 unfiltered young white wines that had been fermented with different commercial yeast strains. The samples were split into two aliquots, one of them containing the original yeast and the other one being filtered to serve as a blank.

After oxygen supply by aeration, the DO decrease in both aliquots at 20°C was plotted against time. Yeast concentration in the wines ranged from 8 to 310 NTU, initial free SO_2 from 0 to 57mg/L, and the age of the wines from 2 to 26 weeks after alcoholic fermentation. In most of the samples, regardless whether they were filtered or unfiltered, the plots took the form of a more or less convex curve fitting a negative exponential function. Figure 5.20 gives an example.

In the unfiltered wines containing yeast lees, both DO consumption by the yeast and DO consumption due to chemical binding by intrinsic wine compounds accumulate to a total, which changes over time according to the instantaneous DO concentration. A mathematical treatment of the equation of both curves provides the percentage and the absolute amount of DO consumed by yeast, with the remaining part corresponding to the DO consumed by chemical oxidation of the wine matrix (Schneider et al 2016).

In this field trial, DO consumed by yeast ranged from 0 to 47 per cent. This range confirmed the large impact of yeast strain, yeast concentration, yeast age and free SO_2 observed in the model solutions. However, the combination and interaction of the various oenological parameters do not allow for a reliable prediction of yeast reactivity towards DO in a given wine: it is hard to forecast how much of the DO is consumed by yeast lees and how much by chemical oxidation of the wine matrix.

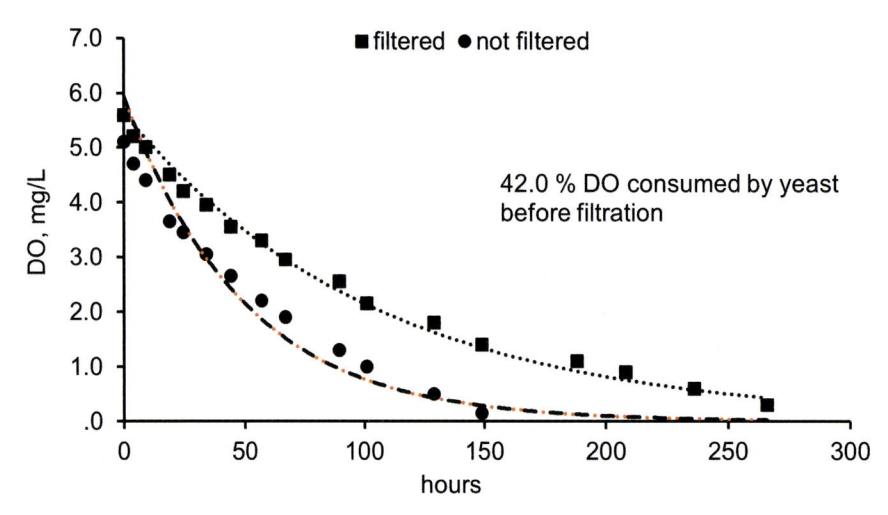

Figure 5.20: DO consumption in a white wine (43mg/L initial free SO_2) with suspended yeast at a concentration of 50 NTU (not filtered) and after filtration, two months after fermentation.

Deciding Between Yeast Lees and SO$_2$

In the course of standard winery operations such as racking, fining, filtration, blending and so on, wines pick up variable amounts of oxygen ranging from 0.5 to 4.0mg/L DO upon each treatment. Furthermore, an uncontrolled oxygen uptake occurs through the liquid surface when containers are not thoroughly topped (section 7.2).

As shown in Figure 5.19, common amounts of suspended yeast lees in unfiltered wines are able to consume several saturation concentrations of oxygen at a rate of 0.5–1.0mg/L DO per hour. However, the yeast lees are not able to entirely consume the DO, since a part of it is concurrently undergoing irreversible reactions with intrinsic wine compounds. These DO decrease reactions are mutually competitive. A similar competitive behaviour is shown in section 5.1 for SO$_2$ as a reducing agent.

The faster DO is consumed by yeast lees, the less DO is available for wine oxidation. However, the rate at which yeast lees consume DO becomes practically insignificant when free SO$_2$ exceeds some 20mg/L (Figure 5.17). Therefore, the reducing effects of SO$_2$ and yeast lees cannot be used simultaneously for the purpose of protecting wine against oxidation. Figure 5.21 illustrates that when a wine displays 40mg/L free SO$_2$, the presence of yeast lees does not affect the DO consumption kinetics in a meaningful way as compared to the sterile filtered lot. Only when no free SO$_2$ is present do the yeast lees consume DO much faster.

Since DO consumption by yeast lees is strongest at low levels of free SO$_2$ or in its complete absence, it is a valuable oenological tool during elaboration and ageing of wines without added SO$_2$ (section 6.3). Furthermore, it explains why barrel ageing of white wines is traditionally associated with low SO$_2$ levels and periodic stirring of the yeast lees (section 6.2). Barrels are gas-permeable containers (section 7.2), allowing for oxygen uptake to an extent that would otherwise cause premature oxidative ageing in filtered white wines.

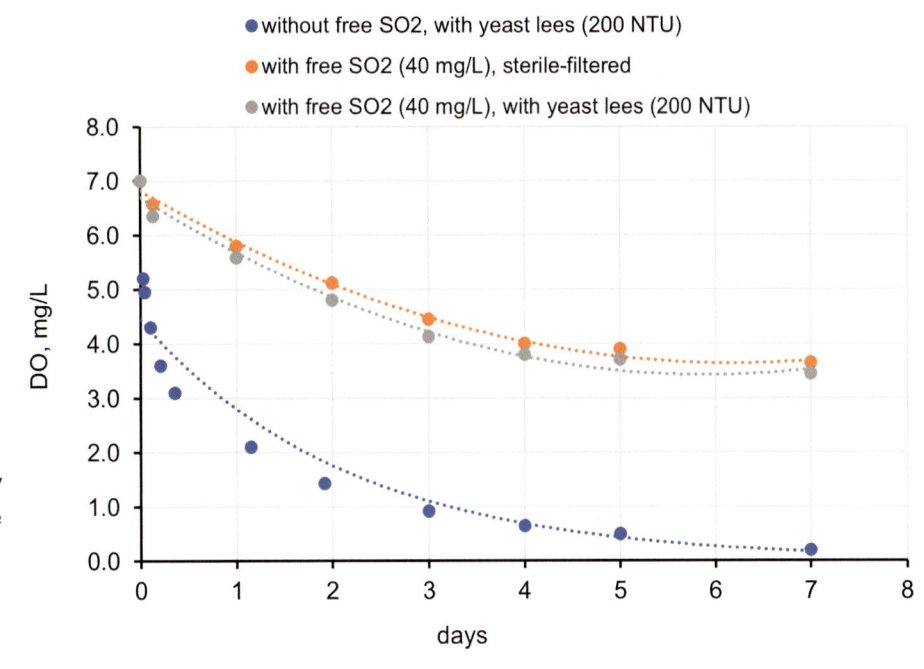

Figure 5.21: Effect of suspended yeast lees, filtration and free SO$_2$ on DO consumption in a white wine three months after fermentation.

USE AND EFFECT OF REDUCING AGENTS DURING STORAGE

ROMFIL
FILTRATION · GASMANAGEMENT · FLOTATION
ROMFIL.COM
KAES
CLASSIC 320

CHAPTER 6

PRACTICAL USE OF YEAST LEES

Apart from the effect of yeast lees as a reducing agent described in the previous chapter, they have many other properties that have a positive impact on wine quality, provided it is actually clean yeast and not dirt remaining after poor juice clarification. Therefore traditional interventions on the wine, such as unnecessarily early rackings and filtrations, need to be questioned, thus opening the way to less interventional, minimalist winemaking. The multifaceted influence of yeast is sought especially during barrel ageing. Well-known oenological keywords such as sur-lie and the stirring of the yeast by bâtonnage come into play. The practical implementation of these measures is described here, as well as the sensory influence of the different woods used in barrel building and the interaction between wine, wood, yeast and oxygen.

Last but not least, the importance of yeast lees in the production and storage of wines without added sulphites is also addressed. In fact, the production of these hotly debated wines is possible without flaws derived from oxidation or microbial spoilage. However, achieving this requires advanced oenological knowledge and a high level of technical equipment that is out of reach of small wineries, which is in contrast to the romantic image surrounding such wines.

6.1 Avoiding Counterproductive Interventions on Fruity Wines

In Chapter 5, post-fermentation yeast lees were shown to directly consume DO, which is thereby excluded from wine oxidation. Other than oxygen, yeast lees also partially absorb further undesirable compounds such as surplus copper required for the treatment of reductive off-flavours (section 8.2) as well as hydrolysable tannins originating from the wood of oak chips or barrels (section 6.2). All these properties are much more pronounced in suspended yeast cells than in settled yeast bottoms. Moreover, when yeast cells start autolysing in the post-fermentation stage, they release colloidal polysaccharides and mannoproteins that add beneficial texture, palate weight and creaminess as a result of bridging the sensations of acidity and alcohol, thus aiding in wine harmony and integration.

Autolysis is the self-destruction of yeast cells by their own enzymes. However, when yeast autolysis proceeds too far, leesy aromas reminiscent of toasted bread, brioche, hazelnuts and almonds will develop. Although these aromas are an intrinsic flavour characteristic of some still and sparkling white wine styles, they are usually not desired when trying to create a very

OPPOSITE: **Cross-flow filter, a filtration technology allowing for sterile filtration of very cloudy wines in a single pass without the use of filter aids.**

delicate, fruit-driven wine just highlighting the gossamer essence of the grape. At the latest, when leesy aromas start to develop, clarification and filtration of this kind of wine become advisable. Provided wines are stored cool (<15°C), this rarely happens before the summer of the year following harvest. Hence, traditional steps such as early racking and filtering need to be scrutinised more closely to establish whether they are really necessary.

The Question of Racking

Racking means the transfer of the wine above its sediments into another container. This operation by no means implies that the transferred wine would undergo any clarification to make it less turbid than it was before, though this assumption is still widely upheld.

In former times, winemakers used to differentiate between heavy lees and light lees. Heavy lees were defined as those that settled within the first week post-fermentation, and were composed of large particles consisting of bitartrate crystals and grape solids that had not been removed by juice clarification. Light lees were considered as all those that required several weeks or months to settle more or less; they comprised essentially yeast cells. As the grape solids contained in the heavy lees were assumed to contribute to off-flavours, wines were racked off them several times before storage with the fine lees started.

In more recent times and in conjunction with technical progress towards the production of highly fruity wines, this perspective has changed. The reason for this lies in the vigorous clarification most juices are subject to (section 2.5). As a result, heavy lees considered detrimental to wine quality no longer exist in wines obtained from those juices. Their solids, be they settled or suspended, consist essentially of yeast cells. Furthermore, the total volume of these yeast cells is considerably less, often only a mere fraction of that found in wines obtained from less clarified juices, because yeast reproduction is reduced in the absence of grape solids. Consequently, there is a tendency to postpone or simply skip racking after fermentation. The less turbid the juice before inoculation, the more post-fermentation racking can be delayed or abandoned, at least as long as the bottoms do not produce any serious reductive off-flavour. Dispensing with traditional rackings after fermentation means less strain derived from pumping with all its sensory drawbacks on sensitive white wines (section 7.3). Whenever possible, it is reasonable to combine the racking with the filtration in one single step, sucking the wine from above the bottoms directly into the filter.

The Question of Early Filtration

An even more effective way to take advantage of the positive properties of suspended yeast lees is to delay filtration as long as possible. As a consequence, the wine is better protected from oxidation when oxygen is inevitably picked up upon treatments like acidity corrections, finings, blendings or trivial storage in poorly topped vessels. Premature filtration within the first two or three months post-fermentation conflicts with the goal of producing fruity white wines. It is only justified for microbiologically unstable wines like those stored at high temperatures (>15°C), with residual sugar, high pH or deleterious bacteria populations developing.

It might be tempting to make use of the widespread availability of modern filtration equipment just to get clear wines, but polishing a young wine only for aesthetic reasons does not contribute to quality. Compelling very cloudy white wines to pass through filter media stresses and causes the wine to fall apart. When wines are filtered much later, they pass through the filter much more easily, causing less pressure difference between filter inlet and outlet. Thus they suffer less mechanical strain, turbulences in the outlet pipe and filtrate tank, oxygen uptake, and stripping out of fermentation aromatics by CO_2 escaping from the filtrate (section 7.3). Gentle self-clarification versus wearing mechanical clarification is a major decision that will heavily impact the quality of sensitive white wines characterised by fruitiness and freshness.

Opened diatomaceous earth filter after cleaning. Such filters are used to filter very cloudy wines, but never provide a sterile filtrate.

Small sheet filter. Such devices are multi-purpose filters, which, after insertion of appropriate cellulose filter sheets and sterilisation with steam or hot water, even allow sterile filtration.

6.2 Barrel Ageing, Sur-Lie and Bâtonnage

Dispensing with rackings and delaying filtration as described in the previous section are measures that make moderate use of the positive properties of yeast lees. In contrast, ageing on the lees means going a step further and maintaining the total of lees in suspension by periodic stirring (bâtonnage) over a longer period, sometimes more than a year and in barrels. In doing so, the sensory influence of the yeast and its autolysis is more emphasised in conjunction with the impact of the barrel, while the wine style moves away from the fruity kind to a more robust one. Barrel ageing, especially in new barrels, is inseparably linked to ageing on the lees (sur-lie) and stirring, because otherwise the wines' character would be excessively marked by wood, oxidation and astringency. Storing clarified wines in barrels is a typical beginner's mistake.

Oxygen Uptake in Barrels

Oxygen uptake in barrels occurs through the inherent porosity of the wood, through the joints between the staves, via the ullage around the bung when barrels are not hermetically sealed, and upon periodic topping. The annual rate of oxygen ingress into barrels is expressed as mg/L O_2 per year and refers to filled barrels of 225L. For new barrels, variable oxygen uptake rates (OTR) exceeding 10mg/L/year O_2 have been reported. As the number of wines aged in a barrel increases, the wood pores and stave joints become increasingly clogged with microorganisms, bitartrate

When there is a lack of space, it is a good idea to stack the barrels on appropriate racks.

crystals and other precipitated wine material, so that the oxygen uptake decreases over time to considerably less than 10mg/L O_2 per year.

However, OTR data referring to new barrels can be misleading because they show a dynamic behaviour, which depends on the wood moisture and the progression of the moisture front from inside the barrel to the outside. In new barrels, the wood pores still contain air, through which oxygen diffuses much faster than through the wine subsequently filling the pores when the wood becomes wine-saturated after some period of wine storage. Thus, under conditions of continuous OTR monitoring, a marked decrease was reported, from 44mg/L/year at day 1 to 22mg/L/year at day 10, to 16mg/L/year at day 30, and finally stabilising at 7.3mg/L/year after one and a half months. These results allowed estimation of the real value of the annual OTR in four barrels, which was 11.3mg/L/year. As a result of the evolution of the OTR, after two months of storage, a new barrel has already supplied nearly 40 per cent of all the oxygen it would provide to the wine in a year. Ultimately, the impact of wood moisture on oxygen diffusion is so dramatic that moisture seems to be the key factor leading to very low OTR conditions in wine barrels just one to two months after filling (del Alano-Sanza and Nevares 2018).

Hydrolysable Tannins Released from Oak

Hydrolysable tannins of oak are also referred to as ellagitannins, and are more abundant in European than in American oak. They are highly astringent. However, they are degraded with increasing toasting level, which in turn confers less astringency to the wine. Nevertheless, their extraction from the wood of new barrels always leads to a strong increase in astringency during the first three to four months of storage. Subsequently their concentration starts to decrease by hydrolysis, leading to a mitigation of their astringency. While tannins play a fundamental role in red wine ageing, their presence in white wines is undesirable due to their astringency. However, if the yeast is stirred with sufficient frequency, they are almost completely adsorbed by it.

Volatile Aroma Compounds Released from Oak

While wood species other than oak show only a limited impact on wine aroma, oak is able to substantially modify or completely mask it by the volatile compounds it releases. Indeed, an unmanageable diversity of different molecules responsible for oak aroma has been identified. The majority of them are produced during seasoning and the toasting process (Pérez-Coello et al. 1999). By varying the temperature and duration of toasting, it is possible to respond very individually to the specific wood, the type of wine and customer requirements. For wine ageing, medium-toasted barrels are generally preferred because they confer the best sensory balance to the wine.

There are major differences between American and European oak. The latter is frequently referred to as French oak, even though an appreciable amount of it originates in southeastern European countries. In a nutshell, while American oak releases fewer ellagitannins, it imparts more aroma intensity, sweeter notes, vanilla and coconut than European oak, which instead provides more aroma complexity with spicier notes. With some experience, such differences between European and American oak are clearly traceable in wine by tasting, though there might be exceptions since wood composition is highly variable and displays differences between trees of the same species and location. These differences can manifest themselves in barrel-to-barrel variations (Towey and Waterhouse 1996a, b). Such compositional differences between individual trees, due to forestry conditions and anatomical localisation of the wood, can have more impact than differences due to the botanical or geographical origin of the oak. It is one of the main tasks of cooperage to minimise them.

Sensory Features of Bad Oak

When sourcing oak barrels, their quality is frequently rated as a function of the cooperage's reputation and their price level. In many countries, French manufacturers or French oak are favoured. However, each cooperage also has batches of bad oak that is supplied to less reputed clients. Table 3 gives an overview of the sensory features of bad oak.

Lightly toasted barrels are occasionally promoted with the claim that they better preserve the original wine varietal aroma by masking it less with oak aroma compounds. This is not true, because even lightly or untoasted oak releases a distinct aroma, which is reminiscent of freshly cut wood, sawdust and green walnut shells. When the intention is to better preserve the original wine aroma, using fewer new barrels and blending back with a portion of the wine stored in stainless steel or old barrels is a better solution than ageing in poorly toasted ones.

Barrel Age and Size

All compounds extracted from wood as well as their sensory impact decrease as a consequence of their progressive depletion when barrels are used repeatedly for successive batches. Assuming that wines spend twelve months on average in barrels, the sensory impact of oak is reduced by approximately half with each wine, but with the most drastic decrease occurring during the first year of use. After the third wine, the aroma and tannin potential of the oak is largely exhausted. Then the function of the barrel is limited to oxygen supply. While such barrels are still useful for red wine ageing, their exclusive use for white wines is less reasonable. On the other hand, the exclusive use of new barrels leads to a one-sided emphasis on oak, behind which the actual wine disappears. This can certainly be done within the context of oenological freedom and options, but such wines are not highly valued. The highest-scoring barrel-aged wines are made from a blend of different barrels.

Some winemakers opt for using larger barrels than the standard ones of 225L to reduce the inner

Table 3: Sensory properties of bad oak as perceived in wine

Sensory feature	Causes
Smell reminiscent of pencil shavings and sawdust	Elevated levels of (E)-2-nonenal caused by insufficient toasting or inappropriate wood
Smell reminiscent of green wood and green walnut shell	Bad oak, sometimes aggravated by insufficient toasting
Aggressive, lingering astringency	Elevated levels of ellagitannins caused by deficiencies in wood quality, seasoning or toasting
Complete absence of oak aroma in the first and second wine	Unsuitable wood

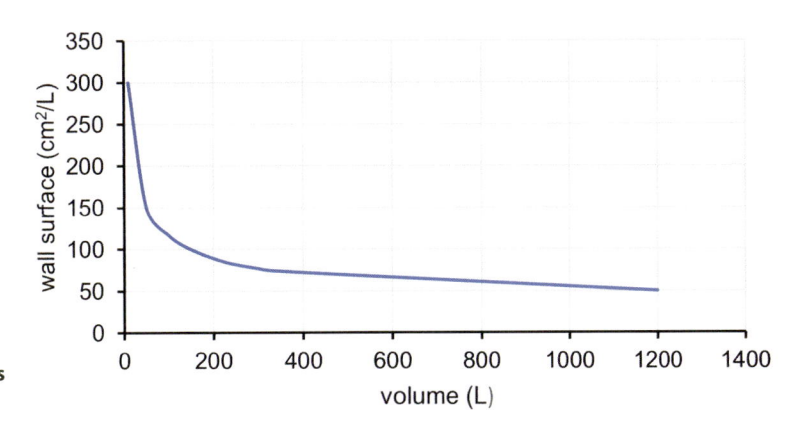

Figure 6.1: Barrels: wall surface area as a function of volume.

surface per volume unit and, thus, the transfer of oak compounds into the wine. Figure 6.1 shows that beyond 225L there is not much to gain with this approach.

The Interaction Between Wood, Wine and Yeast Lees

Under cool-climate conditions only a few varieties are suitable for this kind of cellaring, among which are Chardonnay and Pinot gris. The essential variables that shape the sensory outcome of barrel-aged white wines are:

- The wine
- The age of the barrel and the quality of its wood
- The volume of yeast lees
- The frequency of yeast stirring
- The yeast strain
- The duration
- The use of SO_2

During ageing on the lees, polysaccharides and mannoproteins are released in high amounts from yeast and lower the sensory perception of astringency, sourness, fruit and oak, while increasing the wine's body, volume and protein stability. The stirring causes an oxygen uptake able to change the sensory balance between fruit, yeast and wood, but it does not necessarily induce oxidative ageing because the yeast lees consume a considerable, though highly variable, amount of that oxygen (section 5.5). Hence the redox regime also varies between wines and individual barrels.

This picture is further complicated by rackings and SO_2 additions. Early additions increase the number of components that bind to subsequent SO_2 additions, but hamper the onset of malolactic fermentation generally sought in that kind of wine. It is quite possible to run ageing on the lees over more than a year without any SO_2 and without any signs of oxidation, relying only on the reducing capacity of the yeast lees kept in suspension by regular stirring. At the latest, SO_2 should be added when the wine is removed from the barrel or when it starts browning from the surface downwards.

Barrel storage area in a large winery.

This usually happens when stirring is stopped to prepare the wine for filtration, blending or bottling. Browning indicates the beginning of irreversible oxidation reactions and should be prevented in any kind of white wine.

Generally, stirring frequency depends on the time suspended yeast needs to settle. The faster it settles, the more often it should be stirred in order to prevent oxidation of the topmost liquid layer. Thus stirring frequency typically ranges from once every three days to once per month. The settling rate strongly depends on the individual wine and its oxidation-reduction regime. Figure 6.2 illustrates how both SO_2 (50mg/L) additions and oxygen supply by racking increase the yeast lees settling rate and accelerate clarification. It explains why yeast lees settling is much slower in stainless steel tanks than in wooden barrels allowing oxygen uptake.

Also depending on stylistic goals, the duration of lees contact is highly variable. One year is a very general rule when it is performed in barrels in the traditional way. During that time, it is often associated with the occurrence of malolactic fermentation. Addition of exogenous ß-glucanase accelerates yeast autolysis, the release of mannoproteins, and their sensory consequences. However, it cannot perform miracles when there are not enough yeast lees available or when fermentation was run with a yeast strain that releases low levels of polysaccharides. Differences between yeast strains are considerable, and some commercial strains are marketed specifically for the purpose of enhancing polysaccharide levels during fermentation and subsequent lees contact. When there is a deficiency of yeast biomass, some winemakers add supplementary yeast bottoms obtained from other containers. Clearly, stirring does not make any sense when there is a yeast shortage.

Most winemakers prefer the wine to be already in the barrel for fermentation, especially if it is new oak. This approach is expected to improve the sensory integration of oak, which is achieved by a reduction of oak components by the integral yeast. Comparable results can be achieved if fermentation takes place in tanks and the wine is transferred to barrels immediately afterwards, including all the yeast lees.

6.3 Wines Without Added Sulphites

Consumer health concerns are one of the reasons why wines without added sulphites are produced here and there. However, conventional wines only contain a minimal fraction of the amounts of SO_2 found in many other foods, while less than 1 per cent of the population is reported to be affected by a sulphite allergy. It is debatable whether such an allergy can exist at all, since the human body produces and metabolises more than a gram of sulphite per day, which corresponds to approximately ten times the amount contained in a bottle of wine. Ethical considerations might play a greater role – dispensing with SO_2 additions is frequently associated with organic and biodynamic winegrowing. This explains why there is a small market for wines without added sulphites, and these wines require preservation by other means.

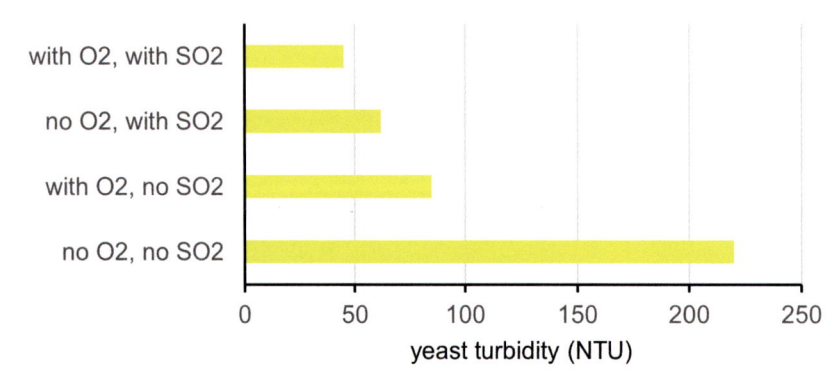

Figure 6.2: Impact of oxygenation by racking and SO_2 (50mg/L) addition on settling of post-fermentation yeast lees.

Wines without any SO_2 do not exist. During primary fermentation, yeasts commonly produce 10–30mg/L SO_2 with deviations upwards and downwards (Figure 4.2). A level of 10mg/L total SO_2 is the upper limit below which the warning 'contains sulphites' need not be stated on the label. There are only a very few selected yeast strains producing SO_2 below this limit under optimal nutritional conditions. Indigenous yeasts performing spontaneous fermentation rarely do so.

In principle, white winemaking without added SO_2 is feasible – that is, it should be possible to produce such wines that do not display oxidation flaws or the smell of free acetaldehyde (section 5.1). However, to achieve this objective and prevent oxidation, much more knowledge and technical input are required than for conventional winemaking with SO_2. Winemaking without added SO_2, while maintaining quality and hygiene standards, requires control of virtually every facet of production from the crush pad to the bottled wine. It is important to emphasise that the basic issue in producing such wines is not so much the microbial stability SO_2 additions would provide. Microbial safety can easily be obtained by physical means such as sterile filtration and cooling, and technical facilities for that purpose are widely available. Rather, the issue is first and foremost about oxidation.

White wines without free SO_2 require consistent and rigorous protection against oxidation as soon as alcoholic fermentation comes to an end. Storage with the yeast lees and delaying filtration until shortly before bottling are essential tools for this purpose. Additionally, post-fermentation oxygen uptake during storage, stabilisation treatments and filtration is systematically prevented by the use of inert gas, be it nitrogen or argon. This is a common and indispensable procedure in the brewing industry, as beer is even more sensitive to oxidation than white wine, but it still needs getting used to in the wine industry. At bottling, headspace inertisation and the use of bottles closures with a low oxygen ingress rate (section 8.4) are an essential element in this approach. Working with a DO meter is highly recommended to check the amounts of DO picked up and understand where it comes from (section 7.2).

Prior to fermentation, deliberate must oxidation and thorough clarification are recommended to lower the phenolic fractions that would otherwise substantially contribute to the sensory consequences of oxidative ageing of wine (sections 2.2 and 2.5). Primary fermentation must run smoothly with a yeast strain producing less than 10mg/L SO_2 and under conditions of satisfactory nutrient supply. Otherwise, total acetaldehyde levels in the wine would exceed 5mg/L. As long as they are lower, they are bound by the SO_2 produced by yeast. As a reminder: 1.0mg/L acetaldehyde requires 1.45g/L SO_2 in order to be bound as an odourless adduct. When there is less SO_2 than required to bind acetaldehyde, free acetaldehyde would strongly affect aroma quality. In conventional winemaking, the usual step to overcome this problem is adding more SO_2 (section 5.1).

Another approach to minimise acetaldehyde contents is malolactic fermentation (section 4.1). It is suitable for lowering total acetaldehyde to less than 5mg/L. When it is completed and malic acid is less than 0.2g/L, wines are stored cold at not more than 5°C, perfectly topped without any liquid surface until they are sterile filtered just before bottling. Under commercial winemaking conditions, headspace blanketing with inert gas is not a reliable enough means to protect against oxygen uptake to the extent that is required for such wines.

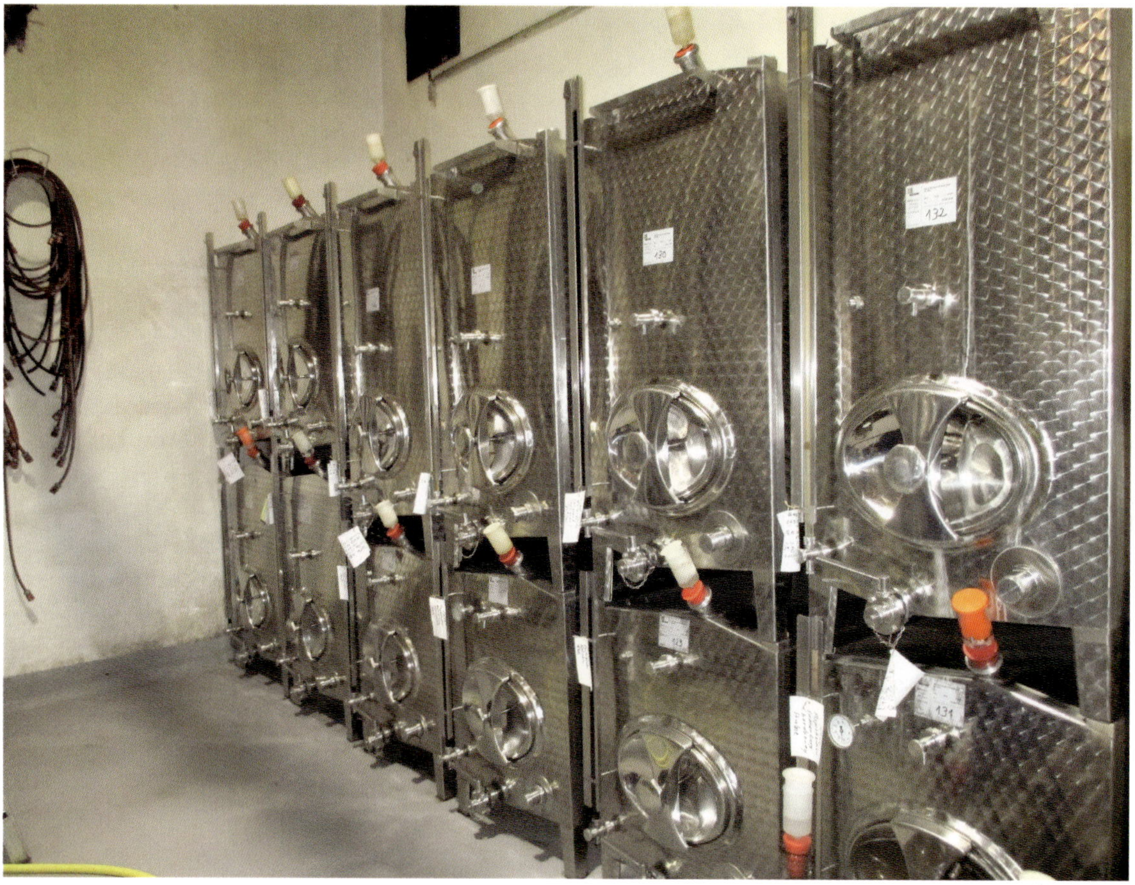

CHAPTER 7

LIMITING OXYGEN UPTAKE

Winemakers are used to quantify and adjust sulphite levels in their wines, but in contrast to the brewing industry, they are still far from being ready to evaluate the amounts and sources of oxygen the wine picks up, which is decisive for white wine evolution post-fermentation. In this very practical chapter, the amounts and various routes of oxygen uptake through container walls, through the wine surface from the container headspace, and upon wine treatments are illustrated along with their sensory consequences. Based on this, recommendations for daily practice follow for reducing oxygen uptake during standard winery operations such as pumping and filtration. They eventually constitute a long list of craft skills for the handling of fruity white wines in the cellar, each an apparently minor measure, but whose sum is crucial for quality and shelf life of these wines; they are much less relevant for the more robust barrel-aged or red wines. They are building blocks of the much advocated low-intervention winemaking and finally culminate in the appealing yet effective concept of 'minimal treatment by controlled idleness'.

7.1 Sensory Impact of Oxygen Uptake in Filtered Wines

When wine picks up oxygen, two consecutive processes occur:

1. The transfer of oxygen from the atmosphere into the liquid and its dissolution therein. This is a purely physical process. At normal pressure and 20°C, wine can dissolve up to 8mg/L O_2, which is the oxygen saturation point. The oxygen dissolved as a gas (DO) can be measured by analytical means. It does not have any taste or odour properties, so there are not yet any sensory consequences.
2. The gradual chemical binding of DO on oxidisable wine compounds. This reaction causes sensory changes. Binding causes oxygen to be consumed and disappear, hence it cannot be measured any more.

The rate of chemical binding of DO, also known as oxygen consumption rate, is proportional to its instantaneous concentration. It depends on wine composition and is difficult to predict. Figure 7.1 gives the example of two wines.

OPPOSITE: **Stainless steel tanks best preserve the freshness of white wine and protect against oxygen uptake when properly topped.**

Temperature accelerates the DO consumption rate in an exponential way. This effect is shown in Figure 7.2. It is of importance when wines are stored in contact with air, because the faster DO is consumed, the faster it is replenished from the atmosphere. Air in combination with heat leads to the rapid oxidative destruction of white wines. Conversely, wine in opened bottles will keep for a long time if stored at a very low temperature in the refrigerator.

Since the DO consumption curves approach zero asymptotically, DO can require several days or weeks until it completely disappears. This behaviour explains why full sensory effects of oxygen pickup can only be observed after this time delay. However, there is an exception: when a stinky reductive taint is present, it can under certain circumstances disappear within a couple of minutes of contact with air, because the volatile sulphur compounds responsible for it require only tiny amounts of oxygen to react and degrade.

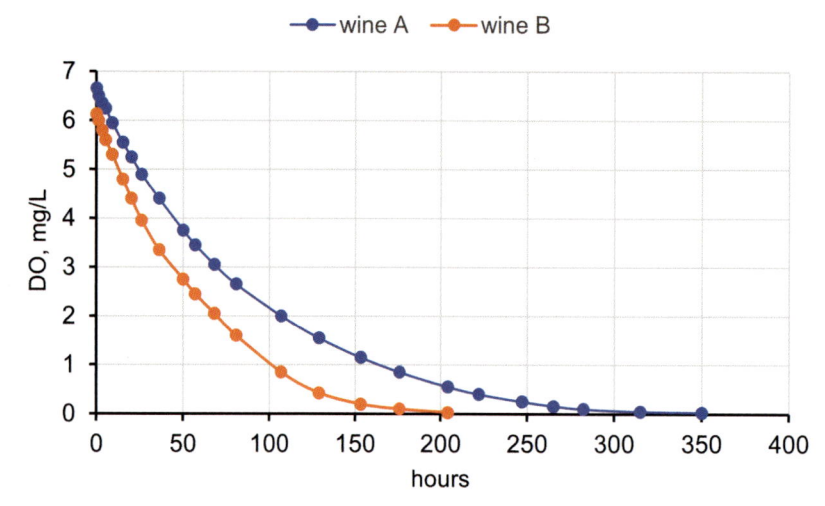

Figure 7.1: DO consumption of two sterile-filtered white wines. No ascorbic acid, initial free SO_2 = 40mg/L, T = 20°C.

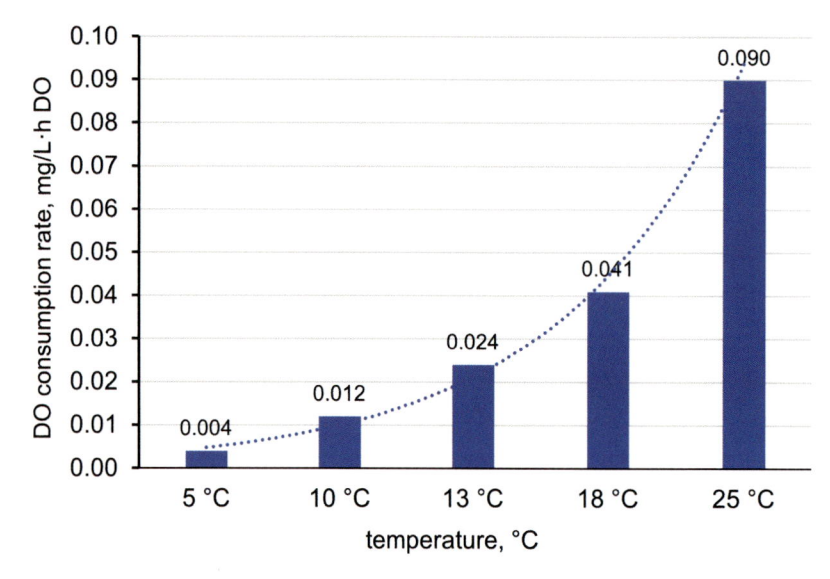

Figure 7.2: Effect of temperature on the DO consumption rate of a sterile-filtered white wine.

How Much Oxygen does a Fruity White Wine Tolerate Without Quality Losses?

There is anecdotal evidence that white wines stored under experimental conditions with absolute exclusion of air remain fairly closed by smell without developing the fruity aroma one expects to find in young wines. However, under standard winemaking conditions, it is inevitable that wine will absorb at least small amounts of oxygen until it is bottled. The sensory consequences after its consumption are stronger in the filtered wine, because then there are no longer yeast lees able to consume a part of the oxygen (section 5.5) and SO_2 does not fully protect against oxidation (section 5.1). Figure 7.3 reports the intensity ratings of ageing as perceived by smell of various cool-climate varietal wines after supplying different amounts of oxygen. The sensory evaluation took place after two months of bottle storage under airtight screwcaps and complete DO consumption.

Depending on the individual wine, 10 or 20mg/L O_2 were sufficient to obtain a significant increase of oxidative ageing or, conversely, a decrease of fruity varietal aroma. Similar results were obtained after bottling with 11.5mg/L O_2 picked up from the air-containing bottle headspace (Morozova et al. 2015). As a conclusion, it can be stated that control and limitation of oxygen uptake post-filtration are of primary importance for preserving white wine quality.

From this perspective, it is desirable that the wine industry attach the same importance to DO control as it does to controlling free SO_2. The brewing industry sets an example by showing how rigorous DO control works.

7.2 Sources of Oxygen Uptake

Inadvertent oxygen pickup and oxidative flaws of filtered white wines are a serious concern in the wine industry. Otherwise, the use of antioxidants would not be such an important topic. The problem can also be seen from a different perspective, trying to tackle the causes instead of relying on the limited effectiveness of antioxidants added.

Oxygen Uptake Through the Container Wall

While winemakers are aware of the oxygen picked up in wooden barrels (section 6.2), they are less aware of the oxygen diffusion permitted by plastic materials. The various polyethylenes (PE) in particular are highly permeable to atmospheric oxygen with precise permeability rates depending on the PE specification. This disqualifies the numerous small and cheap tanks made of this material and frequently found in wine cellars for long-term storage of white wine. Experience has shown that they severely affect white wine quality

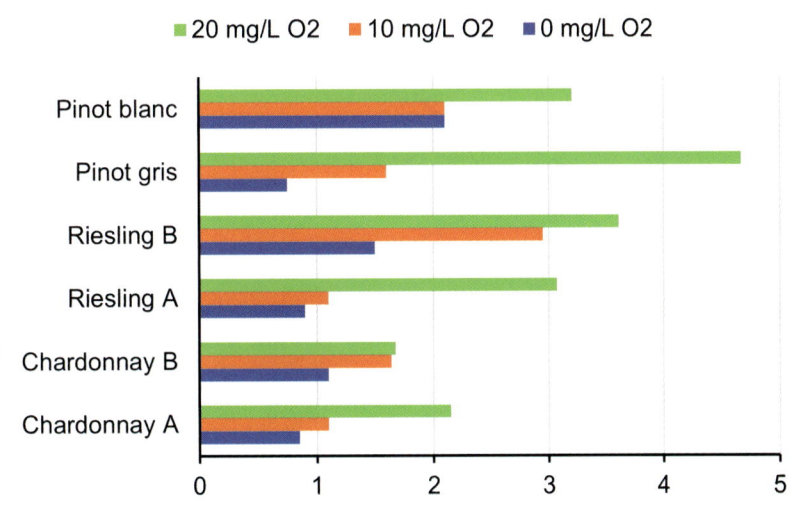

Figure 7.3: Intensity ratings (0–5) of oxidative ageing perceived by smell as affected by oxygen uptake after filtration of white wines. Initial free SO_2 = 27 to 46mg/L, means of fourteen tasters.

within a few weeks' storage. In contrast, they can be useful for storing robust red wines or lees.

Materials such as stainless steel and glass are at the other extreme and absolutely impermeable to oxygen. This qualifies them for long-term storage under oxygen exclusion on condition that the containers are really topped to the brim. The oxygen permeability of the newly rediscovered traditional containers such as clay amphorae or egg-shaped tanks is the decisive factor that distinguishes them from other storage containers, apart from their esoteric aspects. It depends essentially on their inner coating.

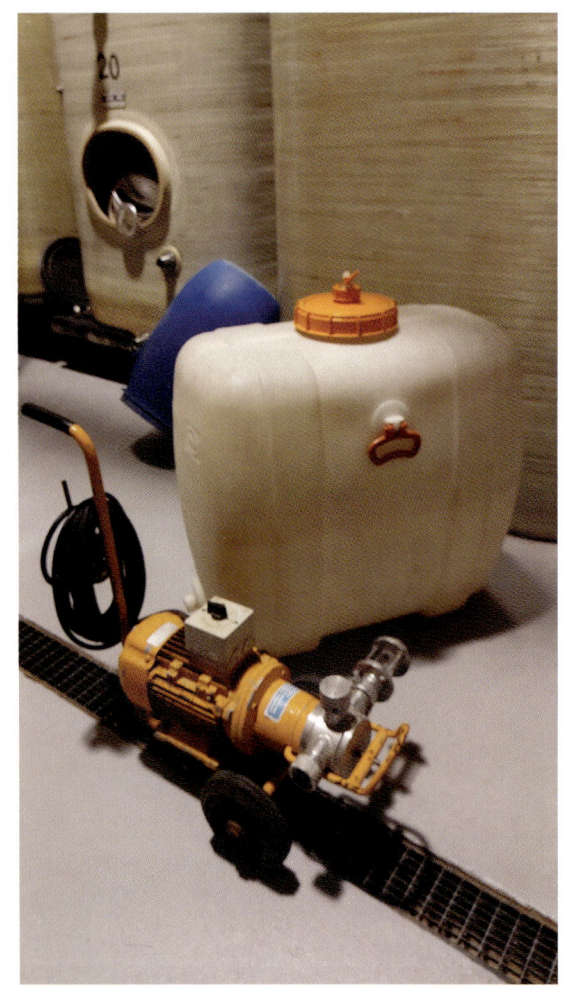

Storage in small plastic tanks made of HDPE frequently found in small wineries is the best way to rapidly destroy white wines due to their enormous oxygen transmission rate.

However, the oxygen permeability of the container material is not the only criterion. It is also crucial to consider the wine volume that absorbs the oxygen provided by a given container wall surface area. This leads to the surface-area-to-volume ratio, which increases with decreasing volume. Storing wine in a small container with a high oxygen permeability easily causes overoxidation.

Oxygen Uptake Through the Wine Surface

Uncontrolled oxygen uptake frequently takes place through the wine surface, which can be undisturbed or agitated. An undisturbed (static) surface occurs when wine is stored in containers that are not completely topped. Upon stirring of such a wine, the surface becomes agitated. Such turbulent surfaces can also be observed when wine flows through hoses, filters, and pumps containing air pockets because they have not been carefully vented.

Gases dissolve in liquids to a certain degree. When a liquid becomes saturated with a gas, no more can be dissolved in the liquid. The gas solubility increases when temperature decreases. At normal pressure, wine can absorb up to 8mg/L O_2 at 20°C and even 11mg/L O_2 at 10°C. Although a cold wine can hold more dissolved oxygen (DO) than a warm one, this general rule is not related to the speed at which wine takes up oxygen from the atmosphere. Measurements in real wine are meaningless because the oxygen escapes them by binding. Instead, measurements of the oxygen uptake through the surface require model solutions containing only alcohol and ascorbic acid at wine pH. Under these conditions, oxygen picked up is consumed by ascorbic acid in a stoichiometric relationship (section 5.2). The decrease of ascorbic acid over time allows direct calculation of the amount of oxygen (in mg $O_2/m^2/h$) passing through the liquid surface. Figure 7.4 reports some of the results.

The undisturbed liquid stored at 20°C picks up 20.2mg $O_2/m^2/h$ or 484.8mg $O_2/m^2/day$. This value increases sixteen-fold when the same solution at 20°C undergoes constant stirring to generate an agitated surface. The latter value depends on the intensity of stirring and turbulence, obviously. The impact of temperature is also crucial. The better oxygen solubility

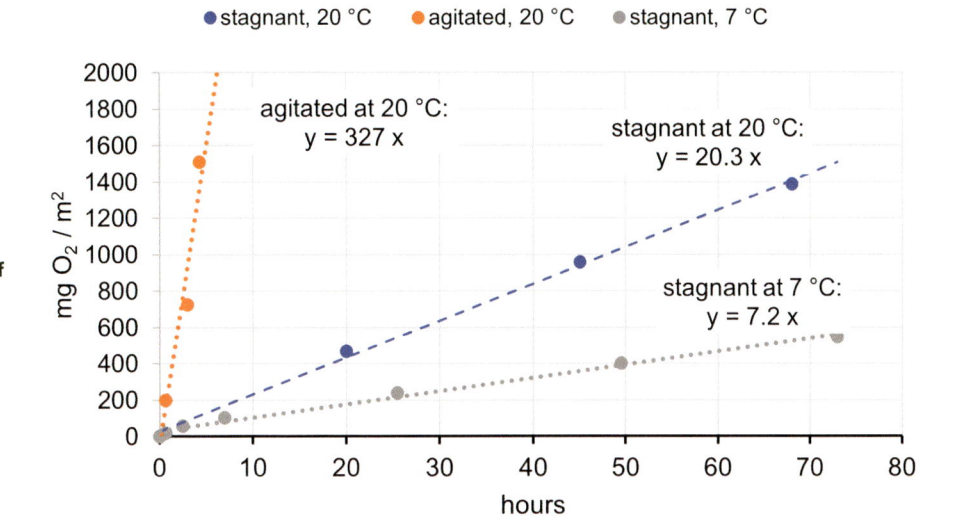

Figure 7.4: Diffusion of atmospheric oxygen through the surface of a wine-like model solution at normal pressure: effect of surface agitation and temperature.

Legend: stagnant, 20 °C; agitated, 20 °C; stagnant, 7 °C

- agitated at 20 °C: y = 327 x
- stagnant at 20 °C: y = 20.3 x
- stagnant at 7 °C: y = 7.2 x

Axes: mg O_2 / m² vs hours

at low temperatures might lead to the careless assumption that oxygen diffusion from the atmosphere into the liquid also increases under these conditions. However, direct comparison of the diffusion rates of the undisturbed aliquots at 7° and 20°C proves the opposite (Figure 7.4): decreasing temperature from 20°C to 7°C lowers the diffusion rate 2.8 times from 20.2 to 7.2 mg O_2/m²/h. This result might appear surprising at first glance but has a simple physical explanation. The uptake of a gas by liquid proceeds in two steps:

1. Passive diffusion of the gas from the atmosphere through the liquid surface into the upper boundary layer of the liquid. This process is almost spontaneous and only active over a small distance. At a given pressure, its rate depends on temperature and the saturation degree of the gas in the liquid.
2. Transportation of the gas into the liquid's interior. Its driving force is the continuous renewal of the boundary layer, for example by mixing. As a result, low-oxygen liquid is transported from below towards the surface, where it absorbs more oxygen. This step becomes more and more rate-determining with increasing distance from the surface.

As a basic principle, the diffusion of a gas within the liquid decreases with decreasing temperature.

Although the solubility of oxygen in wine is higher in the cold, low temperature slows down its distribution in the undisturbed wine and, consequently, all downstream reactions of oxidation. However, when cold and surface agitation interact with one another, oxygen uptake reaches extreme values. This is what happens when wines undergo fining in the cold cellar in winter. On the other hand, oxygen uptake in the cold is reduced when the liquid surface is undisturbed as oxygen diffusion within the liquid slows down. In this way, the effect of a higher oxygen solubility at low temperature is cancelled out. Hence wines not completely topped and stored in the cold oxidise more slowly, though oxygen solubility is higher.

Tank Geometry and Specific Surface Area

In practical cellar work, it is vital to be aware of the high and barely controllable amounts of oxygen a wine can pick up from the headspace when the container is not completely topped. This oxygen uptake is a diffusion process controlled by temperature and the wine surface area. The headspace height or the missing wine volume are without importance, though many practitioners see it differently. Expressed in mg/L O_2, wine stored or processed under an air-containing headspace in small containers has to withstand a many times higher oxygen load than wine in large containers. Along the same line of thinking, tall, slender tanks are preferred to short, wide tanks because taller tanks have less exposed wine surface area. These considerations take us to the concept of the 'specific surface area', expressed in cm²/L. A simple example makes clear what is meant by this: a surface area of 1m² above 1,000L imparts ten times more oxygen (in mg/L) to the wine than if above 10,000L.

Variable-Capacity Tanks
Stainless-steel variable-capacity tanks with a floating lid are generally used to store smaller wine volumes of up to 2,000L. The lid is simply inserted into the tank and then allowed to float on the wine surface. The lid is equipped with an inflatable bladder around

Variable-capacity tanks have a movable lid designed to float on the wine surface to reduce oxygen uptake when a container cannot be completely topped.

its circumference, which is inflated using a PE tube connected to a hand air pump to create an airtight seal on the inner circumference of the tank to protect the wine from air. The bladder pressure can be adjusted at any time to maintain the seal's tightness. The pump has a release valve to deflate the bladder when the lid is to be removed. This apparently perfect solution has been conceived for storage of variable wine volumes without oxygen uptake from the headspace through the liquid surface. It would even work for that purpose if the frequently used vinyl bladders and the air pump gasket did not have a common problem in forming a good seal in the long term. Therefore these tanks usually do allow for some oxygen uptake during extended storage – the problem is that one cannot predict how much.

Headspace Purging with Inert Gas
In the hope of minimising wine–air contact, headspace inertisation with an inert gas, usually nitrogen, attempts to drive out headspace oxygen and maintain an inert gas layer above the wine surface. In order to prevent the growth of aerobic microorganisms on the wine surface, the oxygen concentration must be reduced from 20.9 per cent O_2 found in air to 0.5 per cent or less above the wine surface. A similar level is required to prevent wine oxidation. This is not an easy task. Effective blanketing requires more than just shooting some inert gas into the headspace because the gas flow creates a churning effect, causing the nitrogen to mix with the air. Thus most of the gas is lost to the outside of the vessel, while the gas inside becomes diluted. Effective headspace inertisation with nitrogen requires an appreciable amount of gas – three to five times the headspace volume – and a gas flow rate comparable to a gentle bleed, as provided by the lowest setting the regulator can be set to and still flow.

In order to check whether all oxygen has been driven out, the flame of a lighter is often used and expected to extinguish when the oxygen in the gas coming out of the tank has been successfully removed. This creates a false sense of protection from oxygen, because the limiting concentration of oxygen below which combustion is not possible is 11.5–17.0 per cent for mixtures of air with nitrogen and CO_2, thus far away from the 0.5 per cent required (del Barrio-Galán et al. 2023).

Despite its frequent use, nitrogen (N_2) is actually poorly suited for blanketing, because it has a similar density to air and mixes with it, thus diluting its oxygen rather than displacing it. In contrast, both argon (Ar) and CO_2 are heavier than air, but pure CO_2 is not useful for this purpose because it dissolves in the wine within one to two weeks. Mixtures of $CO_2:N_2$ (20:80) or $CO_2:Ar$ (20:80), as well as pure Ar, are best suited for blanketing because they form a stable gas blanket.

Instead of purging the headspace of wine already transferred into a tank, it is recommended to first purge the empty receiving tank. For this purpose, only 25 per cent vessel volume Ar is sufficient to achieve useful inerting, provided that both Ar and wine enter the destination tank through its bottom valve. In doing so, Ar accumulates as a layer in the lower part of the tank, from which it is pushed upwards by the wine flowing in and finally remains in the headspace as a layer covering the liquid service. In this way, the wine is already protected against oxygen uptake through its agitated surface during its entry into the tank. N_2 is clearly not suitable for this purpose (del Barrio-Galán et al. 2023).

Inert Blanketing Does not Prevent Aroma Losses Through Evaporation
The aroma of young white wines comprises highly volatile compounds resulting from yeast metabolism to an extent that does not happen with red wines. Their relatively low boiling point and high vapour pressure easily enable them to make their way up to the olfactory epithelium located in the nose. They also cause aroma losses by volatilisation as soon as there is a surface. For that reason, oxygen uptake through the liquid surface is always associated with a decrease of volatile aromatics. The inevitable escape of these molecules into the atmosphere adds to aroma losses caused by oxidation. In some wineries these effects can be dramatic and explain why some white wines are bottled when they are already exhausted.

When there is a headspace, an inert gas blanket to drive off the oxygen can prevent oxidation when it is properly done, but it can never impede aroma losses by evaporation into the headspace. Evaporation is a mass transfer from the liquid phase into the gas phase and requires a concentration gradient of the evaporating compound. Concentration balance is reached when the partial pressure of the compound in the gas phase corresponds to its partial pressure in the liquid phase: only when that state of equilibrium is reached does aroma evaporation come to a halt. Hence it is clear that a headspace filled with inert gas can take up as much aroma as a headspace filled with air. The sole fact that oxygen is driven out and air replaced by an inert gas does not have any impact on the evaporation of volatile wine compounds through the liquid surface into an atmosphere regardless of its composition. Therefore headspace blanketing is not a fully fledged substitute for perfect topping of white wines. When working on very small wine volumes, as frequently happens in micro-vinification trials, adding glass beads to make up the missing volume can be a good solution.

Oxygen Uptake upon Wine Treatments

Apart from container headspace, wines also pick up oxygen when they are treated in the winery by racking, fining, filtration and so on, because there are variable amounts of air in the machinery and pipes. Each of these operations results in an oxygen uptake ranging from 0.1 to more than 4mg/L (Vidal et al. 2001, 2003, 2004, Castellari et al. 2004, Calderón et al. 2014). Two phenomena help us understand this large range:

- Oxygen pickup strongly depends on the carbon dioxide dissolved in the wine when the treatment takes place. When a container is filled from the top, more oxygen is picked up when the wine has already lost the largest portion of its CO_2 resulting from fermentation. In contrast, less oxygen is picked up by young wines because they release CO_2 upon entering the receiving tank, which purges its headspace and removes a part of the oxygen it contains. When young wines with high CO_2 levels are transferred by filling the container from the bottom, there is almost no measurable oxygen uptake because oxygen is largely stripped by CO_2 or rapidly consumed by post-fermentation yeast lees.
- The wine volume treated plays a crucial role: the dissolution of oxygen occurs preferentially at the beginning of a transfer when the pipes are still filled with air, and at the end of the process when the pipes are drained. At these stages, the highest oxygen uptake occurs when a wine is filtered, due to a larger liquid surface, turbulent wine flow and filter pressure. In this way, small wine volumes are exposed to a higher oxygen uptake, expressed in mg/L O_2, than large wine volumes. Small-scale winery operations are clearly disadvantaged.

Aroma losses going along with oxygen uptake are difficult to quantify, but they are associated with losses of CO_2, which are much easier to detect. To the extent one succeeds in preserving some fermentation-derived CO_2 until bottling, this is also a substantial contribution to preserving white wine aroma and overall quality. In many fruity white wines, low levels (< 1.5g/L) of CO_2 are accepted and sometimes even expected as long as there is no distinct perlage. Early and heavy CO_2 losses post-fermentation are a clear indication of too robust wine processing. It is useful to identify the point in the production sequence where this happens.

7.3 Importance and Measures of Gentle Wine Treatment

The importance of the wine's surface for oxygen uptake and aroma losses as discussed in the previous section is especially pronounced when the surface is agitated, as occurs during wine treatments. Although the effects might be negligible after a single treatment, the issue is what their cumulative effect might be after many consecutive treatments from racking to bottling. Their extent depends predominantly on the cellar staff's craftsmanship and some practical experience. Mitigation of the effects of treatment requires a closer look at details of the real-world way of working in a winery. Everything essentially comes down to performing any treatment that might be necessary as gently as possible. From this perspective, traditional white wine countries are clearly better performing than red wine regions, because red wines are much more robust, rendering these precautions and considerations hardly necessary.

Operating Pumps

Since each pumping cycle is considered one too many, the use of gravity flow grows in importance worldwide when new wineries are designed. However, moving wine by gravity flow is not automatically the perfect solution. When the downward pipes are not filled with wine across their entire cross-section, a turbulent flow with air pockets will be produced. This results in the dissolution of oxygen and evaporation of aroma compounds. Moving wine by slightly pressurising the headspace of the source tank with nitrogen can be a good alternative to strenuous pumping operations.

In a more realistic scenario, wines will still be moved by pumping, and choosing the appropriate pump is one of the main concerns in any winery. Pumps should be self-priming, have deadhead capabilities, and generate enough pressure to force the wine through a filter. In the particular context of sensitive white wines, they should avoid aeration and minimise agitation and shearing. Centrifugal pumps do not fulfil these requirements under all conditions. Due to the absence of self-priming capabilities, they must be placed below the level of the tank outlet. When there is an air pocket in the sucking pipe, they tend to homogenise air in the wine.

Screw pumps, also referred to as progressive cavity or mohno pumps, minimise shearing and agitation. They are also highly tolerant to sediments and solids. Flexible rubber impeller pumps strike a good balance of features for most wineries, though they can be a little physically rough on the wine when they are run at full speed. Therefore many of them feature a bypass or are operated by variable-frequency drivers to adjust flow rates. Both screw pumps and rubber impeller pumps cannot run dry. Furthermore, they continue working against a closed valve on the discharge side. To ensure the safety of the pump and pressure hose, they frequently feature dry-run and deadhead auto-stop capability.

At least as important as the kind of pump is what happens in the hoses on the suction and the pressure side. Section 7.2 deals with the quality losses related to a turbulent wine surface. Turbulence can also occur in a transfer line. When this happens, there is even more turbulence produced in the receiving tank. Consequently, degassing of CO_2 and volatile aroma compounds occurs, along with oxygen uptake. Laminar flow in the transfer lines prevents turbulences.

The flow is laminar when the wine moves slowly in parallel layers without disruption of the layers, transverse flow or mixing. To keep a flow laminar, flow velocity must not exceed 1.5m/sec, corresponding to the speed of a walker. This can only be achieved when the pump delivery rate does not exceed 3,000L/h for 25mm, 7,000L/h for 40mm and 11,000L/h for 50mm nominal tube diameter respectively. The narrowest point of the whole tubing system is decisive. Since the default tubing diameter is hardly ever changed in a winery, variable-frequency drivers allowing pump capacity adjustment are of great benefit.

Operating Filters

The question of the gentlest filtration technique – diatomaceous earth, pad, membrane or cross-flow filtration – is re-evaluated at periodic intervals of little more than every ten years. However, the way a filter is operated often exerts more sensory impact on the wine than the device itself. Some examples may help to clarify the reasons for this.

On its way through the filter, the wine is under pressure. At some point pressure relief must take place, at the latest when the wine flows into the receiving tank. At this point, degassing of CO_2 entraining volatile aroma compounds occurs, facilitated by the wine surface, which is more or less agitated. Figure 7.5 illustrates this effect.

Considerable agitation of the wine surface in the receiving tank occurs at the beginning of any wine transfer, magnifying the surface area several times as well as oxygen uptake and aroma volatilisation associated therewith. This is the reason that tall, slender tanks are preferred; their low surface area in relation to their volume causes less mass exchange. Further improvement can be achieved by dispensing with filtering in the high pressure range.

When the outlet hose of a filter or any other tubing runs downwards, suction is produced, creating a pressure drop as a function of the height difference. If

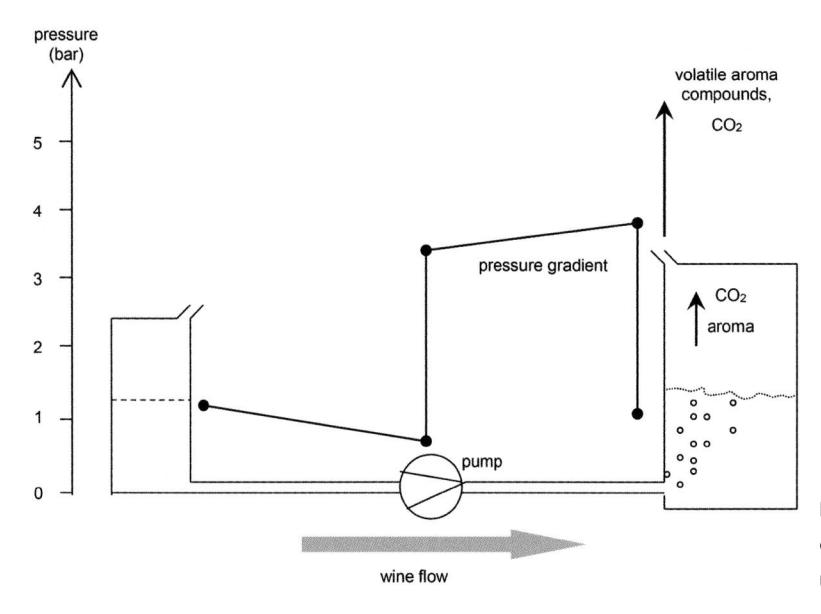

Figure 7.5: Pressure curve in the course of wine transfer; pressure release and aroma losses.

the pipe is not filled with wine over its entire cross-section, there will be an agitated wine surface causing aroma losses, which will be further reinforced by the locally negative gauge pressure above the wine. The aroma compounds accumulate in the pipe's gas phase and are stripped out altogether with CO_2 in the receiving tank, where considerable splashing and bubbling occur each time a turbulent wine flows into it. In the worst case, the effect is comparable with wine degassing upon vigorously shaking it in a half-full bottle. Each time a pipe is not completely filled with wine and contains gas pockets, venting is urgently required to create a laminar flow.

When a filter starts fouling, throughput reduces and the wine surface in the filtrate tank, related to a given wine volume, remains agitated for longer. There will probably be no quality losses on red or barrel-aged white wines. However, when a fruity white wine is split into two fractions during filtration, a first one provided by fast filtration and a second one resulting from slow filtration at high pressure difference, quality losses are likely to be observed in the second fraction forced though the filter. As a general rule, it can be assumed that the lower the filter pressure difference and the higher the filter throughput, the less will be aroma losses and oxygen uptake during filtration. Moreover, low temperatures help to reduce aroma evaporation through an agitated wine surface.

Good cellar craftsmanship suggests the following guidelines for gentle handling.

Gentle White Wine Handling in Practice

Complete topping Carefully and completely top all containers until they spill over. The quality of topping depends on the remaining wine surface area (in m^2) in contact with the headspace atmosphere. It does not depend on the missing wine volume or the height of the headspace. The mass exchange is exclusively controlled by the wine surface area. An increase of cellar temperature can cause some overflow, but many winemakers prefer losing a bucket of wine to any ullage.

Early topping It is useful to commence topping containers by the end of fermentation, when foaming over is no longer possible, and thus remove any liquid surface. In most cases this is possible when two-thirds of the initial sugar has disappeared. Under these conditions, yeasts continue producing fruity fermentation-derived aroma compounds, which cannot escape any more through the liquid surface. The outcome is an aroma accumulation. Although oxygen supply from the headspace or by other means is reputed to improve yeast fermentation activity (section 3.1), that ceases to be effective in the very final stage of fermentation.

Considering blending When wines are topped and racked, it is useful to consider in advance which wine can be used to completely fill the container. When distinct varietal wines are to be produced, the addition of a small percentage of another variety can be less detrimental to varietal style than leaving a headspace. However, not all varieties are compatible, and extreme caution is advised when topping with aromatic varieties such as Bacchus or Schönburger.

Headspace inertisation This is the next best solution when no adequate wine is available for complete topping. When doing so, it is vital to consider that an inert gas volume corresponding to three to five times the headspace volume is needed to reduce headspace oxygen satisfactorily. CO_2 is less useful for that purpose as it dissolves in the wine within two to three weeks, thus creating a negative gauge pressure and thereby sucking in atmospheric oxygen. Both nitrogen and argon are suitable for headspace blanketing (*see* section 7.2 for details).

Appropriate storage vessels Tall, slender tanks are preferable to wide tanks as they allow for less wine surface area in proportion to the wine volume.

Short tubings When wine is racked, blended, filtered and so on, the lengths of hoses should be limited to what is strictly necessary.

Hose connections Loose hose connections must be avoided, as they would suck atmospheric oxygen into the wine flow.

Pump seals Leaky pump seals must be secured; they would act just as loose hose connections.

Purging hoses with water Purging transfer lines with an inert gas to displace oxygen has limited effect unless tremendous amounts of gas are used. Additionally, filter pads are easily damaged by high gas pressure. Instead, before transfers and filtrations, it is appropriate and easy to first pump water throughout the whole system in order to remove any air pockets in tubings and the filter, draining the water on the floor. When the system is vented, connect the inlet hose to the wine without sucking air. Taste on the fly using a three-way valve fixed to the receiving tank. When the cut is ready to be made, switch the valve to connect to the receiving tank. When finished, repeat the operation, pushing through with water to displace the wine in the system. This way of running water through the whole system for venting is faster and more efficient than gas inertisation provided you can distinguish wine from water when tasting on the fly. Simultaneous cleaning is a pleasant side-effect.

Adjusting pump capacity Pump output should be adjusted to match tubing diameters to avoid turbulence in hoses and in the receiving tank. Wine flow should be laminar. *See* the Operating Pumps section above for data.

Tubing diameter for diatomaceous earth (DE) filtration When wines are filtered with DE, it is particularly important to match filter performance and tube diameter to one another. DE filters require a flow rate of at least 1,500L/h per $1m^2$ filter surface, otherwise the DE would be unevenly distributed on the filter plates, causing a breakthrough of solids or early fouling of the filter. Thus hose diameter becomes the limiting factor for laminar flow in gentle filtration when high-performance filters are used. Hoses are frequently too small in diameter or filters too large. A filter area of $5m^2$ requires a minimum flow rate of 7,500L/h, which in turn requires a 40mm diameter in the feeding hose and outlet hose. On the other hand, when the nominal hose diameter is only some 30mm, the filter area should be limited to roughly $3.5m^2$. Both components must be carefully adjusted for gentle filtration.

Filling tanks from the bottom For racking, filtration, or any other transfer, it is good practice to fill the receiving tanks from the bottom. Splashing wine through air causes an enormous and agitated wine surface, enhancing oxygen uptake and aroma evaporation. One splashing of a white wine conceived to be fruity is the best way to transform it into a simple wine for easy drinking!

Purging the receiving tank When white wines are filtered or subject to further transfers after filtration, it is useful to purge the receiving vessel, especially when working on small wine volumes. Purging, though never perfect, is best accomplished by introducing the inert gas at the tank's bottom draw. This ensures more complete displacement of oxygen out of the top. Details are given in section 7.2.

Mixing using appropriate mixers The use of compressed air, inert gas, or pumping over, though useful for red wine, should be avoided for mixing white wines: too much aroma would be stripped or oxygen dissolved. Tank-mounted propeller mixers screwed onto a tank fitting, for example a shut-off racking valve near the bottom of the tank, provide the most efficient and gentle mixing with minimised oxygen uptake. Frequency-controlled mixers afford additional benefits as they allow for adjusting the stirring intensity to the wine volume.

Preserving some dissolved CO_2 Oxygen pickup during wine treatments correlates with losses of CO_2 and volatile aroma compounds by evaporation. The longer natural CO_2 is preserved, the less burdensome cellar operations are for the wine. Moreover, CO_2 provides a tactile sensation, magnifies the sense of acidity, enhances the fruit character and enlivens the palate. Thus it is a stylistic tool in most white wine production today, though it must be carefully controlled. Some wineries add CO_2 before or during bottling, but sensory and legal limits must be respected. CO_2 is perceptible in wine at about 0.4g/L. Fruity white wines with lower levels taste flat, while levels greater than 1.0g/L can cause undesired bubble formation and a spritzy sensation on the palate, which is rejected in most markets.

Controlling residual CO_2 prior to bottling In view of the key role of residual CO_2 in the sensory perception of fruit-driven white wines, the use and monitoring of CO_2 prior to bottling by Carbodoseur or similar devices is beneficial in adjusting concentrations up or down accordingly to style. These simple gadgets involve a glass tube measuring the amount of CO_2 out-gassed from a fixed wine volume by shaking. Comparing results with a calibration curve provides the concentration of CO_2 in mg/L or g/L of wine.

Avoiding sparging Nitrogen sparging is sometimes used to strip DO or volatile sulphur compounds, causing reduction in flavour. The procedure may be effective but it is even more effective in stripping positive aroma compounds from fruity white wines. Treating reductive notes with copper salts is more specific (section 8.3).

Low storage temperatures Low cellar temperatures reduce evaporation of CO_2 and aromatics. However, they require careful avoidance of turbulence and air pockets in pipes to keep oxygen uptake under control.

Reconsidering cold stabilisation by artificial cold Apart from the high energy costs of this process, it is a very strenuous intervention on sensitive white wines, especially when it is used in conjunction with additional filtration steps, crystal seeding and stirring. Not only is there considerable oxygen uptake during the process, but the removal of unstable potassium bitartrate causes noticeable losses of volume on the palate. As an alternative, the addition of crystallisation inhibitors (section 8.3) preserves quality and money.

Minimising wine movements Succinctly put, each movement of fruity white wine is one treatment too many, so it is vital to limit such movements as much as possible. This approach underlines the oenological concept of minimal treatment. It critically examines traditional treatment steps, for example scrutinising to what extent traditional racking is still necessary under conditions of drastic juice clarification (section 2.5). In wines considered microbiologically stable, the concept of minimal treatment gives preference to self-clarification by sedimentation over early forced clarification by filtration. Furthermore, it advocates the combination of racking and filtration in one single step (section 6.1).

Minimal Treatment by Controlled Idleness

Without doubt, quite a few of the preceding recommendations cannot be considered in a real-world case because of operational constraints. However, when all of them are neglected, it will be difficult to produce a serious white wine. Even if only a few are respected, new ways to improve will emerge.

Great wines require the best fruit and consistent implementation of juice treatments. In contrast, post-fermentation interventions on non-barrel-aged wines must be used cautiously if one intends to make individual wines full of character that stand out from the crowd. These wines are the result of controlled idleness, with the emphasis on 'controlled'.

Controlling comprises a close sensory monitoring and making use of analytical tests whenever doubts arise. At best, after post-fermentation topping and SO_2 addition, human interventions in the natural development of wine only take place according to the needs of the individual wine rather than simply following a routine. Then the principle of minimal treatment is fulfilled.

Pushed to the extreme, this approach has given birth to many great white wines that have been moved only once between the end of fermentation and bottling. The fundamental prerequisite for such a proceeding is the willingness to question familiar habits and query cherished routines currently deemed indispensable. Above all, it requires logical thinking and sound knowledge of natural sciences. Different white winemaking conditions and a growing body of scientific knowledge justify a rationale that is a departure from the conventional wisdom that evolved decades ago.

07/05/2016

CHAPTER 8

PREPARING WINE FOR BOTTLING

The final steps before bottling a wine involve multiple controls, bench trials and possibly corrections. One of these is the control of protein stability to avoid post-bottling haze formation. Two methods are proposed for that purpose. The effect and application of bentonites to achieve that stability is discussed in detail. This is particularly important from the point of view that crystallisation inhibitors of plant origin, whose addition is largely used to avoid the appearance of bitartrate crystals in the bottles, cause even minor amounts of proteins to generate cloudiness. However, these inhibitors have the advantage of not affecting wine quality as much as the cold stabilisation that was common in the past.

Corrections of taste and flaws are also possible and even common at this stage. They comprise minor acidity corrections, the removal of reductive taints or the lowering of astringent phenols by specific finings. The implementation of bench trials to determine the corresponding amounts of material by sensory means are described in detail. Of fundamental importance is the measurement of free sulphur dioxide and assuring its long-term stability, which in turn is closely related to the oxygen uptake to be expected during the bottling process and subsequent bottle storage.

8.1 Bentonite Fining for Protein Stabilisation

All white wines are subject to protein hazes after bottling if unstable proteins are not removed beforehand. Therefore, protein stabilisation is one of the central issues in white wine production. Bentonite fining is the tool for this purpose. As described in section 2.5, an early standard addition of bentonite to the juice is useful. If this is done, subsequent bentonite fining of the wine can be avoided or reduced, thus preventing its widely feared side-effects of aroma adsorption in wine.

Figure 8.1 shows that such an effect can indeed occur to a sensorially significant extent, but is not systematic.

Protein Stability Tests

It is therefore desirable to use as little bentonite on wine as possible. In this context, there are some points to consider that are more important than when it is used on juice. The first point is the evaluation of protein stability. There are appropriate tests for this purpose, which simulate the precipitation of proteins at a correct cool storage temperature over the lifespan of wine. The following two tests are the most commonly used:

OPPOSITE: **Bottling line with bottle steriliser, nitrogen injector, filling machine and screw capper.**

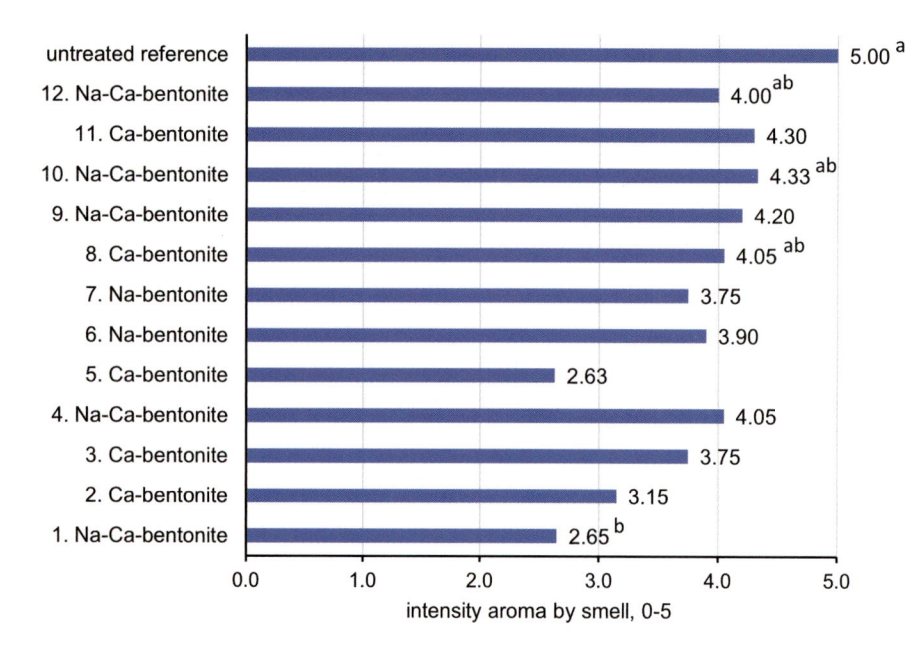

Sample	Intensity aroma by smell (0-5)
untreated reference	5.00 [a]
12. Na-Ca-bentonite	4.00 [ab]
11. Ca-bentonite	4.30
10. Na-Ca-bentonite	4.33 [ab]
9. Na-Ca-bentonite	4.20
8. Ca-bentonite	4.05 [ab]
7. Na-bentonite	3.75
6. Na-bentonite	3.90
5. Ca-bentonite	2.63
4. Na-Ca-bentonite	4.05
3. Ca-bentonite	3.75
2. Ca-bentonite	3.15
1. Na-Ca-bentonite	2.65 [b]

Figure 8.1: Adsorption of wine aroma by bentonites (200g/hL) in a white wine blend. Comparison with the untreated reference = 5.0 aroma intensity by smell. Means of eleven trained panellists. Lots with identical superscript letters = no significant difference within a 95 per cent confidence interval.

Heat test A filtered sample is incubated for two hours at 80°C in a pre-heated oven or water bath. After heating, it is cooled under tap water and set aside for another hour before it is examined for haze formation.

Bentotest™ solution This consists of phosphomolybdic acid prepared in hydrochloric acid to precipitate unstable proteins. One part of test solution is mixed with ten parts of the filtered wine sample at ambient temperature. After three minutes, the mixture is examined for haze formation.

The same evaluation applies to both tests: if the sample remains clear after the specified response time, the wine is protein stable. In contrast, increasing haze formation correlates with increasing amounts of proteins and increasing amounts of bentonite required. Each individual wine has separate dosage requirements. To determine these requirements, bench trials must be conducted with the same bentonite that is used in practice. Since the visual evaluation of the haziness is subjective, a turbidimeter that is also helpful for assessment of juice clarification (section 2.5) can be used for more objective evaluation. The wine is stable when the increase of turbidity does not exceed 1 NTU.

Impact of the Type of Bentonite, Hydration and Wine Temperature

The varying effectiveness of the bentonites must be taken into account. As a tendency, pure Na-bentonites are up to twice as effective as pure Ca-bentonites, but leave twice as large a sediment. Na-Ca mixed bentonites occupy a middle position. Figure 8.2 gives an example of the differences in effectiveness, expressed as the amount of bentonite required to achieve protein stability.

Bentonite is a clay consisting of layers of crystalline silicon and aluminium oxides along with the aforementioned Na^+ and Ca^{++} cations. When it is dry, its lattice structure is closed. When it is dispersed in water, water molecules are absorbed between the layers, which causes them to separate and form an open lattice structure with a large surface area. This area carries a negative charge, which is compensated for by the adsorption of the Ca^{++} and Na^+ cations that are able to be exchanged for the similarly positively charged proteins. For the structure to open, the bentonite must swell. For it to remain perfectly open, swelling must be obtained by hydration in water before use. For this purpose, the bentonite is added under immediate and vigorous mixing to ten times

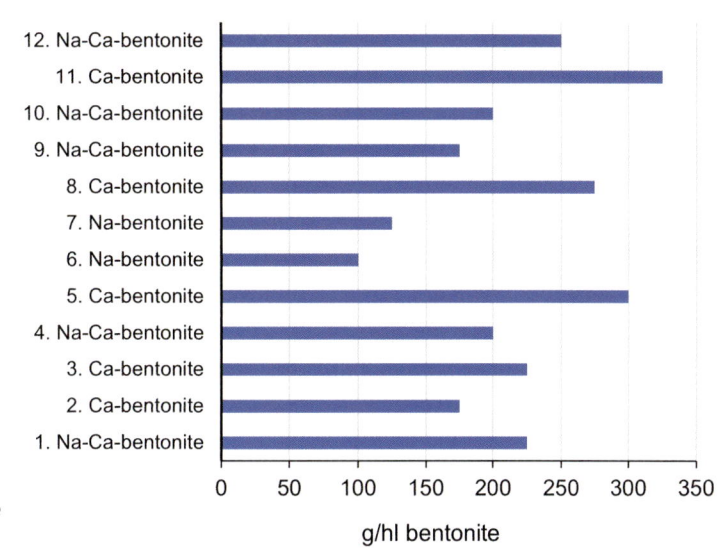

Figure 8.2: Bentonite requirements (g/hL) depending on the type of bentonite to achieve protein stability in a cool-climate white wine blend (pH 3.45) at 20°C.

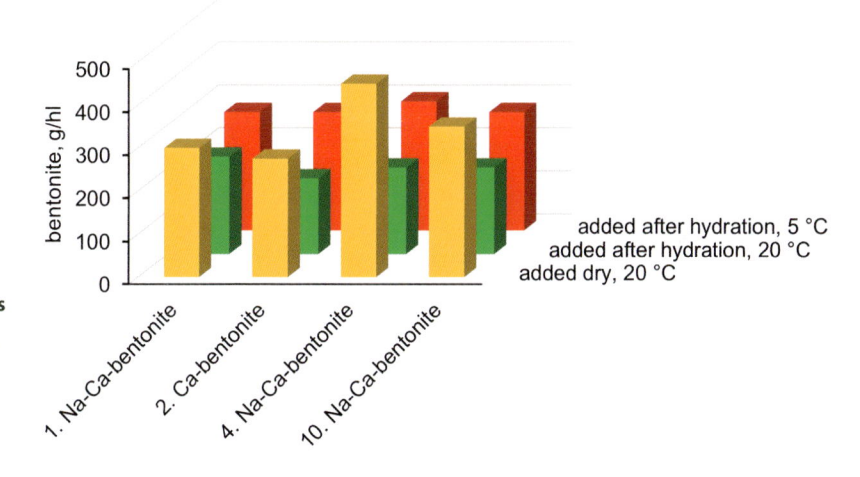

Figure 8.3: Effect of hydration and wine temperature (°C) on the efficiency of four bentonites in a white wine blend (pH 3.45), expressed in g/hL bentonite required to achieve protein stability.

its amount by volume of warm (50°C) water and left to swell for at least four hours. The supernatant water is then poured off and the slurry is added to the wine with constant stirring. After that, the mixer must run for another ten minutes.

Apart from the kind of bentonite and its swelling, wine temperature plays an additional role in dosage requirements. Figure 8.3 illustrates the influence of hydration and wine temperature on four of the bentonites referred to in the previous figure.

Two practical conclusions can be drawn:

- The bentonite dosage requirement in a cold cellar in winter is significantly higher than the requirement determined at room temperature – more specifically, 25 per cent higher on average at a temperature difference of 15°C.
- At identical temperature, dosage requirements increase by approximately 75 per cent when the bentonite is added directly to wine without previous swelling.

Impact of Wine pH

Since the action of bentonite is based on ion exchange, it is inevitably also influenced by pH. The higher the pH, the higher the bentonite requirement under otherwise identical conditions. This is shown in Figure 8.4 using the same bentonites and the same wine as previously, but also increasing its initial pH of 3.45 to 3.90 by addition of sodium hydroxide. As a result, dosage requirements increased by an average of exactly 50 per cent.

After mixing, bentonites settle within one to two weeks, but, in contrast to widespread claims and beliefs, they never leave young white wines less turbid than before the fining. The reason is that bentonites do not react with yeast cells, which are responsible for the cloudiness of these wines. When required, a subsequent fining for clarification combining 15mL/hL silica sol (30%) plus 3g/hL gelatin sediments bentonite within one to two days without sensory effects. However, this has no effect on the turbidity caused by suspended yeast either. Hence, filtration is indispensable for clarifying young white wines.

Iron Release by Bentonites

When bentonite bottoms are left in the wine over many weeks or months, attention should be paid to the iron

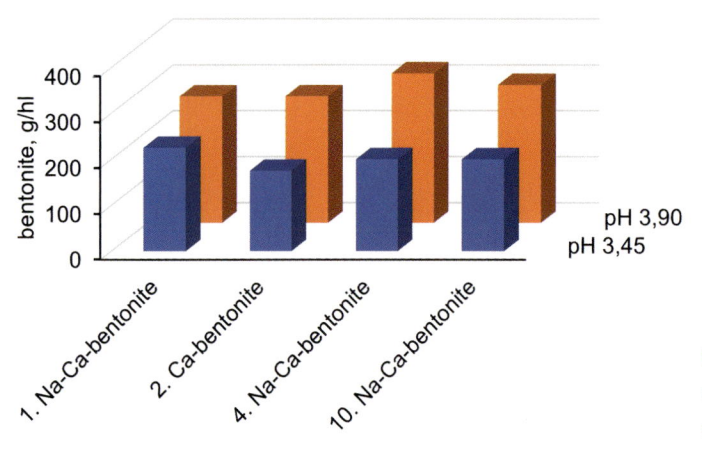

Figure 8.4: Impact of wine pH on bentonite requirements (g/hL) to achieve protein stability of a white wine blend at 20°C.

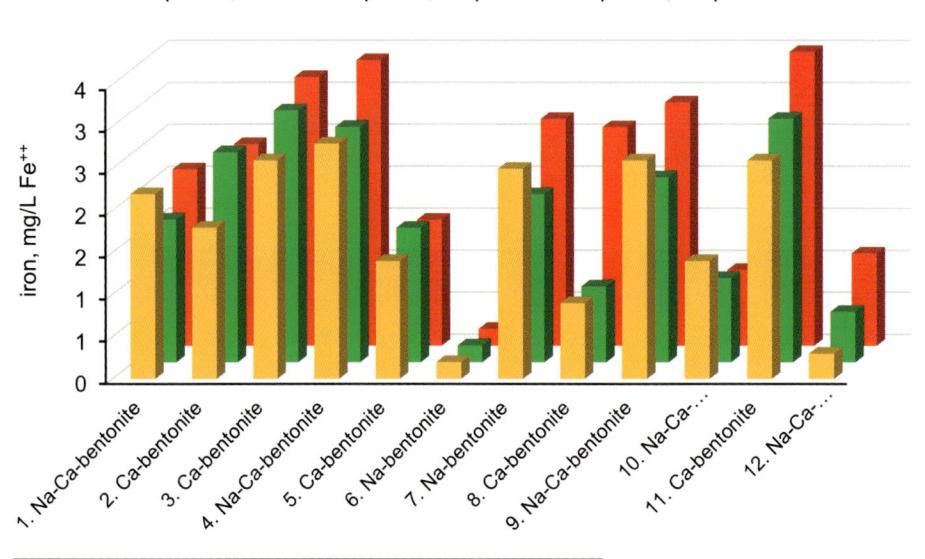

Figure 8.5: Release of iron by bentonites over six weeks as affected by pH and settling.

they are able to release. Most wines contain naturally 0.5–1.0mg/L iron. Its stability limit is about 4mg/L; higher contents can lead to an iron haze if they are not removed by elaborate finings.

Figure 8.5 shows that some bentonites bring the wine into the critical iron range within a contact time of six weeks regardless of whether they are settled or still in suspension. Higher pH slightly increases the iron release. Therefore it is reasonable to use bentonites that are labelled as low in iron.

8.2 Final Corrections of Taste, Flaws and Faults

It goes without saying that each wine should be extensively tasted before bottling, preferably in comparison with the same wine of the previous year and also those of competitors. These tastings should preferably take place at room temperature. Normal consumption temperature (that is, chilled) makes it more difficult to detect sensory imperfections. Wines are known to evolve, and a wine that was pleasing in the cellar a few months previously usually appears quite different in a contextual tasting in the professional environment of a tasting room or laboratory.

Removing Reductive Taints

One of the most common faults found in white wines is reduction flavour. It reminds one of rotten eggs, burnt rubber, rotten onions, sewage and so on. It can appear at any time, both during and long after fermentation (section 3.1) and sometimes even in the bottled wine. It is caused by various stinky volatile sulphur compounds, in particular methanethiol (methyl mercaptan) and hydrogen sulphide (H_2S). Unfortunately, their formation is fostered by the reductive storage conditions that are required for the cellaring of contemporary fruity white wines. Another reason for their increased occurrence is the total absence of traces of copper due to the prevailing equipment of wineries with stainless steel. Luckily, the vast majority of them are easy to remove.

In the old days, reductive taints were removed by pump-overs and splashing. In this process, the stinky compounds were converted into oxidised, less odour-intensive forms, which often reverted later (Vela et al. 2017). Simultaneously, there were significant losses of desired aroma compounds due to their volatilisation and oxidation. Nowadays, the treatment is predominantly performed more gently and specifically by copper fining with copper sulphate ($CuSO_4 \cdot 5 H_2O$). For this purpose, careful bench trials with test solution must be performed to determine how much copper is required. Table 4 explains how such trials are performed. In this context, it must be remembered that copper sulphate contains only 25 per cent pure copper, the concentration of which in the wine, in turn, must not exceed 0.5mg/L Cu^{++} to avoid legal issues and a post-bottling copper haze.

Many professionals are uncertain whether a wine actually displays reduction flavour or not. Therefore, it is recommended to perform a simple test on each wine by adding 1ml of the test solution to 100ml of sample. If the wine smells fruitier after this, it is affected by reduction flavour. Note that the copper takes two to three minutes to react.

Wine treatment with copper sulphate or other copper salts is often regarded with suspicion because copper is a toxic metal. However, toxicity is also a question of quantity. In this context, it must

Table 4: Preparation of the test solution for removal of reductive taints and implementation of bench trials

Preparation of the test solution	Mother solution: dissolve 10g copper sulphate ($CuSO_4 \cdot 5 H_2O$) in water and fill up to 1L. Test solution: take 10ml of the solution above and fill up to 1L with water (→ 100mg/L).				
Application of the test solution on a 100mL sample volume	1ml/100mL wine equals in the tank: + 1mg/L copper sulphate (0.1g/hL)				
	+ 0.5mL	+ 1.0mL	+ 1.5mL	+ 2.0mL	+ 2.5mL
Equals in the tank:	+ 0.5mg/L	+ 1.0mg/L	+ 1.5mg/L	+ 2.0mg/L	+ 2.5mg/L
Equals pure copper (Cu^{++}):	+ 0.13mg/L	+ 0.25mg/L	+ 0.38mg/L	+ 0.5mg/L	+ 0.63mg/L

be remembered that humans have a daily copper requirement of about 2mg that they take up with their diet. Their blood contains approximately 1mg/L, so clearly more than a wine after copper fining.

Lowering Phenol-Derived Astringency by Fining

Astringency is a tactile sensation on the mucous membranes in the oral cavity and pharynx evoking a feeling of desiccation, scouring, shrinking and friction. This sensation is caused by the precipitation of salivary proteins, which leads the saliva to lose its effect as a lubricant. Often but not always, astringency is accompanied by a bitter basic taste. This in-mouth sensation is not much appreciated in white wines and is absolutely rejected in sparkling wines. Its cause is almost always elevated levels of flavonoid phenols as a result of a very reductive winemaking process (section 2.5).

A wide range of fining agents is available for the removal of flavonoids, although their effect is usually described in imprecise sensory terms. Most of them are based on proteins. Figure 8.6 gives an overview of their effectiveness, expressed as the percentage of flavonoid phenols remaining after treatment. Note that the underlying reactions are never stoichiometric. In general, low amounts of fining agent usually induce a sharp decrease of high flavonoid levels, but reducing low flavonoid concentrations requires disproportionately high amounts of fining agent.

Gelatins

Gelatins are expected to remove flavonoid phenols by precipitation and flocculation, as can be easily observed from the cloudiness that their application causes in red wines, whose flavonoids in 100–1,000 times higher concentrations are called tannins. However, this reaction hardly takes place in white wines, because these wines lack flavonoids with the level of concentration and polymerisation required to interact with gelatins. This is proven by the simple fact that the addition of gelatins to white wines does not cause a haze. Instead, the gelatin remains in solution until the system becomes protein unstable. Counterfining with an equivalent amount of silica sol is able to precipitate dissolved gelatin by charge balance. Such combined fining is only useful to bring other fining agents such as bentonite to sedimentation overnight; it hardly removes any astringent phenols from white wine.

PVPP

PVPP (polyvinylpolypyrrolidone) is a synthetic, powdered and insoluble polymer with 'protein-like' characteristics. It has been shown to be the most effective phenol adsorbent for removing both monomeric and polymeric flavonoids (Sims et al. 1995, Barón et al. 1997). Unlike the protein fining agents that preferentially react with high molecular weight phenols, it finds its major application in also removing small and monomeric phenolic species occurring in

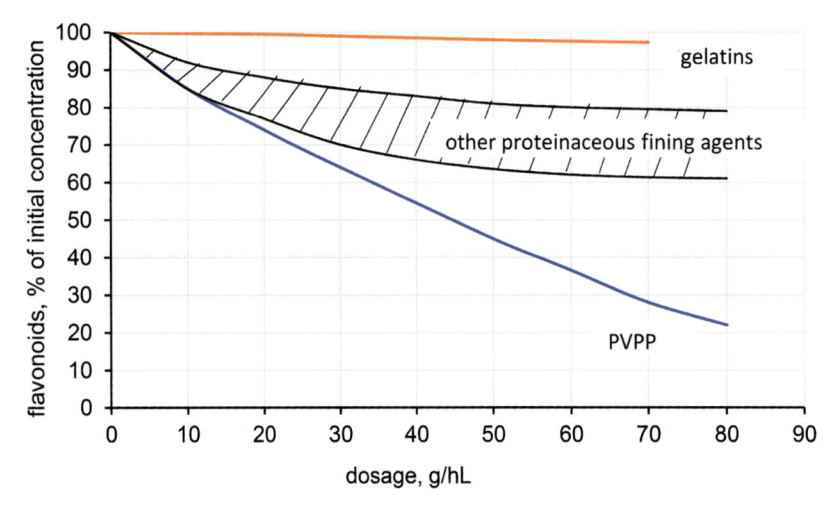

Figure 8.6: Percentage reduction of flavonoid phenols in white wines by tannin adsorbing fining agents. Means of eight white wines.

white juices and wines. With the legally permitted maximum dosage of 80g/hL, the initial content of flavonoids can be reduced by about 80 per cent. However, as the measurement of flavonoids is hardly possible in most wineries, sensory optimisation by previous bench trials is indispensable. When PVPP is carelessly used in high amounts on low-flavonoid wines, it can severely compromise flavour and colour.

It can be used in conjunction with other treatments and does not require previous hydration, but mixing after addition for a minimum of ten minutes. It settles by itself in a time window of two to three weeks, but can advantageously be brought to settle overnight with a fining for clarification combining 15mL silica sol (30%) + 3g/hL gelatin.

Since PVPP is a micro-plastic, with well-known ecological problems these entail, it has now come under criticism for its problematic disposal.

Caseinates

Since pure casein has largely disappeared from the market due to its laborious application in wine fining, it has been replaced by a wide range of easily applicable and differently prepared caseinates. Their effectiveness depends on their variable chemical composition, in particular on their potassium content (Braga et al. 2007). However, from a more practical point of view and in contrast to gelatins, they completely precipitate even in low-phenol white wines apart from residues at trace concentrations with potentially allergenic effects. Of particular interest is their action in mixed commercial preparations generally recommended by the supply industry for lowering phenols and astringency. These preparations consist mostly of caseinates, silicates, isinglass, gelatin and PVPP. Their effectiveness is highly variable and within the hatched area in Figure 8.6. Hence it is indispensable to run bench trials and be sceptical of obscure compositions and promises to tackle all kind of problems.

Plant Proteins

In response to concerns about fining agents of animal origin, extensive research has started to replace them with plant proteins. Currently marketing is more advanced than their development, at least as far as lowering astringency in white juices and wines is concerned. In individual cases, bench trials can confirm their effectiveness.

Practical Considerations

It is recommended to use these fining agents dispersed in a small amount of water. Thorough mixing with the wine is essential. It should start before the fining material is added uniformly and slowly so that it is immediately spread throughout the entire wine volume. Otherwise, it risks exhausting its reactivity before it is completely mixed with the wine, thus reducing its effectiveness. Propeller mixers are preferred, because pump-overs or injecting compressed inert gas easily cause aroma stripping on sensitive white wines.

None of these adjuvants are specific to flavonoids, but they also decrease beneficial nonflavonoids that contribute to weight and volume on the palate. Some of them also adsorb aroma compounds (Moio et al. 2004). Volatilisation during mixing can cause additional aroma losses (section 7.3). Thus, using these fining agents can only be a stopgap measure. It should be one of the primary tasks of future oenological research to help winemakers improve fruit and juice handling and so make these finings superfluous rather than promote their use.

Minor Acidity Corrections

Chapter 4.3 discussed what has to be considered for significant chemical deacidifications by several g/L TA. They are usually performed on juices or young wines, are based on analytical figures and rarely allow the desired in-mouth balance to be adjusted precisely. Under real-world conditions, the question of whether a minor deacidification might be useful frequently arises shortly before bottling, when the wine is tasted in comparison with other ones. In such a situation, the use of calcium carbonate is excluded since it would involve time-consuming calcium crystal stabilisation. Potassium carbonates, on the other hand, can be used to make minor acidity adjustments downwards in the short term, because the required crystal stabilisation can be achieved immediately afterwards by adding the common crystallisation inhibitors, which will be discussed in the

Table 5: Preparation of a potassium bicarbonate (KHCO$_3$) test solution for implementation of bench trials for wine deacidification

Preparation of test solution	Dissolve 100g of KHCO$_3$* in water and adjust to 1,000ml.					
Application of the test solution on a 100mL sample volume	0.1mL/100mL wine equals in the tank: + 0.1g/L KHCO$_3$					
	+ 0.25mL	+ 0.50mL	+ 0.75mL	+ 1.0mL	+ 1.25mL	+ 1.50mL
Equals in the tank:	+ 0.25g/L	+ 0.50g/L	+ 0.75g/L	+ 1.0g/L	+ 1.25g/L	+ 1.50g/L
* 1.0g KHCO$_3$ can be replaced by 0.69g K$_2$CO$_3$. National or regional restrictions on the use of both chemicals must be observed.						

following section. Since such an approach corresponds to a sensory optimisation irrespective of analytical considerations, bench trials are essential. Table 5 gives an example of how such trials can be performed.

When these trials are run, one should observe the following points:

- With wines already containing one of the crystallisation inhibitors referred to in section 8.3 or if such an inhibitor is added to the whole wine volume together with the KHCO$_3$, the trials can be evaluated immediately after the addition of KHCO$_3$. The sensory profile on the palate will remain stable as there will be no potassium bitartrate crystallisation causing an additional decrease in TA and perceived sourness. In this case, addition of 1.0g/L of KHCO$_3$ reduces TA by 0.75g/L. See section 4.3 for details.
- If cold stabilisation instead of crystallisation inhibition is desired, a belated additional decrease of TA must be expected owing to potassium bitartrate precipitation. To accelerate this process and to be able to evaluate the final in-mouth sensations, samples should first be frozen overnight or stored in the refrigerator for several days.

Before bottling at latest, numerous glasses, graduated cylinders and solutions of SO$_2$, KHCO$_3$ and an organic acid are necessary for bench trials for sensory optimisation.

Learning from the acidification trials described, every winemaker would be well advised to always keep a $KHCO_3$ test solution at hand. Its frequent use will show that minor deacidifications can be a powerful tool of sensory optimisation of wines grown under cool-climate conditions. They are even more powerful for balancing wines than the large range of obscure commercial adjuvants recommended for that purpose. Often a change in TA of only 0.2 or 0.3g/L works wonders. The allusion to the increase in pH and associated microbial risks is invalid, as powerful techniques for filtration prior to bottling are ubiquitously available. Despite all their advantages, potassium carbonates are not promoted due to their cheapness and consequent lack of commercial interest.

Depending on variety and year, bench trials for acidification can also be useful. As climate change progresses, they will become more important in cool-climate areas. For this purpose, the procedure is analogous to that for deacidification with potassium carbonates. Lactic acid is preferred because it is microbially stable and does not produce crystals. When citric acid is used, its final amount is limited to 1.0g/L in most legislations. The natural content of citric acid is rarely higher than 0.3g/L, so 0.7g/L can be added before bottling.

8.3 Crystal Stabilisation

Just as with protein hazes (section 8.1), the appearance of crystalline precipitations in bottled wines can be a cause of customer complaints, although it does not affect quality in the slightest. This applies to both still and sparkling wines, albeit the problem has an additional technical dimension in sparklings in that it makes their disgorging much more difficult.

For crystal stabilisation, wines deacidified with calcium carbonate require a special procedure for removal of unstable calcium, which was presented in section 4.3. All other wines, and this is the vast majority, are unstable with respect to potassium bitartrate (KHT) precipitations to a variable degree, but in particular when stored at low temperatures. There are several tests to check for KHT stability or the extent of its instability (Schneider and Troxell 2022).

In the conductivity seeding test, a filtered sample stored at 0 to −2°C is supplied with at least 4g/L finely ground crystalline KHT and continuously stirred during two hours at least. The KHT seed crystals induce the precipitation of unstable KHT, which leads to a drop of the wine's electrical conductivity (in µS) that is monitored. If the drop is less than 30µS, the wine is considered stable.

The measurement of the KHT saturation temperature is based on the fact that when a KHT unstable wine is heated, the KHT it contains becomes completely soluble when a certain temperature is reached. This temperature, also determined by a conductimetric method, is called the saturation temperature. The higher it is, the more unstable is the wine. Considering the effect of wine colloids inhibiting KHT precipitation, most wineries regard white wines as KHT stable at refrigerator temperature when the saturation temperature is below 12°C.

Cold and freezing tests rely on the formation of KHT crystals when the wine is held at reduced temperature for a specified period of time. Due to a lack of industry standards, they are not clearly defined. Most frequently, a filtered sample is stored for four days at a temperature between −4 and +3°C and shaken daily. Sometimes the sample is frozen and then thawed. When sparkling base wines are evaluated, 1.5 per cent of alcohol is added beforehand to mimic the alcohol increase at secondary fermentation. While such tests are only a qualitative assessment of KHT stability, they are widely used because of their speed, low expense and ease.

The use of artificial cooling for KHT stabilisation has largely disappeared, at least for white wines, because of its excessive energy costs and its detrimental effect on wine quality. Instead, additive procedures aiming at inhibiting the KHT crystallisation process by addition of crystallisation inhibitors like metatartaric acid, carboxymethylcellulose, potassium polyaspartate, or mannoproteins are preferred. Such inhibitors act as protective colloids that impede KHT crystal formation. However, they are not able to suppress the crystallisation of unstable calcium tartrate (section 4.3).

Metatartaric Acid

Metatartaric acid is obtained by heating tartaric acid to approximately 160°C to induce its intermolecular esterification. Its addition is limited to 10g/hL. Since it undergoes hydrolysis at wine pH, it is not stable in solution. Hence its effectiveness is limited in time, depending on storage temperature. It is stable for two years at 10–12°C, for one year at 15–18°C, for three months at 20°C, and one month at 25°C. The water temperature used to dissolve it should not exceed 25°C. After it starts decomposing, precipitation of unstable KHT does not occur abruptly, but gradually, with the appearance of sparse small crystals.

Carboxymethylcellulose

Carboxymethylcellulose (CMC) is a poorly defined cellulose derivative obtained from tree wood. Most countries have legalised its additions in amounts of up to 10g/hL. Owing to its cumbersome dissolution in wine, it is commercialised in liquid form of 5% or 10% content. In contrast to metatartaric acid, it does not disintegrate over time or under thermal influence but remains stable for a practically indefinite period of time. In wines showing a high level of KHT instability, however, its effectiveness is somewhat less than that of recently added metatartaric acid, so it should not be relied upon to stabilise grossly unstable wines without some previous cold storage.

Potassium Polyaspartate

Potassium polyaspartate (KPA) is the most recent of the KHT stabilisation additives approved in most countries. It is a polymer of potassium L-aspartate and obtained exclusively from the amino acid L-aspartic acid. The preparation for oenological use is in the form of an odourless brown powder, which is completely soluble and added to wine at a rate of 10g/hL. Its mode of action is based on its negative charge at wine pH, which allows sequestration of the potassium cations required for the formation of KHT crystals. At the time of writing, experience of long-term efficacy is still lacking, but it is assumed to be comparable to that of CMC and almost unlimited.

Mannoproteins

The use of yeast-derived mannoproteins for KHT stabilisation is based on the observation that traditional barrel ageing of white wines on the lees (section 6.2) enhances their mannoprotein content and provides more KHT stability. Thus mannoproteins with a specific molar mass extracted from yeasts are commercialised to improve KHT stability, with recommended additions of 15–25g/hL, depending on the wine. On account of the uncertainties associated with their application and effect, they are not widely used for KHT stabilisation.

Practical Application of Crystallisation Inhibitors

The emergence of CMC and KPA has considerably facilitated crystal stabilisation of base wines for sparkling wines, since they allow for a long-term stabilisation that is not possible with metatartaric acid. Thus, when bottle-fermented sparklings are produced, formation of KHT crystals in the bottles and the consequent technical difficulties at disgorging can be prevented. There is no impact on the future mousseux.

All crystal inhibitors are partially removed by fining agents, especially bentonite, so any finings deemed necessary should be performed before their addition. Furthermore, they also interact with proteins and readily cause a haze when the wine has not undergone rigorous protein stabilisation (section 8.1). This reaction occurs particularly with CMC and KPA even when unstable proteins are present only at trace concentrations. Consequently, wines should be checked carefully for their protein stability. The turbidity induced in protein stability tests (section 8.1) should by no means exceed 1 NTU when these additives are used.

Any filter medium absorbs a fraction of the crystallisation inhibitors until it is saturated, thus reducing their concentration and efficacy. Hence, they should only be added to wines ready for bottling after fining and polish filtration. After their addition, only one final filtration is reasonable, usually the sterile filtration in conjunction with bottling. This filtration should be performed at least five days after addition of the products, thus allowing for their complete dissolution. Otherwise the filter performance could be seriously compromised, filter media prematurely blocked, and membrane cartridges totally clogged. The effect of adsorption is particularly pronounced in filter sheets. When they are used for final filtration at bottling, they should first be saturated by the inhibitor by circulating the wine in a closed loop before starting to feed the filter.

8.4 Adjusting Free Sulphur Dioxide Before Bottling

Most white wines are bottled with 30–60mg/L free SO_2. How much is really required depends on the oxygen uptake during and after bottling. This oxygen is responsible for the free SO_2 decreasing in the bottles. It is crucial that at least 1mg/L free SO_2 remains until the moment of consumption to avoid the smell of free acetaldehyde, also known as premox.

As shown in section 5.1, each 1mg/L dissolved oxygen (DO) consumes between 2 and 3mg/L SO_2, depending on the individual wine. Hence, monitoring the decrease of SO_2 is a rough measure to indirectly monitor initial DO and its consumption in the bottled wines. Direct oxygen measurement is more informative. Using dipping probes, even small and medium-sized operations can measure the DO in the bulk wine before bottling and thus predict approximately how great the resulting loss of SO_2 will be. Non-invasive fluorescence technology can also be used to determine the DO in bottled wine without having to open the bottles.

In detail, the oxygen in bottled wine results from five sources:

- Oxygen dissolved in the wine before bottling
- Oxygen picked up in the course of the filling process
- Oxygen trapped in the bottle headspace
- Oxygen diffusing through the bottle closure
- Oxygen trapped in the cork tissue when natural corks are used

Summarising these five sources, a technical parameter designated as 'total package oxygen' (TPO) is obtained (Figure 8.7). When SO_2 is adjusted prior to bottling, all five sources of oxygen must be considered. Their sum value determines losses of SO_2 post-bottling.

Oxygen Dissolved in the Wine before Bottling

Before filling, the preceding steps of preparing wine for bottling by blending, mixing, filtration and so on (section 7.2) can easily cause the wine to take up much more oxygen than during the actual filling process. Since wine can absorb up to 8mg/L DO, and 1mg/L DO oxidises about 2–3mg/L SO_2 (section 5.1), knowing the amount of free SO_2 before bottling is only valuable if the instantaneous concentration of DO is also known. Many wineries tend to combine SO_2 and DO measurements when a wine is going to be bottled, but the majority of them do not have the opportunity to do so and therefore have to find another solution to the problem. This is to wait for the DO to disappear through binding. As shown in Figure 7.1, it takes about

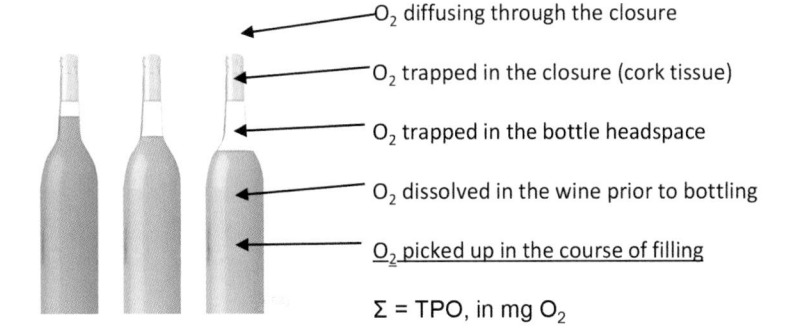

Figure 8.7: Oxygen in bottled wine and the concept of 'total package oxygen' (TPO).

- O_2 diffusing through the closure
- O_2 trapped in the closure (cork tissue)
- O_2 trapped in the bottle headspace
- O_2 dissolved in the wine prior to bottling
- O_2 picked up in the course of filling

Σ = TPO, in mg O_2

a week for 90 per cent of the oxygen to be consumed, provided that the wine is stored motionless under anaerobic conditions in a completely topped container (section 7.2). The free SO_2 measured thereafter is no longer subject to being greatly diminished by DO picked up before filling and hence can be adjusted accordingly. Many renowned wineries would cease having problems with premox if they took these basic facts into account.

Oxygen Uptake in the Filling Process

In many small and medium-sized wineries, wines are still bottled without any protection by inert gas. Under these conditions, wines take up 0.5–3.0mg/L O_2 in the filler bowl and when they flow from the bowl into the bottle. The length of the fill spouts and the type and force of the liquid jet play a role. Oxygen uptake tends to be only 0.5–1.0mg/L O_2 when modern bottling lines are used and when the bottling process runs smoothly without interruptions. However, since most fillers run up to 50 per cent deviation, it is useful to run DO measurements on several bottles and calculate the mean. As a comparison of what is technically possible, it is salutary to remember that average bottling lines in the beer industry operate with 0.2–0.4mg/L O_2 pickup (Crochiere 2007).

Oxygen Uptake from the Bottle Headspace

After sealing the bottle, there is a variable headspace. It may contain plain air causing more oxygen uptake, or it may have undergone a headspace treatment using vacuum or inert gas to remove its oxygen to a greater or lesser extent. Since the oxygen trapped in the headspace has a higher partial pressure than the oxygen dissolved in the wine, it gradually dissolves in it.

Nitrogen injection into a bottle before it reaches the filler.

Some simple calculations are useful to illustrate the importance of headspace oxygen: In standard bottles, 1cm headspace height equates to 2.9mL gas volume. When this gas consists of air, it includes 0.86mg O_2, based on the fact that air contains 20.8 per cent oxygen, which has a density of 1.43mg/mL. When this amount of oxygen is trapped in a standard 750mL bottle, the wine will be exposed to 0.86 : 0.75 = 1.15mg/L O_2. Moreover, when wines are sealed with screw caps, a typical headspace height is 4cm. In the absence of any headspace treatment with inert gas, it contains approximately 11.6mL of air, which in turn contains 2.41mL, or 3.45mg, O_2. The crucial importance of headspace height on the amount of oxygen it contains is shown in Figure 8.8 for standard bottles with no headspace inertisation.

Depending on the bottle size, this amount of headspace oxygen acts upon the wine to a variable extent. As an example, a headspace oxygen of 2.0mg provides 2.0mg/L O_2 to wine in a bottle with 1,000mL filling volume, 2.67mg/L O_2 in a bottle with 750mL, and 5.333mg/L O_2 in a small bottle with 375mL. Clearly, expressed as mg/L O_2, oxygen exposure is higher in smaller bottles than in larger ones.

Possible procedures for lowering headspace oxygen include:

- Flushing bottles with nitrogen before filling
- Flushing the bottle headspace with nitrogen after filling
- Injection of liquid nitrogen (nitrogen dropping) before and/or after filling
- Addition of solid CO_2 (dry ice) before and/or after filling
- Vacuum evacuation of bottles before and/or after filling

There is no lack of sophisticated bottling devices on the market, which allow for an effective lowering of oxygen pickup during the filling process as well as from the bottle headspace. This is crucial to optimise white wines' shelf life. Best results are obtained when bottles are inertised before filling using liquid or gaseous nitrogen. However, regardless of the system used, the time and distance from the filler to the closing machine must be kept as short as possible. This must also be taken into consideration when there is an interruption in the bottling process or when bottles already purged or dosed with liquid nitrogen are left on the conveyor, allowing the inert gas to escape and oxygen to enter the bottle. These bottles are then sealed with additional oxygen if they are not removed and dosed again.

Oxygen Uptake through and from Bottle Closures

Different closure types display variable permeability regarding the diffusion of atmospheric oxygen. This permeability is measured as 'oxygen transmission rate' or 'OTR' and expressed as mg O_2/year or µg O_2/day. Table 6 shows the ranges of OTR data of typical closures.

Obviously, closures with a low OTR are better suited for the oxygen-sensitive white wines. On the

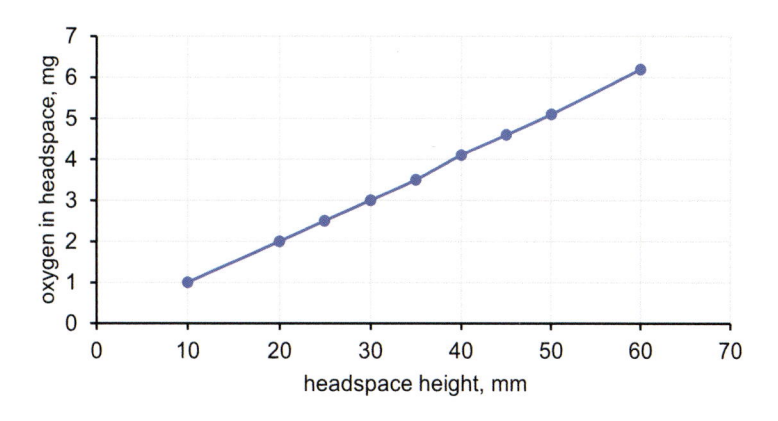

Figure 8.8: Relationship between headspace height (mm) and the amount of oxygen (mg) it contains for the case of standard bottles with no headspace inertisation.

Fluorescence-based measurement technology allows the measurement of dissolved and headspace oxygen through the wall of sealed clear glass bottles into which small sensor spots have been glued before filling.

other hand, absolutely airtight closures (0mg O_2/year) facilitate the occurrence of post-bottling reduction flavour in wines that are prone to develop it. Thus the winemaker must decide whether to drive the wine's evolution more in the oxidative or more in the reductive direction. An OTR around 1mg O_2/year seems a golden mean (Godden et al. 2001, 2005, Lopes et al. 2009, Ugliano 2013, Schneider 2021).

Table 6: Oxygen transmission rate (OTR) of closures used in the wine industry

Closure type	OTR, mg O_2/year	References
Natural corks during the first year	1.0–4.8	Lopes et al. 2006, 2007, Silva et al. 2011, Oliveira et al. 2013
Technical (agglomerated) corks	0.0–1.5	Karbowiak et al. 2010
Synthetic corks	9.3–17.5	Diéval et al. 2011, Karbowiak et al. 2010
Screwcaps with PVC or LDPE inserts	1.4	Müller and Weisser 2002
Screwcaps with Saranex™ liner	1.0–1.5	Vidal et al. 2011
Screwcaps with tin-Saran liner	0.0	Vidal et al. 2011

The behaviour of natural corks is a somewhat more complicated matter. In general, oxygen uptake through bottle closures is understood as a diffusion of atmospheric oxygen through the closure and along the interface between closure and the bottle neck. However, throughout the first year of bottle storage, natural corks provide additional amounts of oxygen, which are initially entrapped in the cork lenticels and gradually forced into the bottle after the cork is compressed upon inserting. Furthermore, as a natural product, they are subject to substantial fluctuations. There are large differences in OTR between cork lots as well as between individual corks within a lot. Examples of cork-to-cork differences within the same lot are given in Figure 8.9, including some 'bad' corks. They explain bottle-to-bottle differences in wine development and ageing.

The relatively high amounts of oxygen released from the cork tissue during the first year post-bottling cause correspondingly high losses of SO_2 during that period. They vary between lots as well as between individual corks. Figure 8.10 depicts an example.

When bottles are properly sealed with airtight closures such as screwcaps fitted with tin-Saran liner, both dissolved and headspace oxygen are consumed after a certain spell of time. From this point forward, SO_2 losses caused by oxidation cease. Figure 8.11 gives an example of the oxygen decrease in a commercial

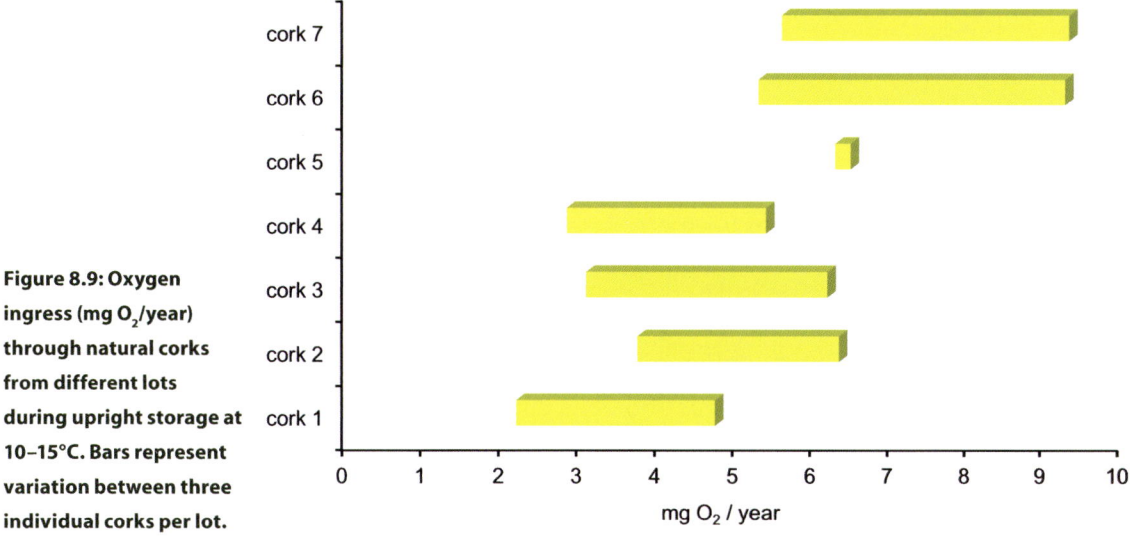

Figure 8.9: Oxygen ingress (mg O_2/year) through natural corks from different lots during upright storage at 10–15°C. Bars represent variation between three individual corks per lot.

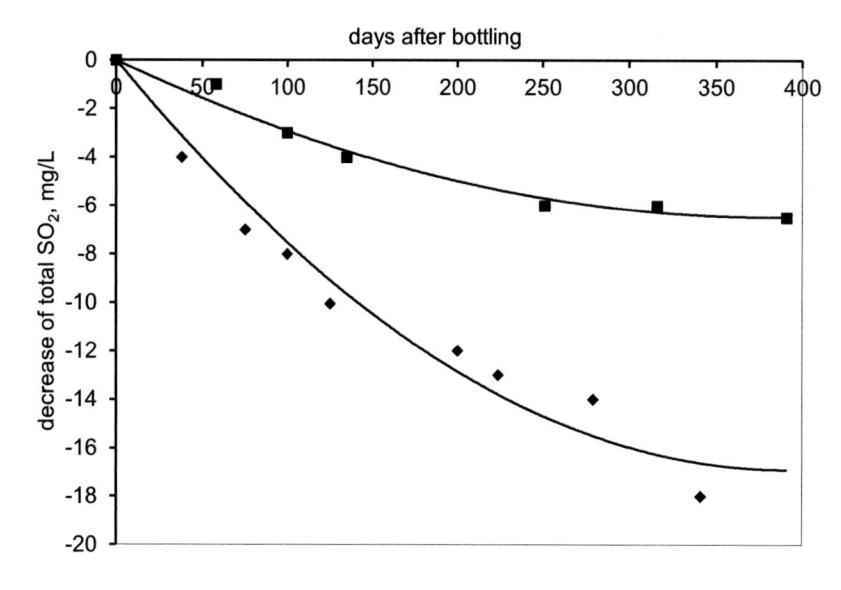

Figure 8.10: Decrease of total SO$_2$ by oxidation during bottle storage of a white wine sealed with two different natural corks.

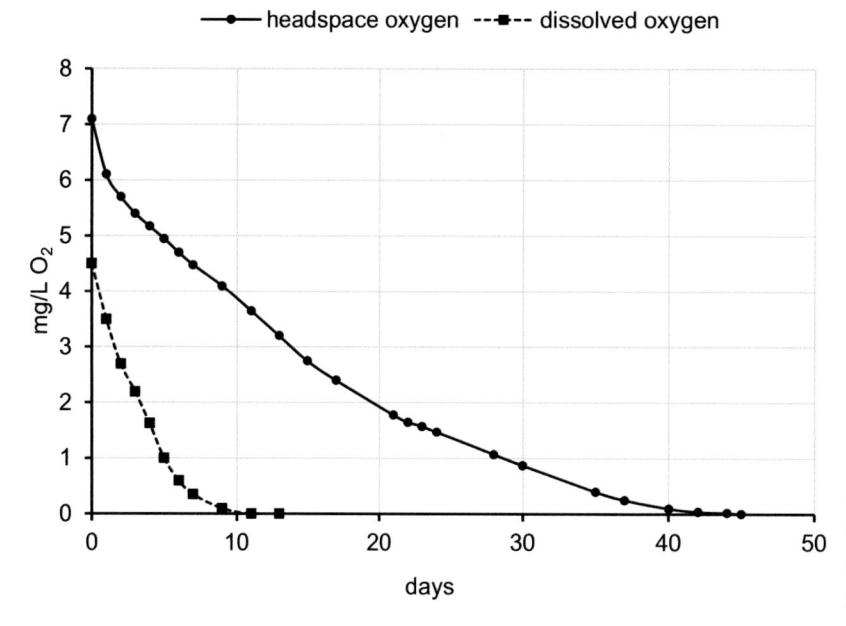

Figure 8.11: Decrease of headspace oxygen and dissolved oxygen after bottling of a white wine sealed with tin-Saran-lined screwcaps.

standard white wine stored at 20°C after filling in bottles of 750mL with air-containing headspace and sealed with tin-Saran-lined screwcaps. In this wine, the initial DO was almost entirely consumed (< 0.1mg/L DO) after ten days, while the headspace oxygen took 45 days to disappear. After expiration of that time, all oxygen contained in the bottle had been reduced to zero and SO$_2$ losses ceased.

Allowing for some variation between wines, more than 95 per cent of the oxygen trapped in the bottle is consumed after two to three months of bottle storage. Accordingly, highest losses of SO$_2$, ranging from 20 to 25mg/L, are commonly observed during this period when the bottle headspace is not inertised. The time required to deplete total oxygen trapped in the bottle is approximately in line with the duration of what is frequently perceived as bottle sickness, if it is possible to perceive it at all.

The behaviour shown in Figure 8.11 will change when closures with higher oxygen permeability supply the wine with oxygen throughout its entire bottle storage. In this case, neither dissolved nor headspace oxygen will drop to zero, because atmospheric oxygen is taken up approximately as fast as it is consumed by the wine. Consequently, the SO_2 decrease will never come to a stop.

The foregoing shows that bottling is an extension of the winemaking process. The varying amounts of oxygen that are picked up during and after bottling affect stability of SO_2 and wine quality in the long term. In any case, we must avoid the situation where free SO_2 completely disappears and acetaldehyde is freed. Therefore, it is useful to monitor SO_2 level during bottle storage in order to be able to better adjust it when future wines are bottled. The reference to wines 'without added sulphites' does not help, since this is a special type of wine whose production is mastered by only a few producers for a limited market.

BIBLIOGRAPHY

Aguera, E., Samson, A., Caille, S., Julien-Ortiz, A., Sieczkowski, N., Salmon, J.M., 'Apport de levures inactivées riches en glutathione en cours de fermentation alcoolique: Un nouvel outil pour la protection des vins blancs et rosés contre l'oxydation', *Rev. Fr. d'Œnologie* (250: 3–11, 2012)

Allen, M.S., Lacey, M.J., 'Methoxypyrazine grape flavor: influence of climate, cultivar and viticulture', *Vitic. Enol. Sci.* (48: 211–213, 1993)

Anastasiadi M., Zira A., Magiatis P., Haroutounian S.A., Skaltsounis A.L., Mikros E., '1H NMR-based metabonomics for the classification of Greek wines according to variety, region, and vintage. Comparison with HPLC data', *J. Agric. Food Chem.* 57 (23: 11067–11074, 2009)

Andújar-Ortiz, I., Chaya, C., Martin-Álvarez, P.J., Moreno-Arribas, M.V., Pozo-Bayón, M.A., 'Impact of using new commercial glutathione enriched inactive dry yeast oenological preparations on the aroma and sensory properties of wine', *Int. J. Food Prop.* (17: 987–1001, 2014)

Antoce, A.O., Cojocaru, G.A., 'Sensory profile changes induced by the antioxidant treatments of white wines. The case of glutathione, ascorbic acid and tannin treatments on Feteasca Regala wines produced in normal cellar conditions', *Agro Life Scient. J.* (6 (1): 19–30, 2017)

Bahut, F., Romanet, R., Sieczkowski, N., Schmitt-Kopplin, P., Nikolantonaki, M., Gougeon, R.D., 'Antioxidant activity from inactivated yeast: Expanding knowledge beyond the glutathione-related oxidative stability of wine', *Food Chem.* (325: 12694, 2020)

Barón, R., Mayen, M., Merida, J., Medina, M., 'Changes in phenolic compounds and colour in pale sherry wines subjected to fining treatments', *Z. Lebensm. Unters. Forsch.* (205: 474–478, 1997)

Barril, C., Rutledge, D.N., Scollary, G.R., Clark, A.G., 'Ascorbic acid and white wine production: A review of beneficial vs detrimental impacts', *Austr. J. Grape Wine Res.* (22 (2): 169–181, 2016)

Bartowsky, E.J., Henschke, P.A., 'The "buttery" attribute of wine-diacetyl – desirability, spoilage and beyond', *Int. J. Food Microbiol.* (96: 235–252, 2004)

Bartowsky, E.J., Francis, I.L., Belloni, J.R., Henschke, P.A., 'Is buttery aroma perception in wines predictable from the diacetyl concentration?', *Aust. J. Grape Wine Res.* (8 (3): 180–185, 2008)

Betés-Saura, C., Andrés-Lacueva, C., Lamuela-Raventós, R.M., 'Phenolics in white free run juices and wines from Penedés by high-performance liquid chromatography: Changes during vinification', *J. Agric. Food Chem.* (44 (19): 3040–3046, 1996)

Blateyron, L. and Sablayrolles, J.-M., 'Stuck and slow fermentations in enology: statistical study of causes and effectiveness of combined additions of oxygen and diammonium phosphate', *J. Biosci. Bioeng.* (92 (2): 184–189, 2001)

Boulton, R.B., Singleton, V.L., Bisson, L.F., Kunkee, R.E., *Principles and Practices of Winemaking* (Chapman & Hall, 1996)

Braga, A., Cosme, F., Ricardo-da-Silva, J.M., Laureano, O., 'Gelatine, casein and potassium caseinate as distinct wine fining agents: Different effects on colour, phenolic composition and sensory characters', *J. Int. Sci. Vigne Vin* (41: 203–214, 2007)

Bradshaw M.P., Cheynier V., Scollary G.R., Prenzler P.D., 'Defining the ascorbic acid crossover from anti-oxidant to pro-oxidant in a model wine matrix containing (+)-catechin', *J. Agric. Food Chem.* 51 (14: 4126–4132, 2003)

Bradshaw M.P., Scollary G.R., Prenzler P.D., 'Examination of the sulfur dioxide-ascorbic acid anti-oxidant system in a model white wine matrix', *J. Sci. Food Agric.* 84 (4: 318–324, 2004)

Calderón, J.F., Del Alamo-Sanza, M., Nevares, I., Laurie, V.F., 'The influence of selected winemaking equipment and operations on the concentration of dissolved oxygen in wines', *Cien. Inv. Agr.* (41: 273–280, 2014)

Carando S., Teissedre P.L., Pascual-Martinez L., Cabanis J.C., 'Levels of flavan-3-ols in French wines', *J. Agric. Food Chem.* 47 (10: 4161–4166, 1999)

Casalta, E., Salmon, J.M., Picou, C., Sablayrolles, J.M., 'Grape solids: Lipid composition and role during alcoholic fermentation under enological conditions', *Am. J. Enol. Viti.* (70 (2): 147–154, 2019)

Castellari, M., Simonato, B., Tornielli, G.-B., Spinelli, P., Ferrarini, R., 'Effect of different enological treatments on dissolved oxygen in wine', *Ital. J. Food Sci.* (16: 387–396, 2004)

Cheynier, V., Rigaud, J., Souquet, J.M., Barillère, J.M., Moutounet, M., 'Effect of pomace contact and hyperoxidation on the phenolic composition and quality of Grenache and Chardonnay wines', *Am. J. Enol. Vitic.* (40 (1): 36–42, 1989)

Cheynier, V., Masson, G., Rigaud, J., Moutounet, M., 'Estimation of must oxidation during pressing in Champagne', *Am. J. Enol. Vitic.* (44 (4): 393–399, 1993)

Coetzee, C., du Toit, W.J., 'A comprehensive review on Sauvignon blanc aroma with a focus on certain positive volatile thiols', *Food Res. Int.* (45: 287–298, 2012)

Constanti, M., Poblet, M., Arola, L., Mas, A., Guillamón, J.M., 'Analysis of yeast populations during alcoholic fermentation of a newly established winery', *Am. J. Enol. Vitic.* (48 (3): 339–344, 1997)

Crochiere, G.K., 'Measuring oxygen ingress during bottling/storage', *Practical Winery & Vineyard* (1: 1–6, 2007)

Danilewicz, J.C., Seccombe, J.T., Whelan, J., 'Mechanism of interaction of polyphenols, oxygen, and sulfur dioxide in model wine and wine', *Am. J. Enol. Vitic.* (59: 128–136, 2008)

Danilewicz, J.C., Wallbridge, P.J., 'Further studies on the mechanism of interaction of polyphenols, oxygen, and sulfite in wine', *Am. J. Enol. Vitic.* (61 (2): 166–175, 2010)

Danilewicz, J.C., 'Reaction of oxygen and sulfite in wine', *Am. J. Enol. Vitic.* (67 (1): 13–17, 2016)

Davis, C.R., Wibowo, D., Eschenbruch, R., Lee, T.H., Fleet, G.H., 'Practical implications of malolactic fermentation', *Am. J. Enol. Vitic.* (36 (4): 290–301, 1985)

Day, M.P., Schmidt, S.A., Pearson, W., Kolouchova, R., Smith, P.A., 'Effect of passive oxygen exposure during pressing and handling on the chemical and sensory attributes of Chardonnay wine', *Aust. J. Grape Wine Res.* (25 (2): 1–16, 2019)

Delcour, J.A., Vandenberghe, M.M., Corten, P.F., Dondeyne, P., 'Flavor thresholds of polyphenolics in water', *Am. J. Enol. Vitic.* (35 (3): 134–136, 1984)

Delfini, C., Cocito, C., Ravaglia, S., Conterino, L., 'Influence of clarification and suspended grape solid materials on sterol content of free run and pressed grape musts in the presence of growing yeast cells', *Am. J. Enol. Vitic.* (44 (4): 452–458, 1993)

De Revel, G., Martin, N., Pripis-Nicolau, L., Lonvaud-Funel, A., Bertrand, A., 'Contribution to the knowledge of malolactic fermentation: Influence on wine aroma', *J. Agric. Food Chem.* (47 (10): 4003–4008, 1999)

De Villiers A., Majek P., Lynen F., Crouch A., Lauer H., Sandra P., 'Classification of South African red and white wines according to grape variety based on the non-coloured phenolic content', *Eur. Food Res. Technol.* (221: 520–528, 2005)

Del Alamo-Sanza, M., Nevares, I., 'Oak wine barrel as an active vessel: A critical review of past and current knowledge', *Crit. Rev. Food Sci. Nutr.* (58 (16): 2711–2726, 2018)

Del Barrio-Galán, R., Nevares, I., del Alamo-Sanza, M., 'Characterization and control of oxygen uptake in the blanketing and purging of tanks with inert gases in the winery', *Beverages* (9 (1): 19, 2023)

Diéval, J.-B., Vidal, S., Aagaard, O., 'Measurement of the oxygen transmission rate of co-extruded wine bottle closures using a luminescence-based technique', *Packag. Technol. Sci.* (24 (7): 375–385, 2011)

Di Lecce, G., Arranz, S., Jáuregui, O., Tressera-Rimbau, A., Quifer-Rada, P., 'Phenolic profiling of the skin, pulp, and seeds of Albariño grapes using hybrid quadrupole time-of-flight and triple-quadrupole mass', *Food Chem.* (145: 874–882, 2014)

Dimitriadis, E., Williams, P.J., 'The development and use of a rapid analytical technique for estimation of free and potentially volatile monoterpene flavorants of grapes', *Am. J. Enol. Vitic.* (35 (2): 66–71, 1984)

Dubois, P., 'Les arômes du vin et leur défauts, Part II', *Revue Fr. d'Œnologie* (145: 27–40, 1994)

Du Toit, W.J., 'Effect of different oxygen levels on glutathione levels in South African white must and wines' (www.wynboer.co.za/recentarticles/200712oxygen.php3, 2007)

Elias, R.J., Waterhouse, A.L., 'Controlling the Fenton reaction in wine', *J. Agric. Food Chem.* (58 (3): 1699–1707, 2010)

Eschenbruch, R., 'The influence of fungicides on the formation of H_2S during the fermentation of grape juice', *De Wynboer* (11: 23–23, 1971)

Fornairon, C., Mazauric, J.P., Salmon, J.M., Moutounet, M., 'Observations on the oxygen consumption during maturation of wines on lees', *J. Int. Sci. Vigne Vin* (33 (2): 79–86, 1999)

Fornairon-Bonnefond, C., Salmon, J.-M., 'The impact of oxygen consumption by yeast lees on the autolysis phenomenon during simulation of wine aging on lees', *J. Agric. Food Chem.* (51 (9), 2584–2590, 2003)

Fracassetti, D., Lawrence, N., Tredoux, A.G.J., Tirelli, A., Nieuwoudt, H.H., du Toit, W.J., 'Quantification of glutathione, catechin, and caffeic acid in grape juice and wine by a novel ultra-performance liquid chromatography method', *Food Chem.* (128: 1136–1142, 2011)

Fracassetti, D., Gabrielli, M., Costa, C., Tomás-Barberán, F.A., Tirelli, A., 'Characterization and suitability of polyphenols-based formulas to replace sulfur dioxide for storage of sparkling white wine', *Food Control* (60: 606–614, 2016)

Godden, P., Francis, L., Field, J., Gishen, M., Coulter, A., Valente, P., Hoj, P., Robinson, E., 'Wine bottle closures: physical characteristics and effect on composition and sensory properties of a Semillon wine. I. Performance up to 20 months post-bottling', *Aust. J. Grape Wine Res.* (7 (1): 64–105, 2001)

Godden, P., Lattey, K., Francis, L., Gishen, M., Cowey, G., Holdstock, M., Robinson, E., Waters, E., Skouroumounis, G., Sefton, M., Capone, D., Kwiatkowski, M., Field, J., Coulter, A., D'Costa, N., Bramley, B., 'Towards offering wine to the consumer in optimal conditions – the wine, the closures and other packaging variables', *Wine Industry Journal* (20: 20–30, 2005)

Goldberg D.M., Karumanchiri A., Soleas G.J., Tsang E., 'Concentrations of selected phenols in white commercial wines', *Am. J. Enol. Vitic.* 50 (2: 185–193, 1999)

Groat, M., Ough, C.S., 'Effects of insoluble solids added to clarified musts on fermentation rate, wine composition, and wine quality', *Am. J. Enol. Vitic.* (29 (2): 112–119, 1978)

Gump, B.H., Zoecklein, B.W., Fugelsang, K.C., Whiton, R.S., 'Comparison of analytical methods for prediction of prefermentation nutritional status of grape juice', *Am. J. Enol. Vitic.* (53 (4): 325–329, 2002)

Houtman, A.C., Marais, J., du Plessis, C.S., 'Factors affecting the reproducibility of fermentation of grape juice and of the aroma composition of wines. I. Grape maturity, sugar, inoculum concentration, aeration, juice turbidity and ergosterol', *Vitis* (19: 37–54, 1980a)

Houtman, A.C., Marais, J., du Plessis, C.S., 'The possibilities of applying present-day knowledge of wine aroma components. Influence of several juice factors on fermentation rate and ester production during fermentation', *S. Afr. J. Enol. Vitic.* (1: 27–34, 1980b)

Houtman, A.C., du Plessis, C.S., 'The effect of juice clarity and several fermentation conditions promoting yeast growth on fermentation rate, the production of aroma components and wine quality', *S. Afr. J. Enol. Vitic.* (2 (2): 71–81, 1981)

Houtman, A.C., du Plessis, C.S., 'Nutritional deficiencies of clarified white grape juices and their correction in relation to fermentation', *S. Afr. J. Enol. Vitic.* (7 (1): 39–46, 1986)

Ingledew, W.M., Kunkee, R.E., 'Factors influencing sluggish fermentations of grape juice', *Am. J. Enol. Vitic.* (36 (1): 65–76, 1985)

Julien, A., Roustau, J.-L., Dulau, L., Sablayrolles, J.-M., 'Comparison of nitrogen and oxygen demands of enological yeasts', *Am. J. Enol. Vitic.* (51 (3): 215–222, 2000)

Karbowiak T., Gougeon R.D., Alinc J.-B., Brachais L., Debeaufort F., Voilley A., Chassagne D., 'Wine oxidation and the role of cork', *Crit. Rev. Food Sci. Nutr.* 50 (1: 20–52, 2010)

Kinzurik, M.I., Herbst-Johnstone, M., Gardner, C., Fedrizzi, B., 'Hydrogen sulfide production during yeast fermentation causes the accumulation of ethanethiol, S-ethyl thioacetate and diethyl disulfide', *Food Chem.* (209: 341–347, 2016)

Kotseridis, Y., Beloqui, A.A., Bayonove, C.L., Baumes, R.L., Bertrand, A., 'Effects of selected viticultural and enological factors on levels of 2-methoxy-3-isobutylpyrazine in wines', *J. Int. Sci. Vigne Vin* (33 (1): 19–23, 1999)

Kritzinger, E.C., du Toit, W.J., Stander, M.A., 'Assessment of glutathione levels in model solutions and grape ferments supplemented with glutathione-enriched inactive dry yeast preparations using a novel UPLC-MS/MS method', *Food Addit. Contam., Part A* (30 (1), 80–92, 2013)

Kudo, M., Vagnoli, P., Bisson, L.F., 'Influence of pH and potassium concentrations as a cause of stuck fermentations', *Am. J. Enol. Vitic.* (49 (3): 295–301, 1998)

Lampíř L., 'Varietal differentiation of white wines on the basis of phenolic compounds profile', *Czech J. Food Sci.* 31 (2: 172–179, 2013)

Lea, A.G.H., Bridle, P., Timberlake, C.F., Singleton, V.L., 'The procyanidins of white grapes and wines', *Am. J. Enol. Vitic.* (30 (4): 289–300, 1979)

Lee, C.Y., Jaworski, A.W., 'Phenols and browning potential of white grapes grown in New York', *Am. J. Enol. Vitic.* (39 (4): 337–340, 1988)

Lopes, P., Saucier, C., Teissedre, P.-L., Glories, Y., 'Impact of storage position on oxygen ingress through different closures into wine bottles', *J. Agric. Food Chem.* (54 (18): 6741–6746, 2006)

Lopes, P., Saucier, C., Teissedre, P.-L., Glories, Y., 'Main routes of oxygen ingress through different bottle closures into wine bottles', *J. Agric. Food Chem.* (55 (13): 5167–5170, 2007)

Lopes, P., Silva, M.A., Pons, A., Tominaga, T., Lavigne, V., Saucier, C., Darriet, P., Teissedre, P.-L., Dubourdieu, D., 'Impact of oxygen dissolved at bottling and transmitted through closures on the composition and sensory properties of a Sauvignon blanc wine during bottle storage', *J. Agric. Food Chem.* (57 (21): 10261–10270, 2009)

Makhotkina, O., Kilmartin, P.A., 'Uncovering the influence of antioxidants on polyphenol oxidation in wines using an electrochemical method: Cyclic voltammetry', *J. Electroanalytical Chem.* (633: 165–174, 2009)

Marais, J., 'Effect of grape temperature, oxidation and skin contact on Sauvignon blanc juice and wine composition and wine quality', *S. Afr. J. Enol. Vitic.* (19 (1): 10–16, 1998)

Marks, A.C., Morris, J.R., 'Ascorbic acid effects on the post-disgorgement oxidative stability of sparkling wine', *Am. J. Enol. Vitic.* (44 (4): 227–231, 1993)

Martineau, B., Henick-Kling, T., 'Formation and degradation of diacetyl in wine during alcoholic fermentation with *S. cerevisiae* strain EC 1118 and malolactic fermentation with *Leuconostoc oenos* strain MCW', *Am. J. Enol. Vitic.* (46 (4): 442–448, 1995)

Martineau, B., Henick-Kling, T., Acree, T., 'Reassessment of the influence of malolactic fermentation on the concentration of diacetyl in wines', *Am. J. Enol. Vitic.* (46 (3): 385–388, 1995)

Martini, A., Ciani, M., Scorzetti, G., 'Direct enumeration and isolation of wine yeasts from grape surfaces', *Am. J. Enol. Vitic.* (47 (4): 435–439, 1996)

Moenne, M.I., Mouret, J.-R., Sablayrolles, J.-M., Agosin, E., Farines, V., 'Control of bubble-free oxygenation with silicone tubing during alcoholic fermentation', *Proc. Biochem.* (46: 1453–1461, 2013)

Moio, L., Ugliano, M., Gambuti, A., Genovese, A., Plombino, P., 'Influence of clarification treatments on concentrations of selected free varietal aroma compounds and glycoconjugates in Falanghina (*Vitis vinifera* L.) must and wine', *Am. J. Enol. Vitic.* (55: 7–12, 2004)

Morozova, K., Schmidt, O., Schwack, W., 'Effect of headspace volume, ascorbic acid and sulphur dioxide on oxidative status and sensory profile of Riesling wine', *European Food Research and Technology* (240 (1): 205–221, 2015)

Mortimer, R.K., 'Yeast isolated from spontaneous fermentations of grape musts in California and Italy', *Practical Winery and Vineyard* (3: 7–16, 1995)

Mpelasoka, B.S., Schachtmann, D.P., Treeby, M.T., Thomas, M.R., 'A review of potassium nutrition in grapevines with special emphasis on berry accumulation', *Aust. J. Grape Wine Res.* (9 (3): 154–168, 2003)

Müller, K., Weisser, H., 'Gasdurchlässigkeit von Flaschenverschlüssen', *Brauwelt* (142: 617–619, 2002)

Muñoz, E., Ingledew, W.M., 1990. 'Yeast hulls in wine fermentations – a review', *J. Wine Res.* (1 (3): 197–209, 1990)

Nicolini, G., Moser, S., Román, T., Mazzi, E., Larcher, R., 'Effect of juice turbidity on fermentative volatile compounds in white wines', *Vitis* (50 (3): 131–135, 2011)

Oliveira, V., Lopes, P., Cabral, M., Pereira, H., 'Kinetics of oxygen ingress into wine bottles closed with natural cork stoppers of different qualities', *Am. J. Enol. Vitic.* (64 (4): 395–399, 2013)

Panero, L, Motta, S., Petrozziello, M., Guaita, M., Bosso, A., 'Effect of SO_2, reduced glutathione and ellagitannins on the shelf life of bottled white wines', *Eur. Food Res. Technol.* (240 (2): 345–356, 2014)

Pérez-Coello, M.S., Sanz, J., Cabezudo, M.D., 'Determination of volatile compounds in hydroalcoholic extracts of French and American oak wood', *Am. J. Enol. Vitic.* (50 (2): 162–165, 1999)

Pons, A., Nikolantonaki, M., Lavigne, V., Shinoda, K., Dubourdieu, D., Darriet, P., 'New insights into intrinsic and extrinsic factors triggering premature aging in white wines', *Advances in Wine Research*, ACS Symposium Series (Vol. 1203: 229–251, 2015)

Pons-Mercadé, P., Anguela, S., Giménez, P., Heras, J.M., Sieczkowski, N., Rozès, N., Canals, J.M., Zamora, F., 'Measuring the oxygen consumption rate of some inactivated dry yeasts: comparison with other common wine antioxidants', *Oeno One* (55 (2): 147–158, 2021)

Pozo-Bayón, M.A., Andújar-Ortiz, I., Moreno-Arribas, M.V., 'Scientific evidences beyond the application of inactive dry yeast preparations in winemaking', *Food Res. Int.* (42: 754–761, 2009)

Ramey, D., Bertrand, A., Ough, C.S., Singleton, V.L., Sanders, E., 'Effects of skin contact temperature on Chardonnay must and wine composition', *Am. J. Enol. Vitic.* (37 (2): 99–106, 1986)

Revel, G., Bertrand, A., Lonvaud-Funel, A., 'Synthèse des substances acétoiniques par Leuconostoc oenos. Réduction du diacétyle', *J. Int. Sci. Vigne Vin* (23, 1, 39–45, 1989)

Ribeiro de Lima M.T., Kelly M.T., Cabanis M.T., Blaise A., 'Teneurs en acides phénols, catéchine et épicatéchine pour les vins de différentes variétés et millésimes du Portugal continental et les îles des Açores', *J. Int. Sci. Vigne Vin* 40 (1: 47–56, 2006)

Ridge, M., Sommer, S., Dycus, D.A., 'Addressing enzymatic clarification challenges of Muscat grape juice', *Fermentation* (7: 198, 2021)

Robichaud, J.L., Noble, A.C., 'Astringency and bitterness of selected phenolics in wine', *J. Sci. Food Agric.* (53 (3): 343–353, 1990)

Rodriguez-Bencomo, J.J., Andújar-Ortiz, I., Moreno-Arribas, M.V., Simó, C., Gonzales, J., Chana, A., Dávalos, J., Pozo-Bayón, M.A., 'Impact of glutathione-enriched inactive dry yeast preparations on the stability of terpenes during model wine aging', *J. Agric. Food Chem.* (62 (6), 1373–1383, 2014)

Roland, A., Vialaret, J., Razungles, A., Rigou, P., Schneider, R., 'Evolution of S-cysteinylated and S-glutathionylated thiol precursors during oxidation of Melon B. and Sauvignon blanc musts', *J. Agric. Food Chem.* (58 (7): 4406–4413, 2010)

Rosenfeld, E., Beauvoit, B., Rigoulet, M., Salmon, J.-M., 'Non-respiratory oxygen consumption pathways in anaerobically-grown *Saccharomyces cerevisiae*: evidence and partial characterization', *Yeast* (19 (15): 1299–1321, 2002)

Sablayrolles, J.-M., Barre, P., 'Évolution des besoins en oxygène de fermentations alcooliques en conditions œnologiques simulées', *Sci. Alim.* (6 (3): 373–383, 1986)

Sablayrolles, J.-M., Dubois, C., Manginat, C., Roustau, J.-L., Barre, P., 'Effectiveness of combined ammoniacal nitrogen and oxygen additions for completion of sluggish and stuck fermentations', *J. Ferm. Bioeng.* (82 (4): 377–381, 1996)

Salacha, M.I., Kallithraka, S., Tzourou, I., 'Browning of white wines: correlation with antioxidant characteristics, total polyphenolic composition and flavanol content', *Int. J. Food Sci. Technol.* (43 (06): 1073–1077, 2008)

Salmon, J.-M., Fornairon-Bonnefond, C., Mazauric, J.-P., Moutounet, M., 'Oxygen consumption by wine lees: impact on lees integrity during wine ageing', *Food Chem.* (71: 519–528, 2000)

Sauvageot, F., Vivier, P., 'Effects of malolactic fermentation on sensory properties of four Burgundy wines', *Am. J. Enol. Vitic.* (48 (2): 187–192, 1997)

Schneider, V., 'Weinalterung, III', *Weinwirtschaft-Technik* (10: 22–27, 1989)

Schneider, V., 'Must hyperoxidation. A review', *Am. J. Enol. Vitic.* (49 (1): 65–73, 1998)

Schneider V., 'Alterungsverhalten österreichischer Weißweine', *Der Winzer* (07: 12–16, 2009)

Schneider, V., 'Atypical aging defect: Sensory discrimination, viticultural causes, and enological consequences. A review', *Am. J. Enol. Vitic.* (65 (3): 277–284, 2014)

Schneider, V., *White Wine Enology: Optimizing Shelf Life and Flavor Stability of Unoaked White Wines* (Board & Bench Publishing, San Francisco, 2019)

Schneider, V., 'Influence of different screwcaps on wine quality', *Grapegrower & Winemaker* (680: 78–83, 2021)

Schneider, V., Müller, J., Schmidt, D., 'Oxygen consumption by postfermentation yeast lees: Factors affecting its rate and extent under enological conditions', *Food Technol. Biotechnol.* (54 (4): 395–402, 2016)

Schneider, V., Kost, C., 'Routine measurement of flavonoid phenols related to astringency and premature aging of white wines, and technical consequences', *Internet Journal of Viticulture and Enology* (www.Infowine.com, 6/3, 2021)

Schneider, V., Troxell, S., *Acidity Management in Musts and Wines*, 2nd edition (Board & Bench Publishing, San Francisco, 2022)

Silva, M.A., Julien, M., Jourdes, M., Teissedre, P.-L., 'Impact of closures on wine post-bottling development: A review', *Eur. Food Res. Technol.* (233: 905–914, 2011)

Sims, C.A., Eastridge, J.S., Bates, R.P., 'Changes in phenols, color, and sensory characteristics of muscadine wines by pre- and post-fermentation additions of PVPP, casein, and gelatin', *Am. J. Enol. Vitic.* (46 (2): 155–158, 1995)

Singleton, V.L., Sieberhagen, H.A., de Wet, P., van Wyk, C.J., 'Composition and sensory qualities of wines prepared from white grapes by fermentation with and without grape solids', *Am. J. Enol. Vitic.* (26 (1): 62–69, 1975)

Singleton, V.L., Salgues, M., Zaya, J., Trousdale, E., 'Caftaric acid disappearance and conversion to products of enzymic oxidation in grape must and wine', *Am. J. Enol. Vitic.* (36 (1): 50–56, 1985)

Singleton, V.L., 'Oxygen with phenols and related reactions in musts, wines, and model systems: observations and practical implications', *Am. J. Enol. Vitic.* (38 (1): 69–77, 1987)

Skouroumounis, G.K., Kwiatkowski, M.J., Francis, I.L., Oakey, H., Capone, D.L., Peng, Z., Duncan, B., Sefton, M.A., Waters, E.J., 'The influence of ascorbic acid on the composition, colour and flavor properties of a Riesling and a wooded Chardonnay wine during five years' storage', *Aust. J. Grape Wine Res.* (11 (3): 355–368, 2005)

Solomon, E.I., Chen, P., Metz, M., Lee, S.-K., Palmer, A.E., 'Oxygen binding, activation, and reduction to water by copper proteins', *Angew. Chem. Int. Ed.* (40 (24): 4570–4590, 2001)

Somers, T.C., Pocock, K.F., 'Phenolic assessment of white musts: varietal differences in free-run juices and pressings', *Vitis* (30 (3): 189–201, 1991)

Steele, J.T., Kunkee, R., 'Deacidification of musts from the western United States by the calcium double-salt precipitation process', *Am. J. Enol. Vitic.* (29 (3): 153–160, 1978)

Towey, J.P., Waterhouse, A.L., 'The extraction of volatile compounds from French and American oak barrels in Chardonnay during three successive vintages', *Am. J. Enol. Vitic.* (47 (2): 163–172, 1996a)

Towey, J.P., Waterhouse, A.L., 'Barrel-to-barrel variation of volatile oak extractives in barrel-fermented Chardonnay', *Am. J. Enol. Vitic.* (47 (1): 17–20, 1996b)

Ugliano, M., 'Oxygen contribution to wine aroma evolution during bottle aging', *J. Agric. Food Chem.* (61 (26): 6125–6136, 2013)

Ugliano, M., Kwiatkowski, M., Vidal, S., Capone, D., Siebert, T., Dieval, J.-B., Aagaard, O., Waters, E.J., 'Evolution of 3-mercaptohexanol, hydrogen sulfide, and methyl mercaptan during bottle storage of Sauvignon blanc wines. Effect of glutathione, copper, oxygen exposure, and closure-derived oxygen', *J. Agric. Food Chem.* (59 (6): 2564–2572, 2011)

Vela, E., Hernandez-Orte, P., Franco-Luesma, E., Ferreira, V., 'Micro-oxygenation does not eliminate hydrogen sulfide and mercaptans from wine; it simply shifts redox and complex-related equilibria to reversible oxidized species and complexed forms', *Food Chem.* (243: 222–230, 2017)

Viaux, L., Devaux, S., Renaud, S., Robillard, B., 'Comparaison des stabilisations à l'acide tartrique racémique et au tartrate neutre de calcium dans des vins de Champagne. Étude de la solubilité du tartrate de calcium racémique', *Bull. de l'OIV* (781–782: 237–249, 1996)

Vidal, J.-C., Dufourcq, T., Boulet, J.-C., Moutounet, M., 'Les apports d'oxygène au cours des traitements des vins. Bilan des observations sur site. 1ère partie', *Rev. Fr. d'Œnologie* (190: 24–31, 2001)

Vidal, J.-C., Boulet, J.-C., Moutounet, M., 'Les apports d'oxygène au cours des traitements des vins. Bilan des observations sur site. 2ème partie', *Rev. Fr. d'Œnologie* (201: 32–38, 2003)

Vidal, J.-C., Boulet, J.-C., Moutounet, M., 'Les apports d'oxygène au cours des traitements des vins. Bilan des observations sur site. 3ème partie', *Rev. Fr. d'Œnologie* (205: 25–33, 2004)

Vidal, J.-C., Guillemat, B., Chayvialle, C., 'Oxygen transmission rate of screwcaps by chemoluminescence and air/capsule/headspace/acidified water system', *Bull. de l'OIV* (84: 189–198, 2011)

Vos, P.J.A., Gray, R.S., 'The origin and control of hydrogen sulfide during fermentation of grape must', *Am. J. Enol. Vitic.* (30 (3): 187–197, 1979)

Waterhouse, A.L., Laurie, V F., 'Oxidation of wine phenols: a critical evaluation and hypotheses', *Am. J. Enol. Vitic.* (57 (4): 306–313, 2006)

Waterhouse, A., Frost, S., Ugliano, M., Cantu, A.R., Currie, B.L., Anderson, M., Chassy, A.W., Vidal, S., Diéval, J.-B., Aagaard, O., Heymann, H., 'Sulfur dioxide-oxygen consumption ratio reveals differences in bottled wine oxidation', *Am. J. Enol. Vitic.* (67 (4): 449–459, 2016)

Wildenradt, H.L., Singleton, V.L., 'The production of aldehydes as a result of oxidation of phenolic compounds and its relation to wine aging', *Am. J. Enol. Vitic.* (25 (2): 119–126, 1974)

Williams, J.T., Ough, C.S., Berg, H.W., 'White wine composition and quality as influenced by methods of must clarification', *Am. J. Enol. Vitic.* (29 (2): 92–96, 1978)

Williams, P.J., Cynkar, W., Francis, I.L., Gray, J.D., Iland, P.G., Coombe, B.G., 'Quantification of glycosides in grapes, juices, and wines through a determination of glycosyl glucose', *J. Agric. Food Chem.* (43 (1): 121–128, 1995)

Zironi, R., Buiatti, S., Zelotti, E., 'Evaluation of a new colourimetric method for the determination of catechins in musts and wines', *Vitic. Enol. Sci.* (47 (1): 1–7, 1992)

INDEX

acetaldehyde 22–23, 86–88, 115
acidification 15–17, 139
acidity correcions 63–83
aroma 36–37, 66–67
aroma thiols 27
aromatic ripeness 10–11
ascorbic acid 93–6
astringency 20, 96, 136–7
atypical ageing 10, 22, 95

Bacchus 28, 50
barrel ageing 110–4
bâtonnage 110–4
bench trials 87, 135, 138
bentonite 41–2, 131–5
bentotest 132
berries 12–13
biogenic amines 64
Botrytis cinerea 40
bottle closures 143–7
bottling 141–7
bound SO_2 23, 65, 85
browning
    of juice 17–18
    of wine 19–20

calcium carbonate 71–81
calcium residues 82–3
calcium tartrate 72–83
calcium tartrate malate 79
carboxymethylcellulose (CMC) 140
caseinates 137
catechin 18, 89
charcoal 41
citric acid 67, 138
clarification
    of juice 36–43
    of wine 108, 114
CO_2 77–80, 124, 128
co-inoculation 64–65
cold settling 39–41
cold stabilisation 128, 138
cold test 139
colour 19–20
conductivity seeding test 139
containers 119–121
cooling 28, 59, 139
copper 95
copper sulphate 54, 135–6
corks 145–7
cross-flow filter 44
crystal stability 82–3, 139–140
crystallisation inhibitors 137–141
cysteine 97, 100

deacidification 63–83, 137–9
dehydroascorbic acid 93
diacetyl 66–7
diammonium phosphate 48–53
DL-tartaric acid 83
double-salt deacidification 78–81

Fenton reaction 88
fermentability 38
fermentation 37–61
fermentation problems 48–49
filtration 37, 81, 104–5, 108, 125–7
finings 40–42, 131–7
flavonoid phenols 17–35, 89, 136–7
flotation 42–43
free SO_2 23, 34, 58, 65, 85–87, 91, 102–5
free-run juice 34–35

gelatin 41, 136
glucanase 40, 114
glutathione 27, 96–100
glycosidase 40
grape processing 17–35
grape quality 9–13

headspace 123–4, 127, 141–7
heat test 132
higher aldehydes 88
histamine 64
hydrogen peroxide 88–94
hydrogen sulphide 53–54
hydrolysable tannins 96, 111
hydropress 44
hyper-oxidation 24–25
hyper-reduction 24–25

inactive dry yeasts 96–100
inert gas 24, 123–7
inert solids 57
iodine titration 86
iron 134–5

juice bottoms 44–45
juice clarification 36–45, 60
juice treatments 36–45
juice turbidity 37–38
juice unfermented 43–44

kieselsol 41

lactic acid 49, 66, 138
Lactobacillus plantarum 65
lees filter 44
lysozyme 49

maceration 28–30
malic acid 49, 66, 73
malolactic fermentation 63–68
mannoproteins 113–4, 140,
metatartaric acid 140
methoxypyrazines 11–12
mixers 128

molecular SO_2 16, 44, 58, 85–87
must oxidation 18–27

nephelometric turbidity units (NTU) 38, 100–1
non-flavonoid phenols 18

oak 110–1
Oenococcus oeni 64–65
orange wine 29–30
oxidation
    of juice 17–35
    of wine 24–26
oxidative ageing 21–22
oxidative must processing 17–35
oxygen
    consumption rate 99–105
    during fermentation 55–56
    in barrels 110–3
    in juice 17–35
    in wine 88–105, 117–8, 141–7

pectin test 39
pectolytic enzymes 39–40
petrol flavor 22
pH 15–17, 35–36, 65, 90, 134
physiological ripeness 9–11
pied de cuve 61
plant proteins 137
polyethylene 119–120
polymerisation 89
polyphenol oxidase (PPO) 25
polyvinylpolypyrrolidone (PVPP) 136–7
potassium 16, 68, 74–78
potassium bicarbonate 71–78, 138–9
potassium bitartrate 17, 68–71, 139–140
potassium carbonate 71
potassium metabisulphite 86
potassium polyaspartate 140
premox 22
press fractions 32–33
pressing 31–36
pressure 125–6
protein stability 131–5
pulp juice 35

pumps 125, 127
purging 127

quinones 88–89

racking 108
reducing agents 85–105
reductive must processing 17–35
reductive taints 48, 53–54, 135–6
rehydration 47–48
residual sugar 43, 48, 52, 57–60, 66, 108
ripeness 9–13
Ripper method 34, 86, 96
rotary vacuum filter 44

Sauvignon 27, 50, 100
screw caps 145–7
sensory assessment
    of flavonoid phenols 19–22
    of fruit maturity 12–13
    of must oxidation 26–28
    of oxygen uptake 119
sequential inoculation 64
silica gel 41
skin contact 28–30
sluggish fermentation 48–49
SO_2
    at pressing 33–35
    in juice 17–35
    in wine 65, 85–93, 102, 114–5, 141–7
    produced by yeast 65
sparkling base wine 43, 35, 74, 136, 139
spontaneous fermentation 59–61

starter cultures 47–48, 65
stems 12–13, 31
sterols 54–55
stirring 113–4
storage 27–28
stuck fermentation 58
survival factors 49, 54–56

tannins 96
tartaric acid 17, 68–69, 72–75
temperature
    during fermentation 50–52, 57–60
    during MLF 66
    during must processing 39
    during skin contact 28
    during storage 102, 118, 132–3
tirage liqueur 43
titratable acidity (TA) 17, 35–36, 66, 69–80
topping 60, 126
total SO_2 38, 85, 90
tubings 127
turbidity meter 37
typical ageing 22

variable capacity tanks 121–3
volatile acidity 48–49, 60–61, 66

wine surface 68, 119–126

yeast lees 100–5, 110–4
yeast nutrients 51–56
yeast strains 49–50, 59–61, 101–3
yeast-assimilable nitrogen (YAN) 52–53

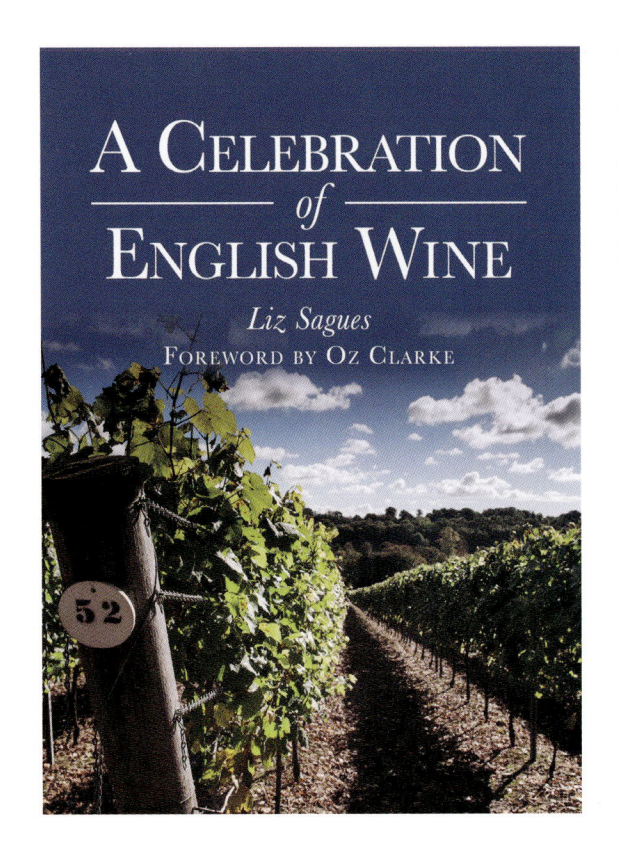

A Celebration of English Wine

Liz Sagues
Foreword by Oz Clarke

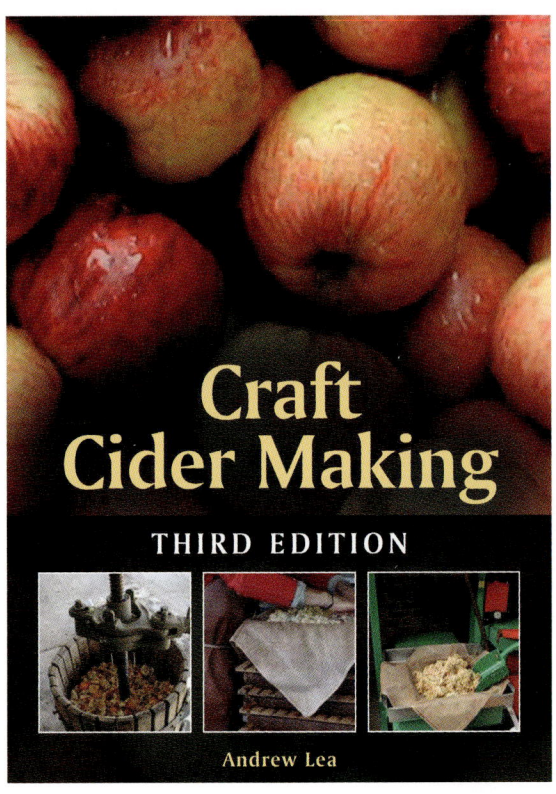

Craft Cider Making

THIRD EDITION

Andrew Lea

CRAFT GIN MAKING

Rachel Hicks and Andrew Parsons

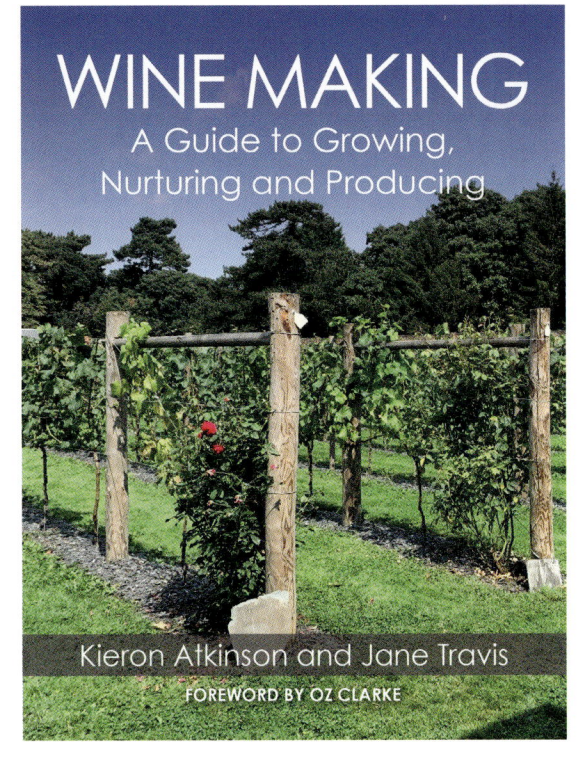

WINE MAKING
A Guide to Growing, Nurturing and Producing

Kieron Atkinson and Jane Travis
Foreword by Oz Clarke